MANUFACTURING WEALTH

Taking Advantage of Your Personal Finance Machine

JOSEPH GALATOWITSCH
with
CHRIS ENGSTROM

NORTHLOOP
BOOKS

North Loop Press
2301 Lucien Way #415
Maitland, FL 32751
407·339·4217
www.northlooppress.com

ISBN-13: 978-1-63505-193-3

Printed in the United States of America

NORTHLOOP
BOOKS

* * *

Dedicated to my wife and family. For their many years of supporting this seemingly endless journey with never a complaint, but only encouragement, constructive critique and love.

—JLG

* * *

To Carol—ever supportive of my many interests, activities, and projects.

—CJE

MANUFACTURING
WEALTH

CONTENTS

FOREWORD

I met Joe about a year ago under somewhat unusual circumstances. My wife Sue and I decided to look for houses in Minnesota. We decided to bid on a house in a suburb of St. Paul. Our realtor informed us that another bidder had made an offer on our chosen house the prior week. After a series of back and forth negotiations, we got the house. Case closed, sort of.

Shortly after we completed the purchase, the house next door went on sale and was purchased. A month or so later, my wife and I were having a glass of wine when we heard a knock at our front door. It was Joe and his wife, Therese. They told us they had bought the house next door. We invited them in for wine. Sometime in the conversation Joe told us that they had been the other bidder on our house! They loved the location so when the house next door was listed, they bought it.

During the conversation I asked Joe what he did for a living; he had co-founded a firm which provided consulting services to major health care product manufacturers. Joe asked me in turn what I did for a living. I told him I was an investment manager, that I had been managing portfolios for over forty years. Twenty years ago I had founded my own firm; we began with about $600 million under management and today we manage about $5 billion. I mentioned that we had written a book a few years ago. He responded that he was writing a book about personal finance.

A quick timeout here. Every good investment manager is born with a skepticism in his or her bones, a skepticism so deep that you never accept anything related to investments at face value. You automatically look under the hood at every company, every idea and every investment. Not to mention there are already a ton of books on personal finance and investing. What could this guy offer that was new or insightful?

It gets worse. I have read nearly every book ever written about investing. My most prized books include those written by Warren Buffett and Benjamin Graham. I hope you can imagine my skepticism when Joe asked me to read his book. After all, Joe had no previous professional training on investing nor had he worked in the investment or personal finance business. But, good neighborliness ruled so I read Joe's book.

To my surprise and delight, I found the book to offer a sound and unique framework for understanding and managing personal finance and building wealth.

First and foremost, I liked that Joe was encouraging the reader to use money as a means to an end, not the end in itself. Throughout my career I have found that the best wealth builders are able to detach from their money. They establish and adhere to sound spending habits and they gradually develop a purpose for their money beyond simple accumulation.

The book also has several unique insights into assets and debt. I encourage the reader to thoroughly understand the different types of assets described.

Unless you are born wealthy, you have to extract money from your income to invest. In a detailed and easily understandable way Joe and Chris provide both a framework and practical steps to convert your income into wealth.

The book highlights the power of compound interest. I have had countless folks ask me what are my favorite books on investing. I always refer them to the writings of Graham, Buffett, and the compound interest tables.

I will leave the discovery of many other powerful insights to you as you read the book. For those who want to develop a sound framework to build financial independence *Manufacturing Wealth* is a great place to begin.

Fred Martin
Founder, Disciplined Growth Investors

AN IMPORTANT NOTE

ABOUT THIS BOOK, THE AUTHORS, AND PERSONAL FINANCE

Background:

This book and website utilize general personal finance examples, models, and measures to describe powerful concepts related to how our personal finances actually work. The Personal Finance Machine and the many unique concepts and perspectives throughout this book are part of an approach to personal financial management developed by Joe Galatowitsch. This fresh approach is designed to provide insight into the mechanics of personal finance and how we can more effectively harness our finances to achieve our goals.

Joe teamed up with Chris Engstrom to write this book. Together, Joe and Chris have over 60 years of combined experience in business management, marketing, and analytics. They have worked in and led complex businesses and functions at large multi-national corporations including Medtronic and Microsoft. They have extensive experience in quantitative analysis and the understanding of complex systems. Joe has also founded and led a highly successful medical technology consulting business. It is these business credentials and experiences in combination with extensive research into personal finance and the management of his own personal finances that enabled Joe to develop such a unique, refreshing and practical approach to understanding the machine that is our personal finances. In addition, Chris has brought a critical, objective, and practical eye along with many unique perspectives to refine the concepts and make the book as clear and compelling as possible.

The Answer Has Always Been Right in Front of Us.

Each person and household has unique personal financial situations, goals, and needs. This book contains a systematic codification of personal finance that helps to explain the potential short and long-term impact of financial decisions we all make every day. We often think financial freedom is beyond our reach, requires some herculean effort, or great sacrifice. There are hundreds of books to tell you how to make money in the stock market, or how to develop a real estate empire, or about all the riches that await in starting your own business. Others will show you how to microscopically budget your way to financial freedom. All this reinforces the idea that financial freedom must come from some great business or financial risk and endeavor, or a lifetime of budgeting every dollar with great personal sacrifice. What we have discovered is that true financial freedom is realistically attainable without requiring some extreme approach or radical change to your life or career. All we have to do is look within our personal finances today with fresh eyes to understand the great opportunity we already have right in front of us. By doing so, most of us can achieve real financial freedom by just doing the things we are already doing today, but with just a bit more insight, control and focus. We know it sounds crazy, but it's absolutely true.

INTRODUCTION:

LIFE ON ELM STREET

A few miles from downtown, if you take exit 37B and turn down Main and take a left at Birch and a right on Lincoln you will find Elm Street. Elm Street in Anywhere U.S.A is tree-lined and well-kept with modest to higher-end homes of working families. As you drive down the street, you see the typical signs of families living the American dream: well-kept homes, nicely landscaped yards, newer cars, and a boat in the garage or drive-way here and there. The homes are all nicely decorated on the inside. They have the latest flat screens, electronics and tech, nice furniture, closets full of up-to-date clothing, and well-stocked kitchens.

If you drive a bit further to the local coffee shop you will find the Joneses, the Smiths, and the Millers sitting together having coffee on a beautiful Saturday morning. They are good friends and they have lived as neighbors for nearly 40 years. They are typical middle-class families and as they advanced in their careers they moved from the more modest homes in the neighborhood to the higher-end homes, but were able to stay close to each other. They know each other well. Their kids played and went to school together, they often vacationed together and now they are in their early-60's contemplating retirement.

Let's listen in on their conversation…

Joneses: *We plan to work full-time for several more years and will need to keep working part-time after that to help with the finances. With all of our commitments and responsibilities along the way, we just could never manage to save much for retirement. We will need to cut back on expenses after we retire and are probably going to sell the house and downsize into a modest condo. No more new* *cars for us, we just won't be able to afford them in the future. We have our hob-bies and the boat and we might take a few driving vacations to someplace warm when we can afford it. Social security is going to be a huge help; we don't know what we'd do without it.*

Smiths: *We are going to quit working full-time in the next few years, but we will also need to do some part-time work after that. We've saved quite a bit, but it just does not translate into anywhere near enough income for us to maintain our lifestyle. We may keep the house, but we aren't sure we can afford it. We plan to take a few vacations, but nothing extravagant. Mostly we plan to stay close to home and keep budgeting and managing our expenses, just like we always have. We're really glad social security is there to help fill the gaps.*

Millers: *We are retiring next year and not going to work after that, though we plan to do some volunteering. We're moving to a luxury 3-bedroom condo in the city overlooking the lake. We also just bought a place down south where we'll be spending the winters. We have some great vacations planned to places all around the world that we've always wanted to visit. We are also planning to buy a used sports car, just for fun. We really enjoy eating out and we love the theatre and football so we are looking forward to having season tickets to both. We like the added income from social security, but we'd be just fine if it's not there in the future.*

Joneses and Smiths to the Millers: *Wait a minute...How can your retire-ment be so different from ours? We all had similar careers and made about the same incomes throughout our working lives. We lived in the same neighborhood, have owned similar houses and cars, shopped at the same stores and yet we spent all our time budgeting, scrimping and working to make ends meet. You guys never seemed to worry about money and always seemed to have money for vacations and eating out and entertainment. And now you've prepared for this great care-free retirement.* **How did you do it?**

This book is about understanding how the Millers achieved what seemed impossible to the other couples. And more impressively, they did it without scrimping, sacrificing, or even worrying about money. They did it by truly understanding how their personal finances worked and then acted on their knowledge to achieve their life and financial goals.

Our Personal Finances Are a Mess

More than 50 percent of US working households admit to having a debt problem.[1] Of the 44 percent of households with revolving credit card debt,[2] the average balance is around $13,000.[3] Forty-six percent of households say they could not cover a $400 emergency expense without selling something or borrowing money.[4] Meanwhile, only 52 percent of households have a formal retirement account (401(k), IRA, etc.)[5] and for those working households approaching retirement who actually have a 401(k) account, the typical balance is only $135,000.[6] Nationally our annual savings rates are in the mid-single digits.[7] Millions of Americans live paycheck to paycheck, and many nearing retirement have had to delay or suspend their retirement plans for lack of sufficient savings. Money is a number one daily concern[8] and a top source of marital conflict and divorce.[9] We spend all this time earning it, worrying about it, budgeting it, managing it, having a love/hate relationship with it, and in the end, we fail to conquer or accumulate it.

Most of us spend a significant amount of time and energy "working" on our personal finances. It's not just paying the bills, but budgeting, saving for long or short-term needs, deciding what to buy and when, managing debt, investing, and endlessly moving money from here to there to cover this or that. Yet there is simply no workable road map, structure, or process to help guide us as we manage our personal finances. Many of us feel we are always one step behind, and every month brings a new expense, a market downturn, a broken this, a needy that. We feel less in control and more like we are being controlled—as if our fate is not in our hands. The to-do list is endless and the effort seems fruitless—so we just try to focus on a few things and hope for the best.

At the same time, we are awash in a sea of financial advice, tools, strategies, and ideas. There are hundreds of books, blogs, radio shows, websites, and financial experts. They seem to be everywhere, bombarding us with their version of the key to personal finance and financial freedom. Frustratingly, much of it makes sense, at least on the surface, but like the latest fad diet, little of it seems to be truly workable or appears to do any good.

Interestingly, there are many similarities between the personal financial advice industry and the weight loss industry. For decades, there has been an endless stream of fads, "quick and easy" weight loss and debt reduction schemes, calorie counting and expense tracking, special diets and budgeting tips. Junk food and easy financing are abundant, but in terms of actual outcomes, sadly, both the diet and personal finance industries can only be judged as colossal failures. In the end, they just don't work, or only work for a short while because they focus on controlling the symptoms (diets and budgets), not the underlying drivers and issues. The real answers to these problems are at a more fundamental level.

What Is Really Going On

We all recognize and appreciate the value of sound financial advice, but why is it so difficult to follow or to integrate into our daily lives?

We wrote this book *because we are not personal finance experts.* Like you, everything we read seemed to make sense, but in the end, it was just an endless stream of advice that simply did not work for us. We kept asking ourselves the same question you keep asking: Why does this have to be so difficult, time consuming, and frustrating? Something has clearly been missing in this equation, and from our perspective it's related to a larger context of how personal finance actually works and how it fits into our lives and lifestyles in a practical way. Said differently, we all want to apply all this good financial advice, but what do we apply it to? This is the fundamental problem. What exactly constitutes *the thing* that is our personal finances?

Our backgrounds are in engineering, business, market strategy, and analytics, so we looked at personal finance from a systems perspective. We found that the complicated mess we call personal finance is, at its most basic level, just a simple system or "machine" that needs to be understood and managed properly. All the advice we hear are just ways of explaining how to run the machine that we don't fully understand or even appreciate *as a thing.* Our goal is simple: Explain how your **Personal Finance Machine (PFM)** works, how to operate it, and how it can be used to achieve your goals and to live your lives in control and on your terms. This is simply what the Millers did.

Today personal finance advice can largely be described by three legs of a financial stool: Cash Management/Budgeting (defining spending limits, tracking expenses, moving money), Investing (optimizing investment returns), and Spending Decisions (deciding what to buy, how much to spend, and whether to finance something). While this seems to make sense, the stool metaphor is missing the most important component—the seat. This book is about *how* the three legs of the stool are connected and entirely dependent on one another. We will show you how your personal finances actually operate and how you can exert control over them. This missing component links the legs of the stool together and creates a comprehensive and functional structure. All four elements work together, but the three legs are nothing without the seat.

You will also soon appreciate that this finance machine we own and control is *really* valuable. Our PFM represents and processes our lifetime earnings and spending, which can easily amount to several million dollars. This makes it incredibly valuable not only to us individually, but to the banking, retail, automotive, and other industries that are trying to wrest control of it from us. Banks and lenders have (literally) spent thousands of years working to understand how our Personal Finance Machine works, and they work very hard, little by little, to get us to turn it over to them. They can't take it from us, but they give us every opportunity to unwittingly relinquish control—and once they control it, it is incredibly difficult to claw it back.

So this is not just a challenge to understand how our personal finances work, it is also a battle to maintain control of them. In fact, it is a hidden battle where the enemy does not want us to see it as an "us against them" struggle because our defenses would go up and we would respond to protect ourselves. The biggest weapon our adversaries have is our misguided belief that they are an ally, our friends, trying to help us achieve our goals. One reason we wrote this book is just to try and make it a fair fight. We want to bring this very real battle out into the open so you can see what is really going on and why our ignorance of how our personal finances work is a significant advantage to them.

Life On Your Terms

This is not only a battle for our money, but also a battle for our lives—the life each of us wants to lead. When we get ourselves on the losing side of this battle, we become trapped in an endless monthly cycle of working to pay bills just to keep our heads above water. We strive for the next level, adding more and more to our plates, and somewhere along the line we lose sight of the fact that our LIFE is being consumed, that our freedom is an illusion, and that we are more and more tightly controlled and limited by our escalating financial commitments. And what is our reward: a few weeks of vacation every year and almost nothing saved by the time we want to retire?

This is not a good deal. A good deal can only be described as one where we control our financial destiny. How many times have you thought "I can't afford to do that" for something that you *should* be able to afford or have to work extra hours, or not be able to leave a job you hate? For many of us, it's just a constant battle that we have gotten so used to that we don't even realize we are in it.

This self-created financial prison is the result of losing the battle for control over our PFM. Like it or not, our lives and our money are inextricably bound. When we give up control of our PFM, we are in effect also giving up control of our lives. This is a big deal.

Take this simple test: [10]

Question 1: *Are you free of credit card debt?*

Question 2A: Answer this if you are more than 5 years to retirement: *Take [(your age - 20) x your pre-tax annual income] then divide by [years to retirement divided by 3]. Do you have at least this much invested/saved for retirement?*

Question 2B: Answer this version if you are less than 5 years to retirement: Take your pre-tax annual income times 15. *Do you have at least this much invested/saved for retirement?*

Question 3: *Do you have at least 3 months of gross monthly income in cash savings/checking?*

If you answered 'no' to any or all of these questions, then you may not have as much control as you think. In fact, you may already be losing the battle.

From the age of 25 to 65, the core of our adult working lives, we have roughly an "inventory" of 480 months and paychecks. How do we want to spend these limited months? Do we want to spend them struggling and budgeting to pay our bills or living our lives where money is just not a problem and not a barrier to the way we want to live? If we squander those months, what will the remaining 20 or 30 years look like? Where are you now? How many months of inventory do you have left: 100, 200, 300?

Regardless of where we are in our financial lifecycle, we need to pay attention to this powerful machine that is our personal finances. Again, the goal of this book is simple: to explain how our Personal Finance Machine (PFM) works, how to operate it, and how to use it to achieve our financial and lifestyle goals.

Who Is This Book For?

This book is written for those at any income level and any level of financial health. However, a critical part of our objective involves a desire to help those motivated to make their personal finances more productive and efficient; to transform a collection of personal finance tasks and parts into a powerful machine that can be controlled and used to make their lives better. Whether you already think you are in good financial shape, or are struggling to keep your head above water, this book can help. At a minimum, it will give you great insight into this wonderful and powerful financial machine that we each own and manage throughout our lives.

Ironically, you will find very little traditional personal financial advice in this book. There is already plenty of generally good advice out there. This book is not meant to provide yet another version of what you can learn from the thousands of existing books, blogs, or websites. What it does provide is powerful insight into your personal finance machinery that will help you understand and harness it to fulfill your needs.

The concepts in the book are very powerful on their own and are immediately useful. In addition, the accompanying website—www.manufacturingwealth.com—is a powerful source of useful information and tools to help you assemble, manage, and optimize your PFM. However, we encourage you to read the book first. It establishes the context and framework for understanding your Personal Finance Machine and the website's related content and features.

This is not just a book about understanding your PFM. It's about being able to see it, interact with it, model it, and refine it. As you read through the book, keep in mind that you will not have to build your PFM by hand. The website (www.manufacturingwealth.com) will help you quickly bring your PFM to life and into focus:

1) We have developed an interactive Personal Finance Machine dashboard into which you can easily and quickly input your key financial information. It takes less than an hour. After which you will have an initial view of your PFM that displays key inputs, outputs, and measures in a way that clearly communicates your financial health and status.

2) You can model and optimize your PFM to better match your short, medium, and long-term goals.

3) You can take your modeled PFM and translate it directly into how you want to manage your personal finances today. No detailed budgets, no tracking every expense, just a simple system for taking control of your finances rather than the other way around.

Think of this book as the *operating/user* manual you never got for the most important, valuable, and powerful machine you will ever own. It will show you how to assemble your PFM, explain how it works, and show you how to operate it to achieve your financial and life goals.

Lastly, we may not be telling you much that you don't already know or at least have a gut feel for. We are simply defining, organizing, and *structuring* all these familiar moving parts into a logical and cohesive system that we can finally make sense of and get our arms around. We titled the book *Manufacturing Wealth* because when we understand and harness our PFM effectively, that is exactly what it does—because that's what it's designed to do!

Thank you for choosing to invest your time and money in this book. We hope it will help you and your loved ones better appreciate and harness the incredibly powerful machine that you have in your hands.

SECTION ONE

UNDERSTANDING OUR PERSONAL FINANCE MACHINE

CHAPTER 1:

MANAGING YOUR PERSONAL FINANCE MACHINE

- A LIFELONG RESPONSIBILITY

What do you think is the economic value of all the money we make over the forty or so years that we spend working—probably a lot, right? It's actually easy to calculate. Take your monthly salary from your first working month to your last and add it all up. Of course, that's not exactly the economic value of our earnings, it is simply just how much money we made. What if we took all that money and invested it in the stock market? Well, the stock market has delivered an average inflation-adjusted return of 6.8 percent/year over the last one hundred years.[11] So if we apply a 6.8 percent compound annual rate of return to earnings, we come up with a number that is actually closer to the economic value of our entire earnings (in today's dollars). As it turns out, this *is* a really big number.

A family that makes the current average annual income throughout their working lives (about $100,000/year[12]) manages a Personal Finance Machine (PFM) worth *millions*. Their Lifetime Economic Value (LEV)—that is, their earnings plus interest—is about $20 million in today's dollars ($20,682,675 to be exact). We calculate this by taking their annual gross income of $100,000/12 or $8,333/month and investing it in the stock market every month at an inflation-adjusted 6.8 percent rate of return for 40 working years. What about those earning the *median* income of around $50,000/year?[13] They have a PFM worth about $10 million in LEV; and, as mentioned above, those making $100,000 have an LEV worth about $20 million; and those at $150,000 have an LEV of $30 million (and so on—roughly $10M in LEV for every additional $50,000 in annual income).

Here is the scary part: Of this incredible economic value that we each generate and manage, after 40 years of working, we only wind up with 1–2 percent of this value in investment assets. Looking across all households, the median value of their investment assets is about $24,000 (0.24 percent of their $10M LEV), with the remainder of their net worth mostly in home equity and other assets.[14] For those households approaching retirement (ages 55–64) the statistics are even more sobering.

A commonly used rule-of-thumb is that at retirement, your retirement assets should be able to sustain a 4 percent annual income distribution throughout your retirement. Table 1-1, shows that of the 59 percent of households age 55–64 with retirement savings, this group has very modest median retirement savings of $104,000. A 4 percent annual distribution from this amount ($4,160) only covers about 5 percent of what is needed to maintain their pre-retirement income level of $86,000).

TABLE 1-1: Pre-Retirement Assets[15]

Households age 55-64	No Retirement Savings	Have Retirement Savings
Percentage of households	41%	59%
Median Income	$26,000	$86,000
Median Net Worth	$21,000	$337,000
Median Retirement Savings	$0	$104,000
Estimated LEV	~$5M	~$18M
% LEV in Retirement Assets	0%	0.6%

For this same group of households (age 55–64 with retirement savings), Table 1-2 shows their retirement assets by percentile. Looking at the 90th percentile, these households have median retirement assets of $718K. While these retirement assets for the top percentile are much higher, a 4 percent annual distribution of their $718K retirement assets ($28,728) only replaces 33 percent of the median pre-retirement income ($28,728/$86,000) for households approaching retirement with retirement assets. What makes this particularly alarming is that this 90th percentile group most certainly has a median income that is higher than $86,000, which stresses how inadequate retirement savings are—even for those with the most savings.

TABLE 1-2: Pre-Retirement Assets by Percentile[16]

Households age 55-64 with retirement Assets	Median Retirement Assets	Percentage of their LEV ($20M)	Estimated Retirement Income from Investments
10th Percentile	$8,760	0.04%	$350/year (0.4%)
25th Percentile	$25,978	0.1%	$1,039/year (1.2%)
50th Percentile	$104,340	0.5%	$4,174/year (4.9%)
75th Percentile	$300,200	1.5%	$12,008/year (14%)
90th Percentile	$718,200	3.6%	$28,728/year (33%)

Said differently, the bottom 41% of households approaching retirement have no retirement savings at all. Those with retirement savings (the other 59%) look like this:

- 75% can only replace 14% of their pre-retirement incomes from retirement assets

- About 15% will be able to replace only 33% of their current incomes

- The rest, only about 10%, can replace more than 33% of their current incomes

Considering households with and without retirement assets, only 2-3% will have enough retirement assets to replace more than 33% of their pre-retirement income.

While we obviously can't keep and invest *every* dollar we make, it does not change the fact that we possess a powerful machine that produces millions. However, most of us manage to keep almost nothing—even though we will need to live about a third of our adult lives on whatever we have saved and invested plus whatever social security may provide in the future.

So if we're not keeping it, then where does all of this money go? Who is taking it from us? The unfortunate truth is that we are to blame. These are, for the most part, self-inflected wounds. We spend it all away, but we have a lot of help.

As mentioned in the introduction, there are organizations that understand our Personal Finance Machinery extremely well—even intimately. They know how much we make, how much debt we have, what we like to buy, where we shop, our tastes and weaknesses, and they most certainly know how financially responsible we are (or are not)—think credit scores. They know everything about us that matters in terms of helping us give them control of our multimillion dollar PFM. And most importantly, they know *exactly* how our personal finances work.

To be provocative, we'll call these organizations (banks, retailers, service providers) the "Debt Merchants." They include not just banks, but any organization that is willing to lend us money to facilitate purchasing their products or services. Our friendly department store offering us easy credit or installment plans, auto manufacturers and mortgage lenders, credit card companies—these are all Debt Merchants. They are in every sense of the word our "frenemies"—organizations who pretend to be on our side, but really do not have our best interests at heart. And in the absence of our direct, ongoing, and effective efforts to understand and control our own PFM, these organizations will take control and in effect own us.

We may not even realize we've become a sort of Financial Drone to the Debt Merchants. We are no longer in control of our finances or our lives, because we serve them. Our future economic potential has become *their* future economic potential.

We may have already been conscripted by the Debt Merchants for years or decades. Sadly, this fact doesn't usually sink in until we're preparing to retire and realize we have given away all but 1 or 2 percent (or worse) of our multimillion-dollar economic machine. Not all of it went to the Debt Merchants, but as we will describe, these entities play a powerful role in our self-destruction.

Debt Merchants have their hands deep into the pockets of a huge portion of U.S. households today. Forty-four percent of families are trapped or at risk of being trapped by revolving credit card debt,[17] and 45 percent of all US households save nothing and are living paycheck to paycheck.[18] They have no excess cash and they are one step away from, or are already doing time in a Debt Merchant's financial prison.

It's not really a fair fight. Like gambling at a casino, the rules favor the house because the house makes the rules. If we think about it, it's clear that Debt Merchants are masters at "helping us" help them. Consider the following:

How easy is it to get a credit card?	Incredibly easy
How easy is it to use it to overspend?	Incredibly easy
How easy is it to make the minimum payment?	Incredibly easy (at first . . .)
How easy is it to buy a new car?	Incredibly easy
How easy is it to afford the monthly payment?	Incredibly easy
How easy is it get financing for almost anything	Incredibly easy
How easy is it to find "no money down" deals?	Incredibly easy

On the other hand:

How easy is it to figure out what this is really costing you?	Incredibly difficult
How easy is it to escape this mounting debt?	Incredibly difficult
How easy is it to understand the total cost of ownership?	Incredibly difficult
How easy is it to understand the impact on our current expenses?	Incredibly difficult
How easy is it to understand the impact on your financial future?	Incredibly difficult

Debt Merchants Have a Very Clear and Specific Plan: help us give them as much of our multimillion dollar PFM as possible. Their strategy for doing so is to keep us off-balance, to prevent us from exerting control over our PFM or knowing the true cost of the things we buy. They don't want us to consider the long-term impact of our decisions; instead, they encourage us to live for today, to immerse ourselves in the pleasure of the instant gratification they've convinced us we so richly deserve. How often do you see advertising for new cars, vacation getaway deals, one-day blow-out clothing sales, easy financing or no money down? They're everywhere! They want to get us working for them as fast and for as long as possible.

Banks and lenders serve a vital role in our economy and are guided by a set of rules and standards. However, over the centuries they have honed their methods and products such that it has become effortless and painless for us to live beyond our means up to the point where the Debt Merchants take control. That is when they can dictate how much we spend, how much we can borrow, and, if we go too far, the terms of our "surrender" (as in bankruptcy).

Debt Merchants fully understand our total lifetime economic value. They understand we collectively spend $12 trillion dollars a year, and that the sooner they trap us, the more valuable we are to them.[19] They fully appreciate the significant lifetime value of a customer.

Debt Merchants do not have our best interests in mind—they have their best interests in mind. They seemingly look at us as valued customers, but in reality, they only see us as the gateway to our PFM. However, with that said, it's just not their job to help us. That's our job.

One of the biggest advantages Debt Merchants have is that they know more about how our finances work than we do. We have simply not figured out how to control our personal finances. We don't fully understand them, don't know how to measure them, don't know how to operate or manage them, and don't know how to use them to achieve our goals. Think about the Joneses, Smiths and Millers. What do the Millers know that the Joneses and Smiths do not?

Personal Finance Is a Simple System (a Machine)

What does the term "personal finance" imply or include? Are we talking about our savings and checking account balances? Are we talking about our investment portfolio and investment strategies; our income and expenses; our credit card debt and mortgage? Personal finance is all these things. Most of us see our personal finances in two simple buckets: Income/Expenses and Savings/Investments (or worst-case scenario, just the first bucket).

When we create and use a budget, we are attempting to gain control over just one part of a system. If we don't understand the whole system or how it works, then creating and using a budget will probably not achieve what we want it to because we can't see how it impacts the overall system. By simply making a budget, we are not understanding how the other decisions we make may undermine the goals we have for creating a budget in the first place.

> This is the stuff that usually comes to mind when we think about our personal finances, but this is part of the problem. These are the *components* or parts of our personal finances, but not the 'system' that _is_ our personal finances.

Our Personal Finances Are Basically a Machine That Manages and Converts Cash. It Includes:

- Inputs (income)

- Outputs (excess cash, changes in asset value)

- Moving parts (the movement of cash into or out of various accounts)

- Hard assets like cash, house, cars, boats, etc.

- Investment assets like stocks, bonds, and mutual funds

- Relationships and dependencies (e.g., buying a car decreases cash and increases expenses)

- Conversion of cash to assets and assets back to cash

- A control panel with levers and dials that impact the outputs, increase savings, decrease spending, increase debt, etc.

The decisions we make are in effect the adjustments we are making to the various levers and dials that influence and control our PFM. There are *powerful* levers and dials (decisions) that have a major effect on the outputs (how much house to buy, new vs. used cars, how much debt to use)—and there are *fine-tuning* levers and dials that have a smaller impact on outputs (spending on clothes or personal care or vacations).

Cash flows through this machine, and the decisions we make about *where* that cash flows either helps our machine run well or causes it grind to a halt. If we don't understand how this machine works, or know when (or in which direction) we are adjusting a "big" dial or a "little" dial, then we will have little ability to understand how our decisions impact our PFM's health or its outputs. Nor will we be able to effectively harness this machine to do work for us in a way that helps us achieve our goals.

We need to know the following in order for our PFM to work for us:

- How the machine **Works**: What are the various parts and how do they interact? What is the theory behind how the machine functions? Unlike a car, where we do not need to know how it works to operate it, successful operation of a PFM requires that we know how it works.

- How to **Operate** the machine: We need to understand what happens when we turn the various dials and levers (i.e., make decisions). We need to know how the machine responds to various inputs and adjustments, and to understand and measure what it is producing.

- How to **Use** the machine to achieve our goals: Once we know how it works and how to control and operate it, we then have the ability to harness it to achieve our objectives.

The Power of Financial Statements

Businesses have been around for thousands of years. But, it was only about one hundred years ago that financial and accounting standards were broadly adopted.[20] Prior to the standardization and broad use of the Profit and Loss statement (P&L) and the Balance Sheet, each business developed and used its own unique system and method to track revenues, expenses, and profits/losses. This wasn't too much of a problem when most businesses were small, but as they became larger and more complex, the lack of standardized accounting and measurement limited how fast and how broadly they could evolve.

It was not until the routine use of the P&L and Balance Sheet that business leaders began to fully understand how their businesses really worked—that is, how to assess their profits (outputs) accurately, how to measure the productivity of their assets, and how to optimize their operations. These tools were developed to define, explain, organize, and measure the core financial dynamics of the business so leaders could use these newly appreciated financial methods to achieve much greater goals and objectives.

Not only did they have a new and powerful set of tools, these tools also became standardized across all businesses. So anyone who understood how the financial tools worked could quickly and easily understand any business, regardless of the type of product or customer or business model.

Imagine if there was not a standard financial structure for businesses to operate within today. Imagine if business leaders ran their businesses the same way we managed our personal finances: no real accounting, no real measures, no real structure, but countless, arbitrary "rules of thumb" like "make a budget" or "spend less than you earn," or "save first." Yes, these are all good maxims, but if the business world operated this way, there would be total chaos. No business or industry today could ever hope to operate and thrive on platitudes and rules of thumb that have little useful context without understanding how the business financial machine really works.

So why, more than one hundred years later, do we not have a standard accounting and financial structure that we can use to better understand, control, and operate our personal finances? The answer is simple: until now, nobody has really taken the time to develop one. For whatever reason, the personal finance industry has been satisfied churning out mountains of advice on every aspect of our personal finances without defining the system that is our personal finances.

And the Debt Merchants aren't going to help since they really don't want us to exert control. They like it when our finances are disorganized, obscured, and vulnerable. They make less money if we are in control. Don't get us wrong. Like lawyers, accountants, and insurance companies, Debt Merchants play a vital liquidity role in the optimal performance of an advanced economy; but their primary job is to maximize *their* revenue and profits. The fact that we have not figured out how to structure and manage our own finances is not their problem, their responsibility, or their fault. However, it does make us multimillion dollar targets. And despite their pervasive and persuasive marketing to the contrary, the Debt Merchants could not care less about our dreams or goals. The last thing they want is for us to realize that we're losing the battle and act to assert control.

So Which Financial Path Are You On?

Regardless of income level, each of us is essentially on one of three financial paths:

Path 1: Financial Drone (The Jones Family)

Based on the 44 percent of households with revolving credit card debt, and the 46 percent that have no savings, we would argue that nearly 50 percent of Americans are "Financial Drones" or on the road to becoming one. Sadly, most these people will live most of their working lives essentially being owned by the Debt Merchants. Financial Drones may think they are in control, but it's only an illusion that the Debt Merchants have created and sustained.

Some characteristics of Financial Drones are that they owe a lot of money. Their monthly payments and related expenses eat up huge chunks of their monthly income, leaving just enough to get by, but not enough to get out from under the thumb of the Debt Merchants. Whenever they get a little extra money, it seems to just disappear. Drones have no cash, feel broke all the time, and are always budgeting and trying to restrain their spending to get by. There is some new expense at every turn. They have little or no savings or investments and try to convince themselves that retirement is not a fantasy and they are one pay raise away from escaping their predicament. There are millions of drones out there *at every income level (just like the Joneses)*.

Path 2: Financial Laborer (The Smith Family)

Financial Laborers see personal financial management as work. While they have some cash reserves, they budget aggressively and worry about monthly spending. They are saving for retirement and new purchases. Unanticipated expenses are problematic, but they work through them. They spend a lot of time and energy on personal finance, thinking about money, budgeting, and making sure they remain in control. They may have a significant amount of debt, but manage to stay one or two steps ahead of the Debt Merchants.

Their hard work and diligence seems to pay off, and they make slow, steady progress, but worry they may be one big "Gotcha" away from the whole thing falling apart. They have to restrain their spending more often than they would like. They wonder why this is so much work and think that if they just made a little more, they could get a better grip on their finances. There are lots of people on this path at *nearly every income level (just like the Smiths)*. They're constantly working hard to be responsible and save for that down payment, and build a retirement by "laboring" through their spending and budgeting every month.

Path 3: Financial Builder (The Miller Family)

Financial Builders have plenty of cash. They don't manage detailed budgets or worry about their monthly spending. They save for college, or other future needs, and retirement, and they have extra money on hand for new purchases. Unanticipated expenses are not a problem. Builders spend little time on personal finances and do not worry about money. They live comfortable and reasonable lifestyles. Their net worth is healthy and growing and they invest for retirement every month.

Others (like the Smiths and the Joneses) wonder about Builders: "How do they do that?" and "How is this even possible?" Once again, there are people like this (the Millers) at *nearly every income level*. They are focused on their *lives*, not their money. To many others they seem like financial wizards.

In fact, Builders (Millers), Laborers (Smiths), and Drones (Joneses) can often live together on the same block. They're neighbors, and their kids play and go to school together. They work at the same companies, make similar incomes, and they share similar lifestyles. Yet they have very different current and future financial situations.

Here is another test for you:

1. Do you live paycheck to paycheck?

2. Do you have less than two months of expenses in cash?

3. Do you carry credit card debt from month to month?

4. Do you NEED to budget to make ends meet?

5. Would an unexpected expense of 20 percent of your monthly gross income be a major issue?

If you answered yes to all five questions, then you are becoming or already are a drone for the Debt Merchants. If you answered no to most or all five questions, then here are three more questions:

1. Do you worry about money?

2. Do you feel like you *have to* spend a significant amount of time working on the details like budgets, tracking spending, etc.?

3. Do you have trouble consistently saving the full amount you think you need for retirement?

If you answered yes to these questions, then you're *laboring* through your finances and probably working harder than you need to. If the answer is no to all eight questions, then you are already operating like a Builder and are ready to take your PFM to the next level.

The key factors that differ between the people on each of these paths are:

1. How well they *understand* how their personal finances work.

2. How much *control* they exert over their PFM (spending discipline).

3. How much time they spend on the *structure* of their finances vs. the details/budget.

Who's Doing the Work Anyway?

Financial Drones and Laborers are doing all the work on their own. They have not taken full control of their PFM. In many cases, the Debt Merchants are using their PFMs against them, trapping them into working harder and longer than they would ever have to if they did gain some semblance of control. Financial Builders on the other hand, are in full control, and consequently, their PFM is doing most of the work—*Manufacturing Wealth*. Builders are just dialing the controls up or down as needed over time. They might make some major or minor adjustments a few times a year, but basically their PFM is just running behind the scenes while they are off living their lives.

The amount we make has less than you might think to do with our ability to establish and maintain a worry-free financial life and to become a Financial

Builder. So how can people who make less than you have more financial freedom and how can people who make much more NOT have financial freedom? They either fundamentally understand how their personal finances actually work—or they don't.

If Financial Drones start making more money, they will ultimately enrich the Debt Merchants even more, because their behavior and lack of PFM control is the underlying problem—not the amount of money they make. If we are Financial Builders and our income increases, we will know how to harness our additional income to further serve our short-term and long-term needs. Our incomes are only part of the equation; the other part involves understanding how the decisions we make affect our PFM.

Your Money and Your Life Are Inextricably Linked

Our PFM is designed to help us achieve two equally important but competing goals: to support the lifestyle we want to have now and to fund the lifestyle we want to have in the future. Taken together, we want our PFM to sustain what we will call a "Balanced Lifestyle."

Each individual, couple, and family needs to tailor this short-term/long-term balancing act to their needs. There is no universal formula or rule indicating where the optimal balance point is for you or your family. Like all financial platitudes, "living below your means" is an inadequate measure to guide our behavior, decisions, or fine-tune our PFM to meet our specific needs. Instead, before we even have a chance to figure out what we really want—or what "living below our means" really means—we unknowingly risk getting sucked into becoming a Drone or Laborer.

Having a Balanced Lifestyle is simply the idea that we want to sustain whatever lifestyle we achieve beyond the short term. Why live beyond our means in the short term if we then must spend the rest of our lives paying the price for our early indulgences and have almost nothing as retirement approaches? This works great for Debt Merchants, but not for us. We all know we need to balance how much of our income we invest in our current lifestyle with the amount we save to be able to sustain our lifestyle, but the key is in how we control—or fail to control—our finances to achieve this.

Unlike a traditional business, our PFM eventually must shift gears and sustain us after we stop earning an income and have to live off of our accumulated assets. But, retirement doesn't mean we want to dramatically downshift our lifestyle; in reality, we may want to up-shift our lifestyle, at least for a while. And we can't do that if we have not prepared for it.

Recall that only about 60 percent of households age 55-64 have *any* retirement savings, and the median amount they have saved is only $104,000. This is NOT establishing a Balanced Lifestyle—and it's why so many people cannot retire, or cannot retire without significantly compromising their lifestyle.

Our income must fund both the "balanced" and "lifestyle" parts of the equation. Our personal finances are the machine we will use to achieve this balance. And when we don't know or don't understand our PFM, we can't possibly measure how our decisions and behaviors affect our lifestyle or its balance. Nor do we clearly understand what dials to turn or in which direction to turn them to achieve the right balance for us individually.

This is what makes our personal finances so frustrating. We know our lifestyle-related decisions have real impact on our PFM, but we just don't know exactly how and what the consequences are in the short or long term. And when things are hard to measure or difficult to see, we throw up our hands and stop trying—or bury ourselves in the details of every transaction and track every dollar, hoping to find an answer. Neither of these strategies is likely to get us anywhere.

We must do the following:

- Know that our money and our lives are inter-dependent and inextricably connected.

- Understand our PFM and how to operate and use it.

- Win the battle to control our money and maintain that control over our lives.

We need to act now.

Your Personal Finance Machine

Our PFM is both complicated and simple. However, we want to start with a straightforward, high-level view of our PFM to introduce some of the key terms and concepts we will be working with. Chapters 2 and 3 will more formally define key terms and go into more detail on how our PFM works while later chapters will discuss how to operate your PFM.

Most of us think about our personal finances as a checking and savings account, a budget, a flow of expenses, and bills to pay. We may also have an emergency fund and investment/retirement accounts. We have cars, furniture, a house, and other stuff. We spend our time balancing the checkbook, saving when we can, paying bills, and trying to stay on budget.

We tend to view our personal finances as activities and events, such as paying bills, shopping, buying electronics, furniture, or groceries, or eating out or funding our activities. We typically don't spend a lot of time thinking about our personal finances as a system or in a cause-and-effect way—and that's where the problem lies.

The whole idea of cause and effect is frequently lost in the process. When we understand our personal finances as a system or a machine, it is much easier to see the interactions and appreciate the cause and effect. Our PFM has several important components and interactions between the components.

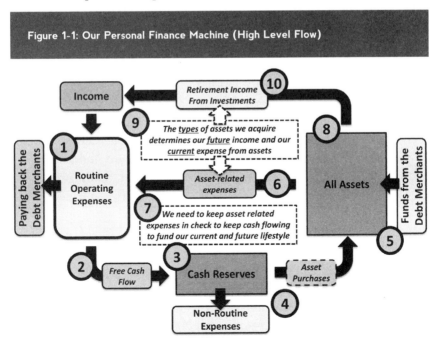

Figure 1-1: Our Personal Finance Machine (High Level Flow)

Figure 1-1 is a high-level representation of our Personal Finance Machine. Let's look at it from the perspective of how money flows through it.

(1) The first step in processing our monthly gross income is to pay taxes and cover our Routine Operating Expenses (ROE)—those that are necessary to routine living and activities such as things like food, clothing, utilities, and house and car payments.

(2) After we cover our Routine Operating Expenses, we have monthly Free Cash Flow (FCF) that contributes to our pool of Cash Reserves (CR).

(3) Cash Reserves is a critically important fund or pool of cash we need to support our PFM's healthy and smooth operation. Though it is not an emergency fund, it can serve as one.

(4) Cash Reserves does two things: it is the source of funds that flow into our Asset Engine (AE) to purchase assets (e.g., cars, furniture, boats) and funds our Non-Routine Expenses (NRE) (including lifestyle expenses like vacations and hobbies and entertainment, as well as "Gotcha" expenses like a new water heater or significant auto repair). We need our Cash Reserves to pay for our Non-Routine Expenses because these can vary widely in amount and are more episodic (less regular) than our Routine Operating Expenses.

(5) When we purchase assets like cars or boats or even our home, we typically use debt. Both the new asset and the debt create new asset-related expenses which impose an increased burden on our Routine Operating Expenses. We have to both pay back the loans (with interest), as well the asset's recurring expenses (like gas, insurance, maintenance).

(6) When we purchase new assets, the impact on our PFM is immediate in that it structurally increases our Routine Operating Expenses, and therefore reduces our Free Cash Flow, making it more difficult to maintain our pool of Cash Reserves.

7 Eventually, if we keep buying more assets and use debt to buy even more expensive assets, our Free Cash Flow continues to get squeezed and can completely dry up. Soon, without Free Cash Flow to replenish our Cash Reserves, it dries up as well. On the other hand, if we keep our asset purchases in check and we maintain a healthy Free Cash Flow, our PFM runs smoothly and effortlessly.

8 By keeping our Routine Operating Expenses low, we also will have the money to fund our retirement accounts or save for other future expenses like a new car, down payment on a house, or college fund. Most of us don't realize that we need a significant amount of cash to support medium (two to five years) and longer-term (ten to thirty year) expenses. If we allow our Routine Operating Expenses to get too large, we will simply not have enough to fund our short and long-term expenses and investment needs.

9 In the end, controlling our personal finances depends essentially upon the decisions we make relative to the assets we buy and how much debt we take on. When we buy more hard assets (like cars and boats) financed with debt, or we buy too much house, we reduce Free Cash Flow. This in turn will limit our ability to protect our Cash Reserves, save or acquire investment assets that eventually provide the money we need to buy a house, replace aging cars, pay for college, or provide the income we need to retire.

10 Finally, after years of managing our PFM, eventually we will retire and have to depend on our accumulated assets to fund our Operations Engine (OE). Accumulating only 1 or 2 percent of our Lifetime Economic Value will not cut it. We must do more.

The difficulty of the "old way" of looking at and managing our finances is that we don't separate our expenses in a way that helps us see our Free Cash Flow or our asset-related expenses. They all get blended together—so all we *see* is an endless stream of fixed and unpredictable expenses and bills, our cars, our house, needed repairs, our debts . . . and our inability to get ahead. If we cannot see the bigger picture or context, then we don't have the information we need to make informed decisions. This is the first problem that the Joneses and the Smiths face—being able to see the inner workings of their personal finances.

The simple act of re-organizing our finances into a PFM can have an immediate and profound impact on our ability to see the dynamics of our personal finances for the first time. It can show us how they actually work and how to exert control like we have never been able to before. This simple view of how our personal finances fit together and how the machine functions provides powerful insight into our finances and how to better manage them.

Like any good system, it is important to categorize things in a meaningful way and then use those categories to help measure, control, and manage the system. This is exactly what's necessary to understand the theory behind our PFM. As we build out the details around this concept, we will encounter and develop several new terms. Throughout this book, we have tried to provide clear descriptions, definitions, and names for each term. But, no matter how deeply we get into the concepts and inner workings, it all comes back to this simply high-level view of our PFM.

There is a whole new language of personal finance that comes from this newfound understanding of our PFM and how to manage and control it. For reference, we have a glossary at the end of the book with the key terms and concepts that we will cover.

So what are the benefits of this new approach? Why learn something new? Why not just keep doing what we are doing now? Think about all those businesses over one hundred years ago that had no standard frameworks or tools to organize and understand their business machines. Where would our society be today if all businesses operated on a few platitudes, some general guidelines, and "Sales - Expenses = Income"?

Understanding and leveraging our PFM can have a profoundly positive impact on our time, our financial health, and our lives, by allowing us to:

- Spend less time managing our personal finances

- Exert more control over our money—and as a result our lives

- Never *have to* manage detailed budgets or track monthly expenses

- Have a greater sense of financial freedom in the short term and long term

- Have the money we need when we need it

- Understand how our financial decisions impact us in the short term and long term

- Retire on our terms with the lifestyle we desire

This is what the Millers discovered early in their lives; to not only enrich their lives throughout their working years, but also to have exactly what they wanted for a long enjoyable retirement.

Chapter Summary:

- We control a multimillion-dollar Personal Finance Machine as represented by our lifetime earnings plus the investment value of those earnings (known as our Lifetime Economic Value).

- Very few of us keep more than 1 or 2 percent of this incredibly valuable machine, in part because we fail to understand how it works, how to manage it, and how to harness it to achieve our financial and life goals.

- There are three fundamental paths *we can chose* to follow: Financial Drone (owned by the Debt Merchants), Financial Laborer (working hard every month to achieve modest financial goals), or Financial Builders (largely letting their PFM do most of the work and achieving most of their short-term and long-term financial goals).

- Like traditional businesses, our PFM has an optimal financial structure.

- Our PFM has important interactions between our incomes, expenses, and assets that we need to understand and manage. If we don't manage them carefully, we can "break" our PFM and lose control.

Personal Finance Machine (PFM) - New Term Review

(Note: A complete list of term definitions can be found in the Glossary.)

- **Asset Engine (AE)** = Your PFM's balance sheet. It contains all your assets and liabilities (debts) and therefore defines your Net Worth. The AE represents the status and actual accumulation of the multi-million-dollar potential associated with our lifetime earnings.

- **Cash Reserves (CR)** = Pool of operating cash required to keep your PFM running smoothly.

- **Free Cash Flow (FCF)** = Excess cash after Taxes, Asset Burden, and Routine Living Expenses are covered.

- **Lifetime Economic Value (LEV)** = The projected value of lifetime earnings compounded over a working lifetime.

- **Non-Routine Expenses (NRE)** = Lifestyle Expenses + Unpredictable Expenses.

- **Operations Engine (OE)** = The part of your PFM that deals with cash flow. This is your P&L or Profit and Loss statement. It is the part of our PFM that all your income and expenses (routine and non-routine) flow through.

- **Routine Operating Expenses (ROE)** = Asset Burden + Routine Living Expenses. These are the core expenses included in the Operations Engine.

CHAPTER 2:
DEFINING ALL THE MOVING PARTS

Understanding How It Really Works

Think of the experience of buying a new car. Though we generally know how to operate it, we read the owner's manual anyway to be sure we understand what each button is for and to familiarize ourselves with the controls and learn new, potentially unfamiliar features. In short, we brush up on how to operate our new car.

If you think about it, the owner's manual is really an operating manual. It tells us how to operate this machine, but it certainly does not tell us how it works. And yet we don't have to have any idea how it works to be a safe and effective driver. We have to know that it takes gas, needs air in the tires, turns left when we turn the wheel left, slows down when we press the brake pedal, and needs service when the service light comes on. But we don't really have to understand any details about what's under the hood.

Lawnmowers, computers, mobile phones, microwaves, and countless other tools are all examples of things we use in everyday life that only need an instruction or operating manual.

Our PFM does not come pre-assembled, nor can we just buy one and start using it. We must build it from scratch with parts we already have access to. The benefit is that by taking the time to assemble it, we also acquire a much deeper understanding of how it works and what we have to do to manage and optimize it.

> Our Personal Finance Machine (PFM) is like any other machine or tool in that it is designed to do the 'heavy lifting' to help us achieve some goal. However, it is *unlike* other machines in that we do need to understand <u>how</u> it works before we can hope to control it and operate it effectively and efficiently to achieve our goals.

This chapter is an overview of all the parts of our PFM. Chapters 3-5 will then describe in detail each part's role in the machine, and finally, it will provide a more thorough review of how the whole machine works overall.

We have always had all the parts necessary to build our PFM. However, it's just that until now, nobody cared to provide the instructions for assembly. As a result, most of us just start organizing our finances in a way that seems logical, or what someone else may have suggested: checking and savings accounts, credit cards, investment accounts, and, of course, cash. However, this is just a collection of parts—not an *integrated*, functioning machine. We must assemble all the parts we already have into something much more powerful and effective than just a random collection of accounts.

Let's begin with the two main structures or "engines" that do the work within our PFM:

- The Operations Engine™ and

- The Asset Engine™

The Operations Engine

The Operations Engine (OE) is the part of our PFM that deals with cash flow. This is our P&L, or Profit and Loss statement. It is the part of our PFM through which all our income and expenses (routine and non-routine) flow. It also houses and maintains our operating cash.

This is also the part of our PFM that can keep us up at night. It pesters us when it's not operating well, and it can make our lives very unpleasant when we ignore it. If we let it, the Operations Engine can be a huge source of anxiety, frustration, and hassle. However, if we manage it properly, it can be our best friend—a smooth-running productive engine that does all the work while giving us years of happiness, freedom, and confidence.

The Asset Engine

The Asset Engine (AE) is our PFM's balance sheet. It contains all our assets and liabilities (debts) and serves as the repository of our net worth. Unlike the Operations Engine, it operates much more quietly and behind the scenes—cranking away in the shadows. Few people even think about it. Most of us focus on income and expenses and don't think about our assets as actively contributing to our financial machine even though it's the Asset Engine that controls almost everything. This component has the greatest influence on our finances and our lives—yet with the exception of our investment assets, we largely ignore it.

In traditional businesses, the Profit and Loss Statement (P&L) and the Balance Sheet are the tools that help business leaders exert control over the operations and drive value generation of the business. It is also the common language used to communicate the status, challenges, and opportunities of a business. For personal finance, the Operations Engine (P&L) and Asset Engine (Balance Sheet) are similar in concept to what is used in traditional businesses, though the structure, components, and measures are very different. As a result, the language is also different. We need different terms, definitions, and concepts to effectively understand and communicate the status, challenges, and opportunities we all face. Together these two interconnected engines form our PFM.

In addition, a traditional business's goals and management focus are far different than those in our personal lives. For example, a business does not need to "live" off its balance sheet/Asset Engine for thirty years in retirement. It is not designed specifically to fund the lifestyle of its owners. Therefore, how these tools work for personal finance is unique and critically important to understand.

The Operations Engine™

The Operations Engine (OE) is your personal finance Profit & Loss (P&L) engine. We introduced it at the end of Chapter 1, but now we are going to dig into more detail. The Operations Engine typically operates on a monthly cycle (like our bills and income) and includes seven elements:

1. Gross Income (GI) (Input)

2. Income Taxes (TX)

3. Routine Operating Expenses (ROE)

4. Free Cash Flow (FCF)

5. Cash Reserves (CR) (this is our operating cash)

6. Non-Routine Expenses (NRE)

7. Asset Engine Contributions (AEC) (Output)

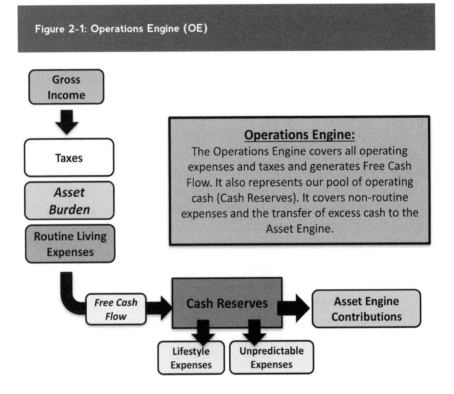

Figure 2-1: Operations Engine (OE)

Gross Income (GI)

Gross Income includes sources, such as your paycheck, government payments, interest, and dividends from income generating assets. Income taxes include all taxes associated with income, including federal, state, social security, and Medicare.

Routine Operating Expenses (ROE)

These expenses are separated into the following categories:

ROE = (Asset Burden + Routine Living Expenses)

Asset Burden™ is one of the most important components of the Operations Engine. This component includes all expenses associated with assets that we own, such as:

- Mortgage interest and principle

- Auto loans

- All other consumer loans (furniture, boats, other toys)

  ○ All non-operating expenses like insurance, property taxes, association dues, etc.

  ○ All operating expenses like gas, utilities, heating/cooling, or routine maintenance

If an expense exists specifically because of an owned asset, it belongs in Asset Burden. Take a minute to complete the worksheet to estimate your own PFM monthly Asset Burden.

Table 2-1 Monthly Asset Burden (AB) Worksheet

Asset Burden	Your PFM	% of GI
Gross Income (GI)		100%
After Tax Income		
Mortgage		
Auto Loans		
Other Loans		
Credit Card Payments		
Non-Operating Expenses		
Operating Expenses		
Total Asset Burden (AB)		

Note your total Asset Burden as a percentage of Gross Income. Does Asset Burden represent more than 40 percent of Gross Income? If so, this is a major red flag that your PFM is structurally unsound and that you may be having to compensate for this excessive level of Asset Burden by budgeting for clothes or food or everyday spending. We will dive deeper into this critical measure later in the book.

Routine Living Expenses (RLE) are expenses we incur that are associated with our basic living needs. These expenses include our basic food, clothes, health insurance, personal care expenses, and other expenses required to manage our households and lives. Routine Living Expenses does not include anything that is discretionary like eating out or entertainment or vacations. We will categorize these expenses a little differently into something we'll call Lifestyle Expenses (LSE).

We will discuss Lifestyle Expenses in more detail shortly, but the key difference between Routine Living Expenses (RLE) and Lifestyle Expenses (LSE) is that our Routine Living Expenses are the basic expenses of living as defined above. In contrast, Lifestyle Expenses are expenses that *enhance our lifestyles*— things like various forms of entertainment, eating out, hobbies, vacations, club memberships, and upscale clothing.

To organize our PFM in a way that maximizes our control, it is critical that we separate our true Routine (unavoidable) living expenses from our Lifestyle (more flexible) expenses. This distinction allows us to assemble our PFM in such a way that we can easily measure, understand, and control the most important moving parts of our PFM.

An important role of the Operations Engine is to help us compartmentalize and manage our Asset Burden and Routine Living Expenses. Both Asset Burden and Routine Living Expenses are relatively stable and consistent from month to month, based on financial commitments we have made or the result of routine behaviors we have established over time.

> A critical differentiating factor in understanding and controlling our PFM is how we compartmentalize or categorize expenses. In fact, how we classify expenses is one of the design elements that make the PFM approach so powerful. This organization is a reflection and codification of how our personal finances actually work.

While Routine Living Expenses vary by definition, they basically occur within a fairly narrow range or go up and down in a fairly predictable way. For example, we will routinely shop at the local grocery store and frequent the same barber or stylist every month. However, we don't generally spend $1,200 on groceries one month and then $400 the next; nor do we spend $30 on a haircut one month and $200 the next. Similarly, our car payment and house payments are consistent. What we spend on gas every month varies, but generally within a reasonably narrow range.

Because these expenses usually vary within a relatively narrow range each month, we don't really care if we spend a little more on groceries or gas one month and a little less on clothes the next, since the average of all our asset and routine living expenses in total should be fairly consistent month to month. *This is important!*

Free Cash Flow (FCF)

Once we have paid our taxes, Asset Burden, and Routine Living Expenses, we can calculate our total Routine Operating Expenses (Asset Burden + Routine Living Expenses), as well as our Free Cash Flow (Gross Income – Taxes – Routine Operating Expenses). Free Cash Flow then feeds and sustains our Cash Reserves. As we will see shortly, Free Cash Flow is an extremely important, but often obscured component of our PFM.

Now take a moment to estimate your Routine Living Expenses. You don't need to be overly-detailed in these estimates; however, they should not include any lifestyle-related expenses. Note that child-related expenses should not include daycare (we'll account for this later). You can now add in the Asset Burden already estimated and calculate your total Routine Operating Expenses and Free Cash Flow. Does this amount of Free Cash Flow surprise you?

Table 2-2 Monthly Routine Living Expenses (RLE) Worksheet		
Routine Living Expenses	**Your PFM**	**% of GI**
Gross Income (GI)		100%
After Tax Income (ATI)		
Groceries		
Everyday Clothing		
Household expenses		
Personal Care		
Healthcare expenses		
Smartphone/Internet		
Child/pets		
Other		
Total RLE		
Total AB (from previous worksheet)		
Total ROE (RLE + AB)		
Total Free Cash Flow (FCF) (ATI - ROE)		

In general, Routine Living Expenses should be a relatively small percentage of your Gross Income. If you are looking at the necessities only, then this may be around 10 to 15 percent or, depending on income levels, potentially less. The key thing we are looking for here is to be able to "see" our Free Cash Flow (maybe for the first time!). As we will discuss shortly, there are a lot of expenses and uses of our cash that happen *after* our Free Cash Flow. Consequently, our Free Cash Flow should be a relatively large number and a high percentage of our Gross Income. Your Free Cash Flow should be on the order of 30 to 40 percent of Gross Income. If it is not, in later chapters we will discuss how to work to adjust the structure of your PFM to get your Free Cash Flow to the level you want and need.

Cash Reserves (CR)

Cash Reserves is the pool of cash that we need to run our PFM. We often hear the advice that we should have about four to six months of expenses in cash as an emergency fund. Cash Reserves is not simply an emergency fund or something that is nice to have. It is an *essential and critical* part of our PFM. Not having a Cash Reserves is like having a car with a gas tank that only holds a gallon of gas. Every time we turned around, we would be out of gas and be at a dead stop, having to divert our attention to getting more gas into the tank instead of focusing on getting where we wanted to go in the first place. Think of how time consuming and frustrating that would be!

> *Without a healthy sustainable Cash Reserves, we can never achieve lasting control over our PFM or our financial lives.*

A fully funded Cash Reserves can also serve the function of an emergency fund—though that is not its primary role and it is certainly not something that is merely nice-to-have. A fully funded Cash Reserves is *the* most important component of a smoothly running PFM.

One challenge we have in running our personal finances as we live our lives is frequently related to the unpredictability of our expenses. This is one of the top sources of stress related to personal finance. While we can't avoid this unpredictability, we can account for and more effectively manage it. This is why we need Cash Reserves—a critical source of funds to cover our non-routine and unpredictable expenses. Without Cash Reserves, our PFM simply does not have the flexibility and resiliency to deal with the unexpected. Unlike the concept of an emergency fund, where it's there "just in case," we are constantly using our Cash Reserves. It helps us manage the unexpected and inconsistent expenses that invariably occur each month.

Non-Routine Expenses (NRE)

What about other kinds of expenses like new tires, replacing a water heater, new furniture, or a vacation? These *are* real expenses that occur frequently and we must account for and manage them. We also need to separate and manage them differently than our Routine Operating Expenses. They have too much variability and can be large relative to typical Routine Living Expenses. In short, without a well-funded Cash Reserves, Non-Routine Expenses can easily blow up our Operations Engine and prevent us from effectively controlling our PFM.

Non-Routine Expenses fall into two categories:

- **Unpredictable Expenses** (UPE):

  o   Replacing a broken appliance, storm damage, major auto repairs, etc.

  o   Other/unexpected expenses like traveling for funerals, significant medical expenses, or other financial surprises of life (things you might use an emergency fund for)

- **Lifestyle Expenses** (LSE):

  o   Vacations, sports tickets, concerts, seasonal expenses, celebrations, holiday travel

  o   Activities, interests, or hobbies, athletic/sporting pursuits, fine dining, or building a wine cellar

  o   Living expenses that are out of the norm and discretionary, such as frequently eating out, high-end shopping, luxury items, etc.

We *choose* to incur Lifestyle Expenses to enhance and reflect our chosen lifestyle. They are unique to each of us, enrich our lives, and help us feel happier and more fulfilled. These are important expenses, but they are also more discretionary and highly flexible in timing and magnitude.

By definition, Unpredictable Expenses are difficult to predict in terms of timing and magnitude. When will we need to replace the water heater or the refrigerator? We can't be sure, but when it happens there is no choice but to replace them ASAP. So it's essential to have excess cash on hand specifically for these types of events. If we don't, then these expenses are highly disruptive to our Operations Engine and frustrate our ability to manage our PFM. This can be one of the most challenging aspects of managing our personal finances—paying for the "Gotcha" expenses.

Separating these expenses from our Routine Operating Expenses allows us to measure and track our spending in each of these categories. This then helps us make important and conscious decisions about our priorities and expenses. Maintaining this distinction can also help deal with the unexpected. If we lost our job, for example, we could immediately reduce Lifestyle Expenses to zero, or near zero, quickly without impacting our ability to pay our bills and cover our Routine Operating Expenses.

Table 2-3: Monthly Lifestyle and Unpredictable Expense Worksheet		
Lifestyle and Unpredictable Expenses	**Your PFM**	**% of GI**
Gross Income (GI)		100%
Free Cash Flow (previous worksheet)		
Hobby/Activities related expenses		
Entertainment		
Eating Out		
Vacations		
Daycare		
Seasonal Expenses		
Lifestyle Clothing		
Lifestyle Personal Care		
Mobile/Cable/Streaming media		
Gifts/Donations		
Total Lifestyle (LSE)		
Unpredictable Expenses (UPE)		
Non-Routine Expenses (NRE) (LSE + UPE)		
NRE as % of FCF (NRE / FCF)		--

Let's come back to daycare expenses. Note that we have designated daycare expenses as a Lifestyle Expense. While there are arguments for daycare being a Routine Living Expense, we designate it as a Lifestyle Expense purely for practical reasons: these expenses can be large, variable, and highly disruptive, but they do not last forever. When we look at what has to give when we have significant daycare expenses, it will largely be *other* Lifestyle Expenses.

Designating daycare as a Routine Living Expense would be analogous to fast forwarding to when our kids are in college and designating any college costs we are paying as Routine Living Expenses. In either case, they are large, disruptive, and short-term (even though they don't feel that way!).

Again, take a few minutes to complete the worksheet above (Table 2–3) for your own Lifestyle and Unpredictable expenses. For expenses that do not occur monthly, such as vacations, estimate how much you spend in a given year and divide by twelve to estimate a monthly allocation. Do the same for Unpredictable Expenses. How do your total Non-Routine Expenses compare to your estimated Free Cash Flow?

> *We need to separate our **non-routine** operating expenses from our **routine** operating expenses and pay these expenses from our accumulated Cash Reserves, NOT from our monthly income stream. This is of critical importance if we want to gain and maintain control.*

An important way to think about the Operations Engine is that it has two stages:

Stage 1: Our Gross Income covers taxes, Asset Burden, and Routine Living Expenses, resulting in Free Cash Flow that pours into our Cash Reserves. Stage 1 should be as controlled, consistent, and "boring" as possible. We should never have big surprise expenses within this part of the Operations Engine. Stage 1 is not flexible and cannot handle random expenses. It has a very clear and simple task: generate an adequate and consistent level of Free Cash Flow.

Stage 2: Stage 2 is dominated by our Cash Reserves. This pool of cash is required to deal with unpredictable, discretionary, and sometimes large Non-Routine Expenses. This is an essential part of the Operations Engine that many of us don't recognize or account for. The overall goal of Stage 2 is simple: protect Cash Reserves by making sure that the outflows from Cash Reserves do not consistently exceed the inflows (Free Cash Flow).

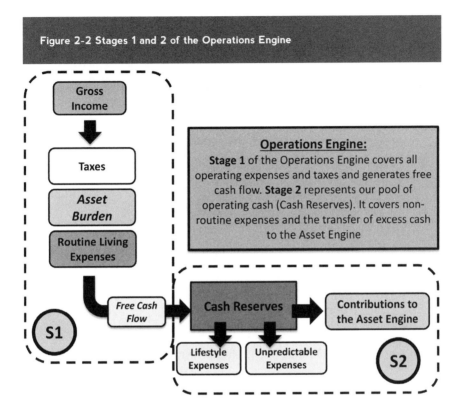

Figure 2-2 Stages 1 and 2 of the Operations Engine

The reason why we define and construct the Operations Engine in this way is to maximize our ability to exert control and create a system that is more or less "self-governing." Why do all this work with detailed budgets and monthly accounting on your own when—as you will see—our Operations Engine can do most of the work for us behind the scenes?

Before completing these worksheets, you might have said something like: "I have absolutely no Free Cash Flow. How can this possibly work for me?" The point is that most of us absolutely *do* have Free Cash Flow; it is just buried in the tangle of all our unorganized expenses.

As soon as we separate and organize our expenses into these important categories, our Free Cash Flow emerges and becomes easy to see and measure. This is a key part of how we need to assemble our PFM in a specific way that helps us exert control and improves our visibility to key components and how they interact.

> A critical requirement to effectively handle our personal finances is to have a *system* that we can easily control, measure, and manage. We are designing, organizing, and building our personal financial 'components' into a Personal Finance Machine (PFM) that we can monitor and track so we can put it to work for us. As we progress through the book, it will become more clear how we can use these expense components to help us spend less time managing our finances, paying bills, and tracking progress—and more time living our lives.

Now that we have a few basics nailed down, let's start to dig deeper into understanding our three families: The Millers (Builders) the Smiths (Laborers) and the Joneses (Drones). Here we will look back at the families when they were thirty-five years old and have been in the working world for the last ten or so years. We will use our three families' finances as examples through the rest of the book to help illustrate how a PFM works, and how these three families with similar incomes and very similar lifestyles can easily be Builders, Laborers, and Drones. And, importantly, how their decisions have a huge impact on their immediate lifestyles and financial futures.

All three families have the same monthly income but very different expense structures. Neither the Smiths nor the Joneses have much organization of their finances. They have a simple checking and a small savings account and pay the bills as they come in. Any excess cash they receive goes into savings, and their unexpected expenses are either covered by savings or go on the credit card. The Millers, on the other hand, have organized their personal finances into a proper PFM.

To help understand and see the similarities and differences between our three families, we have organized all three families' finances into the structure of a PFM, which also helps us communicate more clearly what is actually happening with each family's finances.

In Table 2–4, let's take a moment to study each family's Operations Engine, starting at the top. Each family has the exact same monthly income. Taxes are about the same, and therefore each family's take-home pay is about the same.

When we look at Asset Burden, however, we see that each family is very different. The Joneses' asset-related expenses are about 50 percent of their monthly Gross Income. It's about 40 percent for the Smiths and 30 percent for the Millers. Notice that the Millers do not have any car payments (consumer debt). They paid cash for used cars. Both the Smiths and the Joneses have newer cars that they financed. Another notable difference is that the Joneses have to pay the minimum on their $15,000 in credit card debt, while neither the Smiths or Millers carry any credit card debt.

Each family's Routine Living Expenses are similar. They shop at the same grocery and clothing stores and have similar household and personal care expenses. And while each family's Routine Operating Expenses (Asset Burden + Routine Living Expenses) are very different, they are generally consistent from month to month.

Table 2-4: 3 Family PFM Comparison (monthly)

Operations Engine Summary	Joneses	Smiths	Millers
Gross Income	$8,000	$8,000	$8,000
Taxes	$1,584	$1,520	$1,440
After Tax Income	$6,416	$6,480	$6,560
Asset Burden			
House Payment	$1,288	$1,181	$1,074
Consumer debt payments	$707	$384	$0
Insurance	$430	$330	$251
Taxes and fees	$456	$409	$365
Operating and Maintenance	$760	$809	$708
Credit Card minimum	*$250*	*$0*	*$0*
Total Asset Burden	$3,891	$3,114	$2,398
Percent of Gross Income	49%	39%	30%
Routine Living Expenses			
Phone/Internet	$50	$50	$50
Healthcare	$610	$610	$610
Food	$500	$500	$500
Clothing	$50	$50	$50
Household expenses	$100	$100	$100
Personal Care expenses	$50	$50	$50
Other	$190	$190	$190
Total Routine Living Expenses	$1,550	$1,550	$1,550
Total Routine Operating Expenses	$5,441	$4,664	$3,948
Percent of Gross Income	68%	58%	49%
Free Cash Flow	$975	$1,816	$2,612
Percent of Gross Income	12%	23%	33%
Lifestyle Expenses			
Eating out	$50	$80	$125
Daycare	$0	$0	$0
Vacations	$100	$150	$200
Activities/Entertainment	$25	$160	$200
Cable/Streaming media	$125	$125	$125
Personal Care expenses	$50	$100	$175
Other	$175	$245	$255
Total Lifestyle Expenses	$525	$860	$1,080
Unpredictable expense	*$500*	*$1,500*	*$1,500*
Automatic Savings	$80	$450	$900
Remaining cash *this month*	-$130	-$994	-$868
Initial Cash Reserves	*$2,000*	*$5,000*	*$32,000*
Credit Card Balance	$15,000	$0	$0
Combined CC and Cash Reserves	-$13,000	$5,000	$32,000
New Cash Reserves	*$1,870*	*$4,006*	*$31,132*
New Credit Card Charges	$1,000	$0	$0
New Credit Card Balance	$16,000	$0	$0
Combined CC and Cash Reserves	*-$14,130*	*$4,006*	*$31,132*

The most striking difference between the three families is in the size of their Asset Burden and, consequently, their Free Cash Flow. They all have positive Free Cash Flow, but the Smiths and the Joneses don't see it because they have not organized their finances to be able to see it. On the other hand, the Millers *see* over $2,500 every month flow into their Cash Reserves—and it *feels good* to see that large, positive, and consistent cash flow every month.

We also see some big differences when we look at Lifestyle Expenses. The Millers spend twice as much as the Joneses on things like eating out, vacations, personal care, and club memberships. The Millers are also spending more than the Smiths.

Also note that portions of Lifestyle Expenses are allocations. For example, none of the families are spending $xxx/month on vacations, but they are *allocating* $xxx/month to cover the annual cost of the vacations they plan to take for the year.

Each family also has an automatic monthly savings or investment plan. But again, the Millers are putting away far more than either of the other two families.

To demonstrate a point, we have introduced a significant Unpredictable Expense in this particular month just to see how each family deals with it. Each family has a $1,500 unforeseen Gotcha expense that they must deal with. It might be a major car repair, a medical expense, something to do with the house, or some other event. The cause of the $1,500 expense is not relevant; the point here is the different ways each family handles the expense.

The Joneses handle the situation by paying $500 of the total $1,500 expense and putting the rest on their credit card, basically because they have few other options. Both the Smiths and the Millers pay the entire expense this month. Each family's total expenses exceed their Operating Income this month, thereby forcing all of them to dip into their Cash Reserves to cover the shortfall caused by the unpredictable $1,500 expense.

The Joneses, however, are in a tough spot because they have almost no Cash Reserves to cover their shortfall. The $2,000 that they have is little more than a token buffer against monthly expenses. This is, of course, why they could simply not pay the whole $1,500 expense. The Joneses are loath to drain their limited cash, so they put most of the expense ($1,000) on the credit card, which increases their credit card balance to $16,000 and their minimum payment to $267 from $250.

The Smiths are a little better off, but not much. The $5,000 that they have is about one month's worth of Routine Operating Expenses. While they don't have credit card debt and chose to pay the entire $1,500, it has eroded their cash position pretty significantly.

The Millers however, have about eight months of Routine Operating Expenses in Cash Reserves. Consequently, they barely notice the $1,500 unpredictable expense. They just pay it and move on.

Since neither the Smiths nor the Joneses have organized their finances into a PFM structure, they cannot see all the moving parts—Asset Burden, Routine Living Expenses, or Free Cash Flow—inside of their Operations Engine. Consequently, every month is an adventure for the Smiths and the Joneses. What new expenses will pop up? How will they handle them, given their limited Cash Reserves? Will they maintain their savings or abandon them at the next big unplanned expense?

The Smiths and Joneses are living on a financial roller coaster. They are having a good or a bad month based on whether their total expenses exceed their after-tax income. They will likely begin to panic if they start having several bad months in a row, and their natural reaction will be to start budgeting more aggressively to reduce their spending. However, where are they going to reduce spending? Probably Lifestyle Expenses like eating out, shopping, entertainment (the only things they can realistically cut in the short term). Unfortunately, these things won't help them regain control of their situation. Meanwhile, the Joneses' credit card balance just keeps creeping up.

The Millers, on the other hand, don't even notice the ups and downs of their Lifestyle and Unpredictable expenses. They see their $2,612 in Free Cash Flow every month as it contributes to their $32,000 Cash Reserves. Paying for the unplanned $1,500 expense is not an issue because it just comes out of Cash Reserves. Even if they have several months of excessive Unpredictable Expenses, they wouldn't panic because of their substantial Cash Reserves buffer.

So how did the Millers accumulate $32,000 in Cash Reserves? Simple: They kept their Asset Burden low and funneled most of their Free Cash Flow into building up their Cash Reserves over time. They avoided new cars and car loans and avoided credit card debt. They also focused more of their spending on lifestyle-related activities than on big asset-related purchases.

The Smiths are doing OK. They have no credit card debt, but they are perilously close to the edge. This month alone took a big bite out of their Cash Reserves (-$994) and next month they will probably tighten their belts to see if they can make up the lost ground.

Each of these families is a classic representation of each of the three Financial Paths we introduced in the prior chapter. The Joneses are struggling with credit card debt, trapped by very high Asset Burden, and have literally become Debt Merchant *drones*. The Smiths are *laboring* every month to stay one step ahead and out of reach of the Debt Merchants. And the Millers are *building* the value of their PFM every month without even breaking a sweat. In the end, all three families have the exactly same income every month, but vastly different levels of financial burden and stress. The key differences are: 1) how they managed their asset-related expenses, 2) the size of their Free Cash Flow, 3) how much Cash Reserves they have, and 4) how disciplined they are in maintaining and protecting that cash.

> A fundamental difference between Financial Builders, Laborers, and Drones is the size of their Cash Reserves. When we have very little or no Cash Reserves, we have very little operating margin or buffer and simply cannot handle any financial surprises. Then, when the inevitable "'Gotcha" expenses occur, we have to use our credit cards to cover the expense and thus step onto the path to becoming a Financial Drone.

NOTE: We are assuming that there are no daycare expenses for the three families—either because there are no children, one spouse stays home, or the children are no longer of daycare age. We could have easily included daycare expenses and then adjusted all the rest of the expenses accordingly. However, we chose not to include it because it generally only occurs during one phase of our working lives rather than across all our working years.

In Summary: The Operations Engine

The Operations Engine is a relatively simple part of our PFM. It is really a two-stage "cash flow" engine. Stage 1 takes in our monthly income, pays all our Routine Operating Expenses (Asset Burden + Routine Living Expenses), and generates a fairly consistent level of Free Cash Flow that flows into Stage 2 (our Cash Reserves).

Stage 2 then acts as a giant buffer that absorbs and covers all our highly variable, frequently large, and often random Non-Routine Expenses (Lifestyle Expenses + Unpredictable Expenses). Stage 2 also has another very important function: It connects the Operations Engine to the Asset Engine. In addition to covering our Non-Routine Expenses, our Cash Reserves funds our Asset Engine.

From an input/output perspective, our Operations Engine looks like this:

- Income (Input)

- Free Cash Flow (Stage 1 output/Stage 2 input)

- Contributions to our Asset Engine (Output)

The Asset Engine™

The Asset Engine is similar to a 'balance sheet' in the business world, in that it houses all our assets and debts and is the partner to the Operations Engine. The Operations and Asset Engines work together to form our Personal Finance Machine (PFM).

The Asset Engine has one input, two primary components, and two primary outputs:

- Asset Engine Contributions (Input)

- Assets (Component)

- Liabilities (Component)

- Net Worth Gain (Output)

- Asset Burden (Output)

Assets

Assets can be broken down into four categories:

Dead Assets (DA): These assets depreciate by design. They include anything with an engine, furniture and furnishings, and most other 'stuff' that we own that gets used. We are not making a value judgment about having Dead Assets; we all have them, and they provide great enjoyment, make our lives easier, and may be a key part of our lifestyle choices. They may even be critical to our jobs, but financially speaking, they are still dead (as in going to become worthless over time).

Marginal Assets (MA): Marginal assets include assets that *can* appreciate or have a stable value over time. These include real estate (your house, rental properties, and land), valuables and collectables like jewelry, art, etc. They're not exactly dead, but they aren't really living either. These assets are generally tangible; things that you can hold, use or look at and have a baseline value that can fluctuate. Importantly, they may also have associated expenses to maintain or protect them, but they generally don't wear-out or become obsolete like Dead Assets. They also are typically harder to sell (less liquid) than investment assets.

Living (investment) Assets (LA): This class of assets includes mutual funds, stocks, bonds, REITs, etc. These can be either tax-advantaged (i.e., 401(k) or IRAs) or taxable (i.e., after-tax money invested in a brokerage account). Living Assets generally have three things in common: they're electronic (rights to an asset that you don't actually take delivery of), they have intrinsic value that is intended to go up over time (that is primarily why we buy them!), and they have an active market to facilitate rapid, low-cost transactions or liquidity.

Cash: Cash includes any readily accessible *liquid* funds in accounts like money markets, checking, savings, etc. While cash is certainly an asset and gets counted as part of our Net Worth, we will be *managing* and thinking about our Cash Reserves as part of the Operations Engine.

Liabilities

Liabilities are debts that we are contractually obligated to repay with interest. Liabilities are generally funds borrowed from a bank or other lender to purchase assets. Debt is also frequently tied to specific assets like our house or cars. If we fail to continue payments, we can lose our house or car to help repay the debt. Education debt or consumer debts, like credit cards, are not tied to specific assets, but our legal commitment to pay them off remains the same.

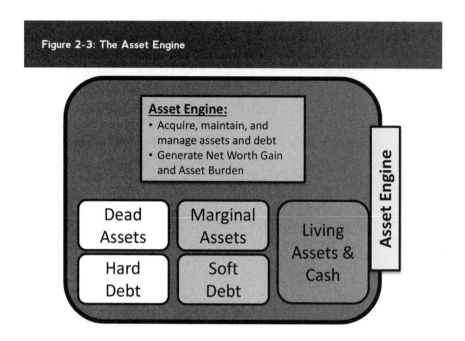

Figure 2-3: The Asset Engine

Liabilities can be broken down into two categories:

- Hard Debt

- Soft Debt

Hard Debt: Hard Debt is all consumer debt, including credit cards, retail charge cards, and auto loans. Hard debt interest is usually much higher than mortgage debt and generally cannot be deducted for tax purposes. We call it *hard* debt because it is usually tied to Dead Assets and the interest cannot be deducted.

Soft Debt: This is generally reserved for mortgage debt. Soft Debt has three features: 1) it is used to purchase marginal or investment assets, 2) its interest is frequently tax deductible, and 3) it typically has a lower interest rate (compared to Hard Debt).

Net Worth: Net Worth is a measure of the current snapshot status of our Asset Engine. It is simply the difference between Assets and Liabilities and includes all types of assets. Net Worth can also be further characterized by the composition or mix of assets that contribute to it:

- Healthy (mostly Investment and Marginal Assets)

- Stable (mostly Marginal Assets and Cash)

- Unhealthy (mostly Dead Assets and Cash)

Net Worth Gain (NWG)

Net Worth Gain is the change in our Net Worth over time, usually from one year to the next. An asset can fluctuate in value from one year to the next, but over time the overwhelming "force" of depreciation or appreciation will move the value of the asset either up or down.

Asset Engine Contributions (AEC) to our assets from the Operations Engine can also increase Net Worth. As we pay off debt or improve assets (redo the kitchen), our net ownership value increases.

Figure 2-4: Net Worth Gain (NWG)

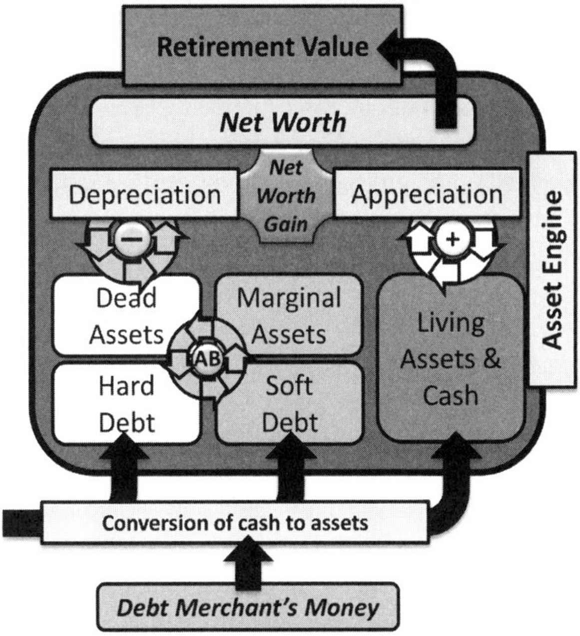

For example, if most of our Net Worth is in cars, ATVs, or boats, the value of these assets will decrease rapidly over time due to intrinsic depreciation. At the same time, our ownership increases as we pay off the debt. However, these assets will eventually become nearly worthless, even though we have paid off the debt and fully own them.

We have all certainly seen plenty of those ten-year-old boats, cars, or ATVs parked along the highway with a shockingly low price or "best offer" sign. Most of our *stuff* simply does not age well.

If most of our Net Worth is tied to our home, then we usually can expect that it will be relatively secure, stable, and may in fact grow over time. As we pay off our mortgage, our Net Worth will generally slowly increase (even if the value of your home is stable, slowly declining, or slowly increasing). As we will discuss later, even if our equity is growing over time, that does not mean that our home has been a good investment.

If most of our Net Worth is tied to investment assets, then we can typically expect significant short and medium-term fluctuations in value; but in most cases, there will be overall positive long-term appreciation.

Retirement Value (RV)

Retirement Value is not the same as Net Worth; it is a subset of our Net Worth and represents the portion of our Asset Engine that can support our lifestyle long into the future. Retirement Value is measured by taking the value of our retirement assets today and projecting them forward on an inflation-adjusted basis to the target date of our retirement. Our retirement assets include all our tax-advantaged investments like 401(k), 403(b), IRAs, or Roth IRAs, plus whatever taxable investments we have dedicated to support our retirement. Typically, this calculation includes the following factors: years to retirement, current retirement asset values, projected annual contributions, and estimated rate of return.

Let's look again at our three families. While we know that they have the exact same income, they have converted their excess cash into very different assets over time. The Millers bought used cars and funneled much of their excess cash into their investments. They have average furniture, appliances, and electronics. The Smiths have newer cars, some high-end furniture, and maybe a boat. However, the Joneses have it all: new cars, a boat, and they have splurged on high-end furniture and electronics for their home. They have a lot of Dead Assets, have almost $33,000 in Hard Debt, and have relatively little invested in Living Assets.

Three families - same income, different asset mix (at year 10)	Joneses (Drones)	Smiths (Laborers)	Millers (Builders)
Table 2-5: Asset Comparison Among the Three Families			
Dead Assets	$51,752	$36,052	$23,118
Home	$337,849	$309,695	$281,541
Other Marginal Assets	$20,000	$15,000	$10,000
Cash	$2,000	$5,000	$32,000
Living (Investment) Assets	$5,000	$30,000	$110,000
Total Assets	**$416,601**	**$395,747**	**$456,659**
Hard Debt	$32,699	$9,624	$0
Soft Debt	$219,237	$200,967	$182,698
Total Debt	**$251,937**	**$210,592**	**$182,698**
Net Worth	**$164,664**	**$185,155**	**$273,961**
Appreciation	$7,477	$8,484	$12,855
Depreciation	-$7,763	-$5,408	-$3,468
Net Worth Growth (NWG)	**-$286**	**$3,076**	**$9,387**
% Change	-0.2%	1.7%	3.4%

We notice that each family's total assets are not that far apart in value; however, this view hides what is actually going on below the surface. While each family's Net Worth is somewhat different, what is important is that their *Net Worth Gain* is very different. The Joneses have a negative Net Worth Gain (-$286). What they have gained in appreciation is more than cancelled by depreciation of their Dead Assets. The $51,752 they have in dead assets is depreciating quickly and relentlessly, and this will only accelerate over time.

On the other hand, the Millers' Net Worth is healthy and growing ($9,387) and will continue to do so because it's largely driven by Living Assets and home equity. The Smiths' Net Worth is growing ($3,076) more rapidly than the Joneses because their depreciation takes a smaller chunk out of their otherwise healthy appreciation. But the Smiths are still nowhere near the Millers in the underlying health and growth of their Asset Engine.

So you may ask, OK, the Millers are in great shape, but we are looking at them at age 35. How did the Millers get to this great spot? Is it realistic that they could have gotten to this point by age 35? The answer is emphatically yes. We modeled all three families from their first jobs starting after college and kept the same approach (Drone, Laborer, and Builder). So that their personal financial situation shown now at age 35 for each couple is a realistic model of what they would have achieved to this point. The Millers could and did get to this spot without any crazy stunts or risks. They just focused early on building their Cash Reserves and avoiding excessive Asset Burden and depreciation. Over time their Cash Reserves grew in natural sync with their incomes and expenses.

Asset Burden (AB)

As discussed previously, Asset Burden is the monthly expenses associated with all the tangible assets that we own. Most of the Marginal and Dead Assets we own have routine expenses associated with their ownership: insurance, maintenance, usage costs, storage, etc. So when we make decisions to acquire new assets, we're not only impacting our Net Worth Gain (through appreciation and depreciation), we also are impacting Asset Burden.

Asset Burden is an output of our Asset Engine and a *negative* coupling factor between our two engines; that is, the larger it is, the more negative the impact it has on the Operations Engine (higher expenses). Asset Burden is the often hidden "feedback loop" from our Asset Engine to our Operations Engine and reflects the decisions we make relative to the assets we acquire and own. By using Debt Merchant money to buy even more expensive assets, we magnify the negative impact Asset Burden has on our Operations Engine.

This is exactly what we see playing out for our three families. The Joneses have the most stuff, the highest Asset Burden, the most fragile finances, and therefore the most stress, time commitment, and frustration relative to managing their personal finances. The Millers, on the other hand, are rarely even thinking about their finances—but when they do, it's with satisfaction, comfort, and confidence.

In Summary: The Asset Engine

Unlike the Operations Engine, the Asset Engine has a variety of internal forces and moving parts that impact how it changes over time. Its role is also very different from the Operations Engine. The Asset Engine must grow over time and eventually become the source of funds in retirement or a new stage of life to support our Operations Engine and our desired lifestyle.

After we retire or are ready for a new stage in life, we will need to rely on our Asset Engine to generate a level of income (combined with other sources like Social Security) to continue the lifestyle we have come to enjoy and expect to continue. This is the central long-term goal/role of the Asset Engine–and it only comes from large and consistent Net Worth Gain.

When we move cash from Cash Reserves into the Asset Engine [Asset Engine Contributions (AEC)], we are often converting our cash into some other type of asset (Marginal, Living, or Dead). If we use debt to increase the "size" of the assets we purchase (like using an auto loan to buy a much more expensive car than we could have afforded with cash alone), then the impact on our Asset Engine as well as on our Operations Engine gets magnified.

While our Operations Engine is not designed or intended to grow in value, our Asset Engine *is* designed to grow in both value and in health. Every year we should have a positive Net Worth Gain that becomes larger and healthier over time (Higher proportion from Living Assets and lower proportion from Marginal and Dead Assets).

This is the first step in understanding how we *Manufacture Wealth* and how we get to the point when we can let go of our jobs and have the necessary income generated from our Asset Engine support us in retirement. The long-term objective for our Asset Engine is to build its Net Worth (especially Retirement Value) until we officially retire, enter staged retirement, or simply decide to do something different.

Putting It All Together: Our Personal Finance Machine

Like any system, the details can get complicated, but our PFM is pretty straight forward. Stage 1 (S1) of the Operations Engine is designed to just chug along, minding its own business and generating a consistent rate of Free Cash Flow (again, because it is only dealing with routine and generally consistent expenses *by design* that flows into our Cash Reserves). At the same time we are managing our Cash Reserves [Operations Engine Stage 2 (S2)] by using it to pay for Non-Routine Expenses that support our lifestyle (Lifestyle Expenses) and cover any Unpredictable Expenses. Excess cash moves into the Asset Engine and is converted it into various assets as we deem appropriate (specific savings or retirement accounts or to purchase Dead Assets or make home improvements).

The Asset Engine generates Asset Burden (from Dead and Marginal Assets) that feeds back into the Operations Engine as a Stage 1 expense. In addition, the Asset Engine is "self-generating" Net Worth Gain via the aggregate depreciation and appreciation of our assets plus any new contributions from our Operations Engine.

So our PFM is comprised of these interlocking engines that both depend on and influence each other. Free Cash Flow, Asset Engine Contributions, and Asset Burden represent the flow of cash through our PFM. They tie our engines together. Asset Burden is a *negative* "coupling" or burden that the Asset Engine imposes on the Operations Engine and directly impacts Free Cash Flow. Asset Engine Contributions are a positive coupling (cash contribution) from the Operations Engine to the Asset Engine. Cash Reserves and the composition of our Net Worth are two pools of assets that we want to make sure we are managing effectively. We want to maintain a target level of Cash Reserves over time and we want to grow the value and health of Net Worth over time.

While it's easy to see how Cash Reserves is a pool or reservoir of funds, Net Worth can also be viewed in this context. There is just a lot more complexity in understanding the dynamics of how Net Worth evolves over time, and therefore we need to pay close attention to the decisions we make that indirectly and directly influence Net Worth over time.

Our personal finances are not just an endless stream of bills to pay, budgets to manage, and accumulated stuff in our house and garage. It is not an impenetrable "black box" that nobody can understand, nor is it an endless stream of fragmented advice and platitudes that nobody can use. We are operating a system—a machine—that we now have a better understanding of how it works. Now we can much more effectively control it, manage it, and *harness* it to meet our financial and life goals.

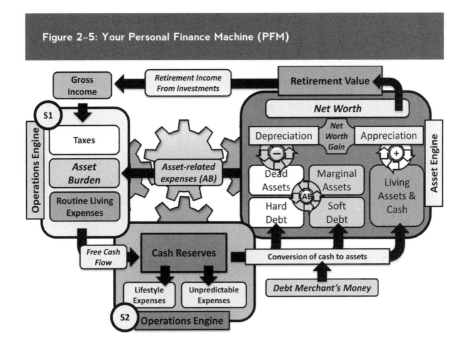

Figure 2–5: Your Personal Finance Machine (PFM)

Chapter Summary:

- Our PFM is comprised of two engines: The Operations and Asset Engines.

- Each engine plays a unique and important role in the overall operation of our PFM.

- There is a unique language, set of definitions, organization, and concepts that are important to understanding our PFM and how it works.

- The Operations Engine has two Stages. Stage 1 deals with income and Routine Living Expenses. Stage 2 deals with Cash Reserves and Non-Routine Expenses (Lifestyle and Unpredictable).

- Free Cash Flow is a critical component of our Operations Engine that is frequently buried and difficult to see.

- Cash Reserves is an essential component of our PFM and represents Stage 2 of our Operations Engine. Maintaining a healthy level of Cash Reserves is a critical responsibility that we have as managers of our PFM

- The two engines are connected by Asset Burden (negative coupling) and AE Contributions (positive coupling).

- Asset Burden is the result of the decisions we make relative to assets and debt and directly impacts Free Cash Flow.

- There are three types of Assets (Dead, Marginal, and Living), and they each play important roles in the operations of our PFM.

- The Asset Engine generates Asset Burden and Net Worth Gain. Net Worth Gain ultimately drives Retirement Value that in turn funds our Operations Engine after we retire.

Personal Finance Machine (PFM) - New Term Review

(Note: A complete list of term definitions can be found in the Glossary.)

- **Asset Burden (AB)** = All expenses associated with assets we own.

- **Asset Engine Contributions (AEC)** = Movement of cash from the Operations Engine into the Asset Engine. Often this includes the conversion of that cash into assets other than cash.

- **Dead Assets (DA)** = All assets that depreciate over time.

- **Gross Income (GI)** = Income from all sources.

- **Hard Debt (HD)** = All consumer (e.g., car loans) and credit card debt.

- **Lifestyle Expenses (LSE)** = Expenses related to vacations, activities, entertainment, etc.

- **Living (investment) Assets (LA)** = All investment-related assets.

- **Marginal Assets (MA)** = Assets that can hold or increase in value, but also have ongoing costs of ownership.

- **Net Worth (NW)** = Total value of assets – liabilities.

- **Net Worth Gain (NWG)** = Year over year change in Net Worth.

- **Retirement Value (RV)** = The projected value of our retirement assets at retirement.

- **Routine Living Expenses (RLE)** = All routine expenses associated with everyday living.

- **Soft Debt (SD)** = Mortgage debt or any other debt where the interest is deductible

- **Taxes (TX)** = Income taxes from all sources.

- **Unpredictable Expenses (UPE)** = All unexpected expenses that are outside of Asset Burden, Routine Living Expenses, and Lifestyle Expenses.

SECTION TWO:
UNDERSTANDING HOW IT WORKS

CHAPTER 3:

THE OPERATIONS ENGINE:

YOUR CASH MANAGEMENT MACHINE

Now that we have defined the various components and how they are assembled into the "Twin Engines" of our PFM, the next step is to more clearly understand how they interact and work together as a powerful tool. This chapter will focus on the Operations Engine to develop an understanding of what happens when we manipulate its various dials and levers.

For simplicity, we will ignore income. While income can vary—sometimes dramatically from month to month—this chapter's goal is to understand how our PFM works. For these purposes, we will assume that monthly income is fixed and steady.

To fully embrace the mechanism of the PFM, we need to let go of how we operate our personal finances today. Many of us are simply mixing all our various monthly expenses into a big blender, paying bills as they come, and then applying what's left to the most urgent project we have.

Some of us may have budgets or special allocations for various expenses. We may use a spreadsheet or financial software or some other product to track expenses. We may be focused on budgeting, tracking our expenses (sometimes even down to the penny), and generally focusing on the details. This is not a bad thing; it's just incomplete and *tactical* instead of comprehensive and *strategic*. This is what Financial Laborers do. They keep their finances in line by brute force, but they miss the larger context and the opportunity to engage their PFM.

While this tactical approach can work for the most disciplined and detail-oriented of us, it frequently fails to live up to its promise. It's a lot of work to manage only a portion of the total equation. It's like counting calories while failing to address the many other components to weight management.

In fact, dieting is something of a "last resort" tactic when we don't understand how the weight management system works; it fails to incorporate the importance of healthy foods, moderation, sleep, stress, exercise, and good habits. If we appreciate and use a *system* of weight management, then dieting becomes a much less important, but also a more effective tool since it's one part of our overall strategy. If all we have is the diet, then we are: 1) working way too hard; 2) likely to fail; and 3) missing an opportunity to achieve an even better result with less effort.

The exact same dynamic is in play with our personal finances. Neither diets nor budgets are bad. They have a place in our toolbox, but they should not be the only tool we use.

> We have all been taught to immerse ourselves in the details of our personal finances—but more often than not, this approach simply doesn't work. We need to immerse ourselves in understanding and controlling the big levers (vs. the little ones). We need to focus on our Personal Finance Machine's structure at the *macro* level. Once the structure is established—either by your design or (sadly) by the Debt Merchants—the details become less important.

By way of another simple analogy, let's say we really care about gas mileage but we own a gas-guzzling SUV that gets only 10 miles to the gallon. No matter how much we try to improve our mileage by driving smoothly and not pounding on the gas pedal, we still feel frustrated every time we drive—because no matter what we do, we might squeeze out 12 MPG, but we will never get to 20 MPG.

Getting that extra 2 MPG (12 vs. 10) will consume a lot of our time, energy, and attention, but it will also generate significant frustration as we are constantly adjusting our driving and our lifestyle to accommodate our "structurally" poor mileage automobile. We simply can't make a gas guzzler into a gas efficient car by how we operate it, and the paltry 2 MPG we gained is nowhere near our goal.

On the other hand, if we own an automobile that is designed to average 40 MPG, we have no need to worry about our driving habits. We stop worrying every time the price of gas spikes; we buy gas where and when it's convenient; we don't worry about how aggressively we drive or whether we can afford to take a longer road trip. In short, we do not let our automobile dictate our life and create unnecessary drama because it structurally gets great gas mileage. And we don't really care if one month we're getting 36 MPG and the next it's 42, because it's on average 4 times higher than 10 MPG!

Now what if we replaced the word "MPG" with "Free Cash Flow" and the word "automobile" with "Operations Engine"? Are our personal finances structured to be a major cash hog, sucking up every dollar, forcing us to budget, shop sales, skip lattes, etc.? Or are they structured to produce a river of Free Cash Flow every month? If our finances are structured to generate significant excess cash, will we feel the need to budget, cut back on lattes, and feel frustrated every time we paid the bills? Of course not.

It's not that designing our PFM to burn through most of our cash and deliver 10 MPG is bad per say, or that being super frugal and generating 40 MPG is good. We should simply make a conscious decision about how we want to structure our PFM and recognize the implications of those decisions on our life and lifestyle.

Said differently: if we are budgeting and tracking our spending and stretching our paycheck every month because we need to, we are operating a "cash hog" PFM. Trying to manipulate it into generating 15 or 20 MPG is exhausting, frustrating, and often impossible. This is the essence of the problem with personal finance today. We are all focused on the details and not on the structure, which means that no amount of budgeting will convert our gas hog Operations Engine into a cash-efficient one.

A better idea would be to restructure our PFM to generate 20 or 30 MPG. If we can restructure our PFM effectively, we can then choose to invest time and energy in detailed expense budgeting (fine-tuning) or not—by choice, not necessity. We also have to change our mindset to focus on the system of our Operations and Asset Engines. It's not difficult; it's just a different way to think and manage, which requires a bit of effort at first.

To better manage our PFM, we need to focus on our cash flow—our MPG, if you will. We want to be crystal clear about this flow, what influences it, and how to keep it flowing in ways that keep our engines healthy, working together, in balance, and working *for* us.

There are three major elements of our Operations Engine that we want to focus on as we think about cash flow.

Cash Reserves

This reflects our capacity to deal with the unexpected. Cash Reserves is our source of flexibility and freedom. When it's empty, our engines are at risk of grinding to a halt at the slightest disruption in our income or from a major unexpected expense. A lack of Cash Reserves makes us vulnerable to becoming Financial Drones, and dramatically increases the risk of sliding into bankruptcy.

Free Cash Flow

This is the source of fuel for our PFM. It represents the rate at which we can replenish our Cash Reserves and reflects the amount of flexibility that we have to redirect our flow of cash to deal with changes in our lifestyle, handle emergencies, replenish Cash Reserves, increase savings, etc. If we squeeze Free Cash Flow down to a trickle, Cash Reserves will inevitably dry up.

Cash Burn (CB)

Cash Burn is the monthly drain of our Cash Reserves. It includes both our Non-Routine Expenses (NRE) as well as Asset Engine Contributions (AEC) to our Asset Engine. This represents the proverbial hole in the bottom of our Cash Reserves bucket. Remember from Chapter 2 that Stage 1 of our Operations Engine covers Asset Burden and our Routine Living Expenses. Our Stage 1 expenses are frequently a large percentage of our total expenses; however, much of our monthly spending may come from Stage 2 of our Operations Engine.

Spending from our Cash Reserves in the form of Lifestyle Expenses or Asset Engine Contributions to our Asset Engine (new asset purchases or savings) can sometimes be larger than our Routine Living Expenses or Asset Burden. We need to effectively manage our Cash Burn since this combined with Free Cash Flow determines if our Cash Reserves are stable, growing, or declining in the short and long term.

Think about Free Cash Flow, Cash Reserves, and Cash Burn as a system comprised of a *river* of Free Cash Flow pouring into a *reservoir* of cash. This reservoir has a *dam* that controls the outflow of cash (Cash Burn). If we open the gates of the dam to allow more flow out than is coming in, our lake of cash reserves declines. If we close off the gates, the lake fills. If we cut off the river of Free Cash Flow, then the lake level can't increase no matter what we do with the dam. To maintain a stable level of Cash Reserves we want to have our average monthly Cash Burn and average monthly Free Cash Flow in balance. If either Free Cash Flow or Cash Burn becomes much higher or lower, relative to each other, then the level of our Cash Reserves will start to change—sometimes dramatically and rapidly.

Figure 3–1: Cash Reserves Flow

From a practical standpoint, Free Cash Flow and Cash Burn are rarely equal. Consequently, the level of our Cash Reserves is rarely the same month to month. However, the *average* Free Cash Flow and the *average* Cash Burn should be fairly equal over time if we want to maintain Cash Reserves within a target range. Measuring and controlling our average Free Cash Flow and average Cash Burn allows us to effectively manage the level of our Cash Reserves. When Free Cash Flow consistently exceeds Cash Burn, our Cash Reserves are growing. When Cash Burn consistently exceeds Free Cash Flow, our Cash Reserves are declining. Consequently, we want to be sure that we are measuring our Free Cash Flow, Cash Burn, and Cash Reserves over time and look at the averages and the trends vs. what happens in any given month.

We can frequently have big negative swings in the level of our Cash Reserves because of a large Cash Burn event like a vacation or new furniture or a remodeling project. However, we have much less ability to create a big positive change in Free Cash Flow because Free Cash Flow is the output of our

Stage 1 Operations Engine which generally does not fluctuate significantly. Though we may sometimes have a big positive cash windfall that adds to our Cash Reserves when we sell something, get a bonus, or receive a tax refund, the more typical situation is that we experience big reductions in Cash Reserves that we need to replenish over time.

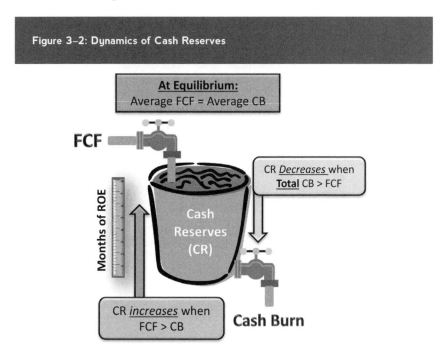

Figure 3–2: Dynamics of Cash Reserves

In part, this is why we need to maintain a relatively large Cash Reserve and consistent Free Cash Flow. Cash Reserves plays the role of a buffer that allows us to absorb big negative Cash Burns events without having Cash Reserves fall to zero.

Months of Cash Reserves

Usually we measure our level of Cash Reserves in months of Routine Operating Expenses (ROE). For example, the Millers have about eight months of Routine Operating Expenses ($32,000 in Cash Reserves vs. about $4,000 in monthly Routine Operating Expenses). This allows the Millers to easily absorb a relatively large Cash Burn event like a vacation or major house repair and still have enough of a buffer as they wait for their Cash Reserves to recover over time.

It is important to restate that our Cash Reserve is NOT an Emergency Fund, nor is it part of our savings or investments (Living Assets). It is much more than that. Our Cash Reserve is our PFM's energy reserve—it's our reserve fuel tank, a *vital c*omponent that we use every day to support and manage our PFM. Cash Reserves represents our capacity to handle the financial ups and downs of life. A healthy and stable Cash Reserve is the key difference between Builders, Laborers, and Drones, which is why we need to understand what impacts it, how to measure it, and how to manage it effectively.

Our Cash Reserves has three essential functions. It must:

- Cover Non-Routine Expenses

    o Unpredictable Expenses (new furnace or a major auto repair)

    o Lifestyle Expenses (vacation or holiday spending)

- Provide contributions to our Asset Engine

    o Help to purchase new assets (e.g., new car down payment, furniture, investments)

- Serve as a financial cushion in case of a major disruption (e.g., unemployment, major medical expense). This is the classic idea of an "emergency fund"

Our primary responsibility in effectively controlling and managing our PFM is to maintain a healthy and sustainable Cash Reserves. When this essential component is depleted or non-existent we have a *broken* PFM that takes all our time and energy to manage. It makes us feel trapped, poor and miserable, and gives us nothing of value in return.

Managing Cash Reserves

Note: This section gets into the weeds of effectively managing our Cash Reserves. Understanding these concepts and dynamics are important, but they are nothing that we have to measure and track by hand. This is one of the key features that will be available on the PFM website. www.manufacturingwealth.com

If we are actively spending from our Cash Reserves, how can we begin to consistently replenish it over time? Let's start by looking at some simple relationships. First, let's consider our Cash Reserves as some number of months of our Routine Operating Expenses. Financial advisors often say that you need four to six months of cash in an emergency fund. Knowing how many months of expenses we have in our Cash Reserves is important, but we also need to have some sense of whether our Cash Reserves is going up or down over time. The measure that we use to determine this is our Replacement Rate (RR)—that is, the number of months it takes to add one month of our Routine Operating Expenses to our Cash Reserves.

Think about Replacement Rate as taking our average monthly Free Cash Flow (money going into CR) minus our average monthly Cash Burn (money going out of CR) and dividing it into our Routine Operating Expenses. This is the Replacement Rate (RR).

> Replacement Rate (in Months) =
> Routine Operating Expenses / (Free Cash Flow − Cash Burn)

This makes sense, but if average Cash Burn is close to, above, or equal to Free Cash Flow (as is frequently the case because over time Cash Reserves should be stable: Free Cash Flow = CB), then the Replacement Rate can be years (vs. months), or even negative. For example, if we use this method to calculate the Replacement Rate for our three families, we quickly see that it will take 5.3 (64/12) to 24.4 (293/12) *years* to replace one month's worth of Routine Operating Expenses for the Millers vs. the Joneses.

If that's the case, then what good is this measure—and how can we use it to understand or control our PFM?

Table 3–1: Replacement Rates by Family

Replacement Rate	Joneses (Drones)	Smiths (Laborers)	Millers (Builders)
Total Routine Operating Expenses	$5,441	$4,664	$3,948
Free Cash Flow	$975	$1,816	$2,612
Cash Burn	$956	$1,754	$2,550
Replacement Rate (months)	**293**	**75**	**64**

We have to step back for a minute and explore Cash Burn a little more closely. As mentioned, our Cash Reserve has three fundamental uses: 1) Lifestyle and Unpredictable Expenses, 2) Asset Purchases and investment/savings, and 3) financial buffer/emergency fund. Up to this point, we have been organizing our expenses into specific categories with the goals of increasing our insight into their role and improving our ability to establish control over our PFM.

So far we have organized more variable and more discretionary expenses into Stage 2 of our Operations Engine so that we can manage them with a pool of cash (Cash Reserves) instead of a fixed flow of cash (after-tax income). We now need to make one additional distinction between our more predictable and stable sources of Cash Burn from the less predictable and more variable.

To do this we separate our Cash Burn sources into two groups:

- **Baseline** Cash Burn (BCB) and

- **Episodic** Cash Burn (ECB).

Baseline Cash Burn is the total of our Cash Burn that is relatively predictable and stable. By definition, some of these expenses are more variable than our Stage 1 expenses (which is why they're in Stage 2), but we still have some level of consistency with some of these expenses. As you can see from the table below, some examples of Baseline Cash Burn include our monthly savings/investing and most of our Lifestyle Expenses (they may fluctuate quite a bit month to month, but they are not usually large relative to our monthly gross income). Just about everything else is a pure episodic expense.

Table 3–2: Baseline vs. Episodic Cash Burn Examples

Cash Burn Examples	Typical Amount	Typical Variability	Typical Frequency	Cash Burn Type
Investments/Savings	10% of GI	Low	Monthly	Baseline
Eating out or entertainment or sporting events, hobbies, etc.	<< 5% of GI	Moderate	Monthly	Baseline
Seasonal/holiday expenses	<< 5% of GI	Moderate	Annual	Episodic
New Dead Assets	Variable	High	Infrequent	Episodic
Vacations	Variable	Mod - High	1-2x/yr.	Episodic
Broken something (car, water-heater, furnace, etc.)	Variable	Mod - High	Unknown	Episodic

Episodic expenses are, in general, one-time or annual and relatively large. Sometimes we get to choose when they occur (vacation or adding a sprinkler system), and sometimes we cannot (broken dishwasher, storm damage, or travel for a funeral).

We will typically have some Lifestyle Expenses every month (weekend getaways or attending sporting events, entertainment, eating out, or expenses associated with our activities). Generally, these expenses will fluctuate, and even quite a bit on a monthly basis; but in total they should be well below our monthly Free Cash Flow.

Another relatively consistent element of Cash Burn is our contributions to our investments or special savings accounts. This includes both tax-favored (401(k)) and taxable investment accounts. Generally, we automatically direct some percentage of our monthly income into our 401(k) or an IRA. We may also be making periodic or even automatic contributions to taxable investment accounts for other purposes (e.g., a college fund).

An important point is that our monthly Baseline Cash Burn must be well below the level of our monthly Free Cash Flow. While Episodic Cash Burn events are more infrequent, they can sometimes be quite large and often exceed monthly Free Cash Flow (or even our monthly income).

Consequently, for most months, Cash Reserves grows (Baseline Cash Burn < Free Cash Flow). We will then need to make infrequent asset purchases or have a larger episodic Lifestyle Expense like a vacation or seasonal expenses that will exceed our monthly Free Cash Flow. As a result, our Cash Reserves will experience a reduction that we then replenish over time by the amount our Free Cash Flow exceeds our Baseline Cash Burn.

> As previously highlighted, the central reason that we have and need Cash Reserves is because we have groups of expenses that are not easy to predict. We must therefore manage them with a pool of cash that is well in excess of the 'worst case' monthly or even quarterly scenario. The alternative, when we don't have the cash is to liquidate assets or rely on credit cards to bail us out.

Think About It as Two Different Cash Flow Dynamics: The Baseline expense dynamic enables a consistent monthly increase in Cash Reserves because Baseline CB is, by design, less than Free Cash Flow. In other words, the amount flowing into our Cash Reserves pool exceeds the amount flowing out. The second dynamic is that there will be episodic withdrawals from Cash Reserves that may or may not be large, but can sometimes far exceed Free Cash Flow and even represent one or more months of Gross Income. This is like opening the floodgates on the dam and allowing much more cash to flow out of our Cash Reserves pool than is coming in via Free Cash Flow.

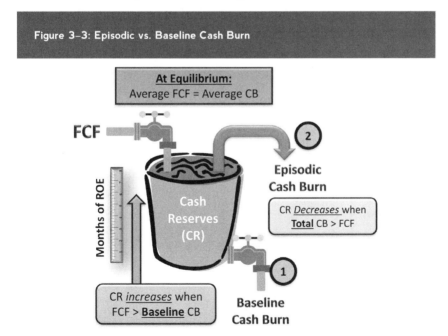

Figure 3–3: Episodic vs. Baseline Cash Burn

At Equilibrium:
Average FCF = Average CB

FCF

Months of ROE

Cash Reserves (CR)

Episodic Cash Burn

CR *Decreases* when **Total** CB > FCF

CR *increases* when FCF > **Baseline** CB

Baseline Cash Burn

This requires that our Free Cash Flow well exceeds our Baseline Cash Burn and Cash Reserves for most months, and methodically grows over time. We will then have a significant expense event every once in a while, but given the combination or average of our Baseline Cash Burn and our Episodic Cash Burn, our Cash Reserves should fluctuate around some average target level that we have decided is right for us (say four to six months of Routine Operating Expenses) over the longer term.

Consider again the calorie relationship between exercise and eating. We can easily consume 2,000 calories of pizza in 20 minutes but it takes hours at the gym to work off those calories. It's even harder than it seems because we still eat every day, adding even more calories (to support our baseline *calorie* burn). Similarly, it takes no time at all to burn $2,000 from our Cash Reserves, but given our ongoing Baseline Cash Burn expenses, it may take us many months to replenish that money—and it will *only happen* if Free Cash Flow consistently exceeds our monthly *Baseline* Cash Burn.

Therefore, the more informative way to look at and measure Replacement Rate (RR) is to only use Baseline Cash Burn in the equation. This allows us to more clearly see how quickly our Cash Reserves are growing monthly (in the absence of any episodic Cash Burn expenses):

Replacement Rate (in Months) =
Routine Operating Expenses / (Free Cash Flow - *Baseline* CB)

Let's revisit our three families to illustrate this important concept: As highlighted previously, Asset Burden is much higher for the Joneses and the Smiths as compared to the Millers. The Joneses have an Asset Burden of 49 percent of Gross Income, the Smiths are at 39 percent, and the Millers are at a more accommodating 30 percent.

	Joneses (Drones)	Smiths (Laborers)	Millers (Builders)
Managing Cash Reserves			
Gross Income (GI)	**$8,000**	**$8,000**	**$8,000**
Net Taxes	$1,584	$1,520	$1,440
Asset Burden	$3,891	$3,114	$2,398
Routine Living Expenses	$1,550	$1,550	$1,550
Total Routine Operating Expenses	**$5,441**	**$4,664**	**$3,948**
Free Cash Flow	**$975**	**$1,816**	**$2,612**
Baseline Lifestyle Expenses (average)	$425	$710	$880
Savings/investments	$80	$450	$900
Baseline Cash Burn	$505	$1,160	$1,780
Baseline Cash Reserves monthly change	$470	$656	$832
Average episodic Cash Burn (last 12 mo.)	$451	$594	$770
Average monthly impact on CR over time	*$19*	*$62*	*$62*
Total Cash Reserves today	$1,870	$4,006	$31,132
Credit Card debt	$16,000	$0	$0
Asset Burden (% of GI)	49%	39%	30%
Free Cash Flow Rate (MPG)	**12%**	**23%**	**33%**
Replacement Rate (mo.)	**11.6**	**7.1**	**4.7**
Cash Reserves (months of ROE)	0.3	0.9	7.9

Table 3-3: Asset Burden Impact on Replacement Rate

The reason the Joneses and the Smiths' Asset Burden is much higher than the Millers is that both have somewhat nicer homes and cars, and certainly have more toys. As a result, each family's Free Cash Flow is significantly different, even though their Routine *Living* Expenses are exactly the same. This nets to different levels of Routine *Operating* Expenses for each family: Joneses = $5,441, Smiths = $4,664, Millers = $3,948. Consequently, the Millers have a Free Cash flow rate (or MPG) of 33 percent. The Smiths are at 23 percent and the Joneses' Free Cash Flow is only at 12 percent—leaving the Joneses with very little room to maneuver, given their relatively low Free Cash Flow.

Note that the Millers' Replacement Rate is 4.7 months. We calculate this by taking their Free Cash Flow ($2,612) and subtracting their Baseline Cash Burn ($1,780) and dividing this into their Routine Operating Expenses ($3,948). This means that every month the Millers are adding about $832 to their Cash Reserves. After about 5 months, the Millers have added one month's worth of Routine Operating Expense to their Cash Reserves ($832/month x 4.7 months = $3,948), assuming they have no episodic expenses during that time. It takes 7 months for the Smiths, and almost a full year (11.6 months) for the Joneses to add the value of one month's Routine Operating Expenses to their Cash Reserves.

Think of Replacement Rate as an indicator of the resiliency or ability of our PFM to bounce back from large Episodic Cash Burn events. The Millers are adding $832 every month to their Cash Reserves net of their average Lifestyle Expenses and what they save every month (the definition of Baseline Cash Burn). In comparison, the Joneses are adding only $470 each month to their Cash Reserves, but they also have a higher Routine Operating Expense number to "Replace" ($5,441), giving them their 11.6 month Replacement Rate. So the Millers' 4.7 months Replacement Rate is a much faster rate (> 2x) than the Joneses' 11.6 months.

By way of an example, let's say the all three families experience a $5,000 Episodic Cash Burn event next month. This event would send the Joneses further into credit card debt, wipe out the Smiths' Cash Reserves, but only put a small dent in the Millers' Cash Reserves.

However, let's look at it from a Replacement Rate perspective—that is, the ability of each family's PFM to recover from this event. The $5,000 is not a meaningful number by itself. We want to look at this (and any other large Episodic Cash Burn event) in terms of impact on Cash Reserves as a 'number of months of Routine Operating Expenses' that just went out the door and how quickly we can replace it. The $5,000 is close to one month's worth of Routine Operating Expenses for each family—0.9 months for the Joneses, 1.1 for the Smiths, and 1.3 for the Millers.

If each family can completely avoid any other new Episodic Cash Burn events during the time it takes to replace one month of Routine Operating Expenses (11.6, 7.0, and 4.7 months for the Joneses, Smiths, and Millers respectively), going forward, then each of their Cash Reserves balances will have all generally recovered from the $5,000 Episodic Cash Burn event.

But how realistic is it that nothing unexpected will come along for almost a year (11.6 months) for the Joneses? The Joneses are highly unlikely to go a full 12 months—and the Smiths 7 months—without experiencing any other significant Episodic Cash Burn event. However, it is much more likely that the Millers can go 4 or 5 months without a significant event, and even if they have another event, their PFM is rapidly recovering based on how it is *structured*. The point here is that a low Replacement Rate helps repair our Cash Reserves more quickly.

The longer our Replacement Rate is, the more vulnerable we are to events beyond our control having a major impact on our Cash Reserves. This risk is multiplied when our Cash Reserve is also at a relatively low level. These are the *mechanics* of the cycle that can frustratingly erode our hard-earned cash and force us into constant budgeting and unnecessary frustrations that never seem to end.

So we always want to avoid being "caught" in long periods of financial vulnerability (low Cash Reserves AND long Replacement Rates) because no one can predict what Gotcha expense might be around the next corner.

Let's step back for a minute and look at the Millers. Because Free Cash Flow is significantly higher for them, they can responsibly spend more on Lifestyle Expenses like entertainment and eating out. They also have the ability to save much more than either of the other families while having the reassurance of a healthier Replacement Rate.

All three families make a positive baseline contribution to their Cash Reserves (Free Cash Flow > Baseline Cash Burn) every month, but the amount is much larger for the Millers. This is true even though they are saving $900 each month as part of their Baseline Cash Burn compared to $450 for the Smiths and only $80 for the Joneses.

Each family's Episodic Cash Burn varies widely from month to month, but has averaged out over the last 12 months to be $451, $594, and $770 respectively for the Joneses, Smiths, and the Millers. Notice that again the Millers have much more to spend every month on episodic events like vacations, concerts, or whatever suits them.

The Joneses are literally living paycheck to paycheck and their options and choices are effectively controlled by the terms of the Debt Merchants. They have no room to maneuver and simply react to whatever comes each month. The Smiths, on the other hand, are master budgeteers. They stay ahead of the game by brute force. They are classic Laborers who are saving, but only because of their exhaustive budgeting and attention to detail. They account for every dollar—an approach that's typical for many families and which is a symptom of having a *structurally vulnerable* PFM, most often due to excessive Asset Burden.

It's important to remember our Replacement Rate is just an ***index*** or a ***measure*** we use to describe the 'structure' of our Operations Engine. The larger the Replacement Rate is in months, the more time it takes to *recover* from significant reductions in Cash Reserves. Our Replacement Rate provides a measure of how quickly our PFM can respond to significant episodic cash burn events.

To illustrate what happens to Cash Reserves over time, let's look at the Millers' Cash Reserves over the last 24 months. This family's Free Cash Flow remains constant at $2,612/month. Cash Burn has a baseline rate of $1,780/month (which can vary, sometimes significantly, from month to month). However, we also have various months that are much larger due to episodic CB events. The resulting Cash Reserves balance experiences significant fluctuations (from $29,000 to $36,000), but over time fluctuates up and down around our target of $32,000. The key dynamic to reinforce is that the Millers' Baseline Cash Burn is well below Free Cash Flow, which means that the Cash Reserve is growing quickly *between* the large Episodic Cash Burn events. We always want that upward pressure on our Cash Reserves to counteract the downward force of our Episodic Cash Burn events (which we can never fully predict). Note the positive baseline trend (see arrows) noted in the graphic below. This is a classic representation of the upward trend or pressure that we want our Cash Reserves to experience for most months.

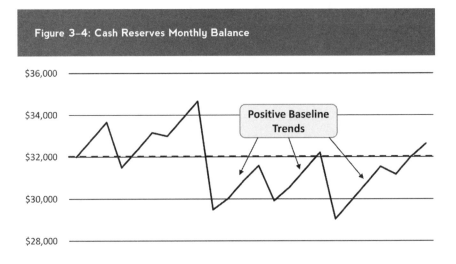

Figure 3–4: Cash Reserves Monthly Balance

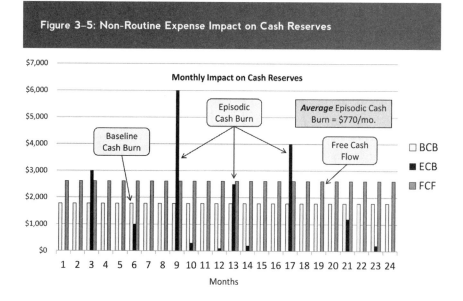

Figure 3–5: Non-Routine Expense Impact on Cash Reserves

So the two key drivers of this Cash Reserve dynamic involve *protecting* a consistent level of Free Cash Flow and *managing* Cash Burn in such a way as to *maintain* Cash Reserves within a healthy range over time.

So as we manage our PFM over time, these parameters (Free Cash Flow, Cash Reserves, Cash Burn, and Replacement Rate) will have a prominent place on our PFM Dashboard.

We now have a clear picture of the *balance* we have to achieve between Free Cash Flow and Cash Burn over time. We also have a better understanding of the spending *dynamics* that impact our Cash Reserves, as well as a set of measures to help us see how our Operations Engine is structured and how it is performing.

The Key to the Successful Management of Cash Reserves Is Free Cash Flow. The higher this is, the lower our Replacement Rate can be. This gives us more flexibility in our target level of Cash Reserves and the frequency and magnitude of fluctuations (Episodic Cash Burn events) in Cash Burn we can safely tolerate. If Free Cash Flow is low, we simply cannot quickly recover from unexpected expenses and our Cash Reserves simply erode over time.

So why do we need to understand all these components, cash flow dynamics, and new measures?

The reason is simple: control. We need to be able to understand, categorize, and *measure* the impact of that beach vacation (Episodic Cash Burn), or the decision to increase our automatic contribution to our 401(k) (Baseline Cash Burn), or buy a new or used car, with or without financing (decrease in Cash Reserves, increase in Asset Burden and reduction in Free Cash Flow). We need to understand the components of our PFM that we can change quickly (savings rate) verses those that are structural and cannot be easily or quickly modified (house payment).

The goal is to be able to *measure* the impact of our decisions and *anticipate* when to make adjustments, what to change, and by how much. We need to assert control and steer clear of avoidable problems and financial pitfalls. If we don't know how it works, we can't understand cause and effect. If we don't understand cause and effect, we can't control it. If we can't measure status, we won't know which direction or how much to turn the dials or move the levers. Our PFM really *is* a machine that we *can* control, but we must keep our focus on the structure and on the most important dials, levers, and gauges.

Managing Stage 1

To this point in this chapter, we have focused entirely on Stage 2 of our Operations Engine. Stage 1 is also extremely important, but much less complex compared to Stage 2. Instead of a flow dynamic, Stage 1 is simple and linear: Gross Income – Taxes – Asset Burden – Routine Living Expenses = Free Cash Flow. Done!

The two keys to effectively managing Stage 1 are Asset Burden (covered in Chapter 5) and Routine Living Expenses.

From the perspective of understanding our PFM, Routine Living Expenses are not that complicated. Many of them are relatively fixed like cell phone and internet services, and life or health insurance premiums. Others are more discretionary like food and clothing, but they are generally tied to our routines and habits. Where we shop for clothes and food and what we like to wear and eat largely defines these routine expenses. If we have young children, there are routine expenses related to them.

One important point about these expenses is that we need to pay attention when we are allocating expenses to Lifestyle Expenses vs. Routine Living Expenses. Eating out at expensive restaurants is not a Routine Living Expense; it's a Lifestyle Expense. Neither is shopping for items at a luxury boutique. Routine Living Expenses are just that—routine and reasonable. We need to allocate anything extravagant (read: we don't really *need* it) to Lifestyle

Expenses. Think of Routine Living Expenses as *need* expenses and Lifestyle Expenses as *want* expenses.

If we have allocated our expenses correctly, there should be little we can do about Routine Living Expenses. These are our fundamental operating expenses and are therefore practically unavoidable and generally predictable. In general, we want to be conservative in what constitutes a Routine Living Expense. This allows us to more easily see the magnitude of our Free Cash Flow and our Lifestyle Expenses and make more informed decisions about the required size of our Cash Reserves and the amount we are spending on our short-term lifestyle vs. longer-term saving, etc.

Erosion of Free Cash Flow

All of this understanding of how to measure and manage our Cash Reserves is great; however, many of us deal with the everyday challenge of how to *maintain* Free Cash Flow. It's not easy and some of us never quite understand what is really happening when the amount we have left over each month seems to get smaller and smaller.

If we don't organize our PFM, most of us don't even see our Free Cash Flow. If we can't see it, we can't manage it. If we can't maintain our Free Cash Flow or our Baseline Cash Burn is staying the same or even growing, then inevitably our Cash Reserves will decline and eventually dry up, putting us at risk of becoming Financial Drones. How do we prevent this from happening? It's all about Asset Burden, which is the topic of the next chapter.

A Word About Measurement

There are several important attributes of our PFM that we want to measure. Like any machine, there are gauges and controls that we want to monitor and adjust. From this Operations Engine discussion, there are several important structural measures to keep in mind:

- **Cash Reserves** is simply a measure of the amount of cash that we have at any given point in time. However, if we put it in context of something important like how many months of expenses it represent, then it can become a useful measure. If we divide our Cash Reserves by our Routine Operating Expenses (ROE), it becomes a measure of the number of months of Routine Operating Expenses we have in our Cash Reserves. This then reflects our ability to deal with both the unexpected and future planned expenses. It is a measure of the safety margin we are operating our PFM within: Cash Reserves / Routine Operating Expenses = months of expenses.

- **Free Cash Flow (FCF) or MPG** (using our Miles Per Gallon analogy) directly measures the output of Stage 1 of our Operations Engine and reflects the fundamental health and flexibility that we have in our PFM. When divided by Gross Income, it can be used to calculate the fuel efficiency or MPG of our Operations Engine: Free Cash Flow / Gross Income = Stage 1 output.

- **Replacement Rate (RR)** measures our recovery rate when we have large episodic hits to our Cash Reserves. It also tells us how resilient our PFM is or how quickly (in months) it can bounce back from a significant cash outlay without disrupting the normal operating flow of our Baseline Cash Burn: Routine Operating Expenses / (Free Cash Flow – *Baseline* CB) *equals* Replacement Rate in months.

Fortunately, you don't have to keep track of all of these measures on a piece of scratch paper or in your head, or run them through a spreadsheet every month. We have developed and made available a simple to input and easy to use PFM control panel and *dashboard* that organizes our PFM. It calculates and tracks the core measures and highlights areas of concern and strength. This customizable control panel and dashboard combined with the website provides a wealth of information and tools to help harness and focus our incredibly powerful and valuable PFM. It can be found at www.manufacturingwealth.com.

Chapter Summary:

- Stage 1 of our Operations Engine is straightforward and designed to be both boring and consistent, generating a healthy level of Free Cash Flow. This is where all our Routine Operating Expenses are covered.

- Stage 2 of our Operations Engine is more complex and has an important flow and pool dynamic that we need to manage. It is designed to deal with Non-Routine Expenses. These expenses are more discretionary (eating out, week-end getaways, etc.) or are large Gotcha expenses (car accident) that we need a reserve of cash to cover.

- There is a steady incoming flow of cash (Free Cash Flow) and two types of Cash Burn (or outflows): Baseline (Monthly Lifestyle Expenses and savings), which happens most every month, and Episodic (vacations, seasonal expenses), which happens infrequently or only once or twice a year.

- Baseline Cash Burn MUST be well below Free Cash Flow to ensure that CR has a positive upward force or trend that drives its recovery from Episodic Cash Burn events.

- Together, Baseline and Episodic Cash Burn need to be less than or equal to Free Cash Flow to maintain our Cash Reserves balance over time.

- There are three important measures that can help us manage or Operations Engine: Free Cash Flow / Gross Income, Cash Reserves / Routine Operating Expenses and Replacement Rate.

Personal Finance Machine (PFM) - New Term Review

(Note: A complete list of term definitions can be found in the Glossary.)

- **Baseline Cash Burn (BCB)** = The sum total of your Cash Burn (from Cash Reserves) that is relatively predictable and stable. BCB example expenses include monthly savings/investing and most Lifestyle Expenses.

- **Cash Burn (CB)** = The monthly drain of your Cash Reserves which includes Non-Routine Expenses (NRE) and Asset Engine Contributions (AEC). CB is the hole in the bottom of your Cash Reserves bucket.

- **Episodic Cash Burn (ECB)** = Infrequent Cash Burn events. These events can sometimes be large and even exceed monthly Free Cash Flow (or even our monthly income). Sometimes you choose when they occur (vacation or new furniture) and sometimes you don't (broken water-heater, storm damage, or travel for a funeral).

- **Miles Per Gallon (MPG)** = Analogy for the rate of Free Cash Flow (FCF/GI). Free Cash Flow relative to Gross Income is like the fuel efficiency (or MPG) of your Operations Engine.

- **Replacement Rate (RR)** = The number of months it takes to add 1 month of Routine Living Expenses to Cash Reserves.

CHAPTER 4:

ASSET BURDEN

- HOW IT CAN ALL GO SIDEWAYS

This chapter focuses on how things can go wrong with our PFM. As discussed in Chapter 2, Asset Burden is the total monthly cost associated with owning Dead and Marginal Assets. It reflects the amount of "structural" cost we have imposed on our PFM. These costs include monthly payments, routine maintenance, insurance, taxes, and operating expenses—all of which are generally large and hard to adjust. Asset Burden is in many ways the opposite of Free Cash Flow; it is financial weight that restricts and reduces Free Cash Flow.

It is like loading up the car for a long trip. It not only slows the car down, but the car becomes more sluggish, harder to maneuver, and gets far less gas mileage. The higher the Asset Burden is, the more difficult it is to maneuver our finances, prepare for the unexpected, provide funds for lifestyle-related expenses or save for future expenses and retirement. A higher Asset Burden means a lower Free Cash Flow. And since we are generally obligated to pay the Asset Burden first, all other expenses tend to be *downstream* from Asset Burden.

As discussed, we can use our Cash Reserves in three ways:

1 Cover our Non-Routine Expenses (LSE + UPE)

2 Invest for the future (Living Assets)

3 Buy Dead or Marginal Assets

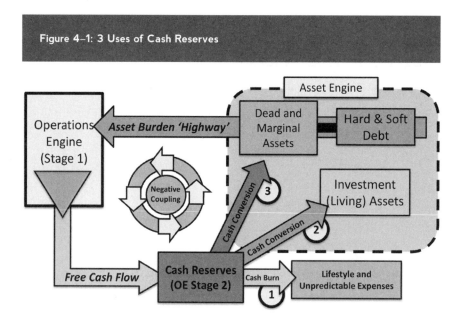

Figure 4–1: 3 Uses of Cash Reserves

Some of what we spend our Cash Reserves on impacts Asset Burden and some of it does not. So when we use Cash Reserves for our Lifestyle and Unpredictable Expenses (arrow 1 in the graphic above), there is no impact on Asset Burden because what we spend at the baseball game or on vacation gets paid directly out of Cash Reserves (or shortly after sitting on a credit card that we pay off each month).

When we have excess Cash Reserves and convert it into an investment or Living Assets (arrow 2 in the graphic), we also do not impact on Asset Burden because there are no operating expenses that can impact our Operations Engine associated with investing in mutual funds or buying stocks. From the perspective of Asset Burden these decisions are "free" relative to our Operations Engine.

However, when we convert excess cash into Dead or Marginal Assets (arrow 3), we *do* create extra burden on our Operations Engine in the form of Asset Burden. In addition, when we take out a loan to finance these purchases, we increase the size of that Asset Burden and *magnify* the negative impact of that expense on our Operations Engine.

The Negative Coupling Effect of Asset Burden: As we use our excess cash to purchase new assets (Episodic Cash Burn) we frequently—and sometimes unknowingly—increase Asset Burden. Every time we acquire a new (or used) Dead or Marginal Asset, we incur additional monthly structural expenses (that flow from our Asset Engine, along the Asset Burden highway, so to speak, directly into our Operations Engine). We can't avoid the new loan or increased insurance payment, and we can't ignore the associated usage and maintenance expenses. If we *finance* things like cars, recreational vehicles, or new furniture, we further magnify the impact on Asset Burden. These expenses all become baked into our operating expenses—and the consequences then ripple through and *structurally* impact our PFM.

For Example: Let's say the Millers are contemplating buying a car and considering two options:

- **Option 1:** Purchase a new $40,000 car using $10,000 from their Cash Reserves and financing the rest; or,

- **Option 2:** Purchase a used car for $10,000 using money from their Cash Reserves

Option 1 includes several important structural and immediate impacts on their PFM:

1. Cash Reserves are reduced by the $10,000 down payment.

2. Asset Burden goes up (e.g., insurance, loan payments, operating costs).

3. Free Cash Flow goes down.

4. Their Replacement Rate gets longer, making it more difficult to replenish their just-depleted Cash Reserves.

5. Their PFM becomes more vulnerable to future unpredictable expenses.

6. They have less to spend on Lifestyle Expenses or to save for medium or long-term financial commitments and needs.

Let's look at the specifics: Asset Burden increases by $700* (4-year loan at 6 percent interest), which has a major ripple effect throughout the Millers' PFM. The $700 represents an 18 percent increase in the Millers' Routine Operating Expenses ($700 / ($6,560 - $2,612)) which causes Free Cash Flow to fall by nearly 30 percent while Free Cash Flow as a percent of Gross

Income drops from 33 percent to 24 percent. In addition, their Replacement Rate increases 7-fold from 4.7 months to 35.2 months (Routine Operating Expenses = $3,098 + 1,550 = $4,648, Free Cash Flow – Baseline Cash Burn = $132, Replacement Rate = $4,648/$132 = 35.2 months)—which significantly magnifies the risk of having other episodic cash burn events further drain the Cash Reserves.

Table 4–1: New Car Purchase Impact on the Millers' Operations Engine

Millers' New Car	Before Purchase	After Buying $40K Car	After Buying $10K Car
Gross Income (GI)	**$8,000**	**$8,000**	**$8,000**
After tax Income	$6,560	$6,560	$6,560
Asset Burden	$2,398	$3,098	$2,398
Routine Living Expenses	$1,550	$1,550	$1,550
Free Cash Flow	$2,612	$1,912	$2,612
% of Gross Income	**33%**	**24%**	**33%**
Baseline Cash Burn	$1,780	$1,780	$1,780
BCB as % of Free Cash Flow	68%	93%	68%
Replacement Rate	**4.7**	**35.2**	**4.7**
Cash Reserves	$32,000	$22,000	$22,000
Months of Cash Reserves	**8.1**	**4.7**	**5.6**

> *Note that we will explore the total cost of ownership of a car later in the book. In this simplified example, we are only looking at the cost of the debt and not the other costs associated with purchasing a more expensive car.

Overall, this seemingly routine decision to buy and finance a new car materially reduces the Millers' ability to maintain Cash Reserves and recover from both expected and unexpected expenses going forward. In addition, reducing Free Cash Flow by $700 also puts a significant strain on Lifestyle spending and savings; Baseline Cash Burn increases from 68 percent of Free Cash Flow to 93 percent of Free Cash Flow. This balloons their Replacement Rate, limiting their ability to quickly replenish Cash Reserves and makes them more vulnerable to future Unpredictable Expenses. As pressure increases on Cash Reserves, both savings rates and lifestyle spending will have to go down. In short, Option 1 *structurally* and *significantly* changes the Millers' PFM, making it weaker and puts pressure on them to adjust both their Lifestyle spending and savings rates.

Now let's consider what happens under Option 2 where the Millers use the same $10,000 to purchase a $10,000 used car. This decision has only one impact on the Millers' PFM: It reduces their Cash Reserves from $32K to $22K and consequently reduces their months of Cash Reserves from 8.1 to 5.6. Both their Free Cash Flow and Replacement Rate remain unaffected, which means that their PFM will be able to quickly replenish the Cash Reserves deficit they just created. In addition, there will be no impact on their lifestyle spending or savings. The same *impact* would be true if they bought a $20,000 or even a $30,000 car; it would directly impact their Cash Reserves balance, but not change the *structure* of their PFM.

Debt Magnifies Asset Burden

As we have just highlighted, Asset Burden is one of the most important factors in controlling and managing our PFM and its impact on our life and lifestyle. A critical element of Asset Burden is how we use debt. Remember that there are two kinds of debt: Soft Debt (tied to marginal assets and where interest is deductible) and Hard Debt (tied to Dead Assets and where interest is not deductible). Generally, mortgage debt and qualified student loans are Soft Debt and all consumer credit and loans are Hard Debt. Consumer credit includes credit cards, auto loans, loans to buy furniture, and installment plans.

When we use debt, we magnify the impact of our asset purchase decision on Asset Burden. So in the example above for the Millers, they can afford to buy a $40,000 car by using a $10,000 down payment and financing the rest. Though without Debt Merchant financing, they might only be able to afford a $10,000 or $15,000 car if they had to pay cash.

Are the Debt Merchants the bad actor in this situation? *No, they are not.* The Millers made the decision, the Debt Merchant simply facilitated the transaction. The Debt Merchants only consideration is whether the Millers can afford the payment. By *afford*, the Debt Merchants' mean: Can they afford to repay the loan? They could care less how the transaction impacts the Millers' Cash Reserves, Replacement Rate, long-term savings rates, or any other aspect of the Millers' PFM. The only calculation the Debt Merchants are making is relative to repayment risk—they absolutely know how the $700/month will impact the Millers' PFM, but they just don't care. It's not their responsibility to care; that's the Millers' responsibility.

Even though we only accounted for the car payment in this example, everything about the $40,000 car is more expensive: insurance, maintenance, operating expenses, and especially the payments (principle PLUS interest). Using consumer debt causes us to significantly *magnify* the impact of our asset purchase decisions on Asset Burden—in this case, at least by a factor of three.

Consumer credit can be very useful, but it is also the most powerful and effective tool Debt Merchants have to draw us in. We must use it with caution and forethought.

The simple and (for most of us) necessary act of buying a car has a much bigger impact on our PFM than we might imagine. We don't usually think about or appreciate EXACTLY what the costs and consequences really are. In this example, we know our monthly car payment is going to be $700, we know we just wrote a $10,000 check, and we know that there will be additional costs associated with the new car; but we have not had the tools and measures necessary to accurately and clearly assess the impact of new asset purchases on our PFM.

As a quick exercise, fill in the chart below for your own finances. For Baseline Cash Burn, consider an average of your lifestyle-related monthly expenses plus the amount you save every month (pre-tax and post-tax).

Table 4–2: Car Purchase Exercise Worksheet

Your New Car	Before Purchase	After buying $40k car	After buying $10k car
Gross Income (GI)			
After Tax Income			
Asset Burden			
Routine Living Expenses			
Free Cash Flow			
% of Gross Income			
Baseline Cash Burn			
BCB as % of Free Cash Flow			
Replacement Rate			
Cash Reserves			
Months of Cash Reserves			

This example demonstrated the dramatic impact associated with a major purchase like a car. But also consider that we make all kinds of smaller, seemingly innocuous decisions that start to have a cumulative effect on Asset Burden, allowing it to creep up in a more slow and insidious manner. Decisions like putting that big screen TV or a big vacation on the credit card with the intention of paying it off over time, or buying a nice used boat with cash and then having the storage, winterizing, tune-ups, insurance, gas, all get added to Asset Burden. In addition, after we buy the boat, we don't exactly let it sit in the garage—*we use it* and incur the incremental expenses associated with our enjoyment of our new asset purchase—including gas, skis, wakeboards, life-jackets, and trips.

There is nothing wrong with buying and enjoying a boat or a new car. We just need to clearly understand the full cause-and-effect on our PFM. If we ignore this, we'll eventually end up with too much Asset Burden and little or no Free Cash Flow. When the inevitable and unavoidable episodic expenses arise, they will drain our remaining Cash Reserves and force us to use credit cards (Virtual Cash Reserves) to bridge the gap, thereby locking us into financial servitude.

Locking Up Our Engines

The big risk we face in managing our PFM is locking up our engines. This occurs when we have virtually no Free Cash Flow and very little or no Cash Reserves. This typically happens when consumer debt-driven Asset Burden has grown so large that it has structurally compromised our Operations Engine. In essence, Stage 2 of our Operations Engine collapses and shuts down.

This pushes us into extreme budget mode, where we watch every dollar and become frustrated because we don't seem to have the resources to cover our Lifestyle and Unpredictable Expenses. This forces us to use our credit cards without having the money to pay them off each month and consequently allowing the Debt Merchants to ensnare us. This kind of "financial prison" can foster a defeatist attitude toward personal finances in just about anyone. In fact, nearly 50 percent of US households are already trapped or on the edge of relinquishing control of their PFM to the Debt Merchants.

This predicament leaves us stuck paying the minimums on credit cards with huge balances that—given their interest rates—we'll likely never be able to pay off. Once our engines are locked, the Debt Merchants have us where they want us—in many cases, for life. We have now joined the ranks of Financial Drones.

To be clear, locking up our engines is a *mechanical* thing. It occurs due to excessive Asset Burden, debt, and lack of sufficient Free Cash Flow and Cash Reserves. Therefore, we can't unlock them without a reboot/restructuring of some sort that allows us to pay off the credit cards and car loans and significantly reduce Asset Burden. All kinds of triggers can drive us to lock up our engines, frequently through no fault of our own. These can involve a tragedy or major disruption in our lives: a medical emergency, long-term unemployment, or some other crisis that demands and consumes all our cash, leaving us reeling and with a mountain of debt.

Being a Financial Drone, on the other hand, is a *psychological* thing—a result of failing to fully understand one's financial situation (locked engines) *and* allowing the Debt Merchants to use us. Financial Drones may even believe they are in control and that this is how people are *supposed to* live. They buy into the illusion that everybody carries credit card debt and are convinced that they don't make enough money to get ahead, or that the next raise will get them out of this mess. They believe that retirement is a pipe dream very few can achieve. It's these beliefs that keep them in a perpetual state of financial enslavement while the Debt Merchants siphon away their multimillion dollar PFM.

Anyone Can Lock Up Their Engines. It can happen as a result of making uninformed decisions, runaway spending, bad circumstances, or bad luck. However, the key to avoid becoming a Financial Drone is to **recognize the situation early and address it quickly**. This is a serious predicament that requires us to take both decisive and aggressive action. The process of locking up our engines usually occurs slowly over time, because we are lulled into the mind-set of a Financial Drone. Like a frog in a slowly heating pot of water, we don't realize we're cooked until it's too late—which is why we need to do something as soon as we see the situation for what it is. Now that we have these newfound measures and tools, we can quickly see right through the clutter and know exactly what's happening.

Becoming A Drone: A Common Story

The road to becoming a Financial Drone is paved, smooth, downhill, and frequently a beautiful drive. Nobody *plans* to become a Drone; some of us just wind up there. Ironically, our PFM is usually in excellent condition before we start down this inviting palm tree-lined road. The journey can start with a significant increase in income from a big promotion, new job, or new working spouse or partner and a surging river of Free Cash Flow. However, for some, the road starts out with our first real job and our first real chance to manage a significant flow of money.

When we first start out or after a big bump in income, we have few expenses relative to our newly-earned income. This new surging river of cash *flows* into the shimmering lake that is our Cash Reserves. Soon we are marveling at the "depths" of our cash and we start to spend it. We may upgrade our apartment, buy a new car, get a boat, etc. As we acquire stuff, we likely use debt to finance these purchases (because we don't want to use all our cash and the financing is so inexpensive and *easy to get*). For a while, we see almost no effect; but over time, this activity starts inflating Asset Burden, which acts like a diverter, siphoning off our river of Free Cash Flow. At first it's not so bad; eventually, however—or even with a single large purchase (like too much house)—Asset Burden grows quickly into a giant drain. As it grows, our sparkling river of Free Cash Flow begins to fall. But we don't really notice because we still have this big beautiful lake of cash.

Meanwhile, we are also elevating our lifestyle and related decisions like going on vacation, going out, enjoying season tickets, buying furniture, a new bike—doing whatever we feel like to just enjoy life. We are simply using our credit cards as a convenience to pay for these things and paying them off every month. But now, suddenly, Free Cash Flow becomes constricted by our ballooning Asset Burden. As a result, we start burning our Cash Reserves—slowly at first, but then much faster. Soon our deep emerald lake of cash starts to drain away, evaporating right before our eyes. We are just about to get really concerned when suddenly we have a big unforeseen expense—say a major home repair, a big medical expense, or a car accident. Suddenly our Cash Reserves are gone, or nearly gone, and we have to use our credit card to bridge the gap.

We tell ourselves not to worry; it's just a minor setback. We will pay off that credit card right away (just like we always used to). But wait. What happened to that flowing river of Free Cash Flow? It's not what it used to be because Asset Burden is now sucking up 40 or 50 percent of our monthly income. So we attempt to manage the situation by starting to "budget" our expenses and making payments on the credit cards instead of paying off the entire balance. This gives us some breathing room for a while, but the unpaid credit card balance and minimum payments just add to our Asset Burden and cut even deeper into our anemic Free Cash Flow. Then, something else happens—because something else ALWAYS happens—and we have no choice but to use the credit card again . . .

In short, we have just locked up our engines and precipitated a PFM meltdown. If we delude ourselves into thinking that "something" will come along to get us out of this mess—or that this is just the "new normal"—we become Financial Drones and effectively hand over control of our multimillion PFM to the Debt Merchants.

Once our Operations Engine locks up, our ability to sustain and enhance our lifestyle is greatly compromised. Now every new dollar goes toward exorbitant interest on a balance we can't ever hope to pay off. This is just a simple, effective, and "soft" form of financial slavery. We might think we're free, but we're not even close.

So what just happened? At the highest level, we made decisions relative to Dead and Marginal Assets but did not appreciate those decisions' cash flow implications over time. We failed to notice the linkages between the Asset Engine and the Operations Engine and the impact on Free Cash Flow and our Cash Reserves. We did not see how unsustainable the combination of our Dead and Marginal Asset purchases and our lifestyle choices were, even though we *seemed* to have plenty of cash. We did not appreciate the impact that our increased Asset Burden and reduced Free Cash Flow would have on our ability to replenish our Cash Reserves as quickly as we had previously. We did not have the *visibility*, insight, tools, and measures to see what was happening so that we could stop it *before* it was too late. We only saw the problem *after* it was too late.

Before we move on, we want to note that there is of course another way we can lock up our engines—and that happens if we let our lifestyle spending get out of hand. Vacations we can't afford, online spending sprees, entertainment and clothes far beyond our means, all charged to those handy little pieces of plastic, can just as quickly and just a completely land us in the hands of the Debt Merchants.

Some of us buy stuff, some buy experiences and some buy both. But no matter which road we take, the Debt Merchants are happy to help.

Are you becoming a Financial Drone?

Do you:

1. Use consumer credit to buy stuff and experiences without regard for ability to pay for them?

2. Fail to recognize the full impact of these decisions on Asset Burden?

3. Ignore how Asset Burden is growing and causing *structural* changes to your Operations Engine?

4. Not measure Free Cash Flow or recognize when it is in decline?

5. Fail to adjust your Cash Burn by maintaining lifestyle spending and asset purchases as if nothing material has changed?

6. Run out of cash and need to use credit cards to fill the void?

7. Budget and cut back on discretionary expenses as you lose the ability to pay off your credit card balance every month?

8. Reluctantly continue using your credit cards, which just adds to the unpaid balance and Asset Burden?

9. Watch helplessly as Free Cash Flow falls to near zero?

10. Witness the total collapse of Stage 2 of your Operations Engine (no more Cash Reserves) and then resign yourself to living pay-check to pay-check, because 'I don't make enough money'?

The Debt Merchants Are Here to Help . . . Themselves

One of the most insidious factors in this dynamic is consumer debt—especially credit card debt. The only real power the Debt Merchants have over us is that which we give them through our use of consumer debt. Consumer debt is the *mechanism* by which the Debt Merchants slide their tentacles into our PFM and effectively divert a significant portion of the millions that we earned and could have otherwise kept for ourselves.

Looking at the graphic below, consider Stage 2 of our Operations Engine—our Cash Reserves. When we use our own cash for Stage 2, we have a well-functioning and healthy PFM. However, when we allow the Debt Merchants to effectively take over our Stage 2, *they* become our "Virtual Cash Reserves." They help create the illusion that we are using our own money, but in reality, we are using their money to "fund" our Stage 2.

This is the core area within our PFM where the Debt Merchants can take control.

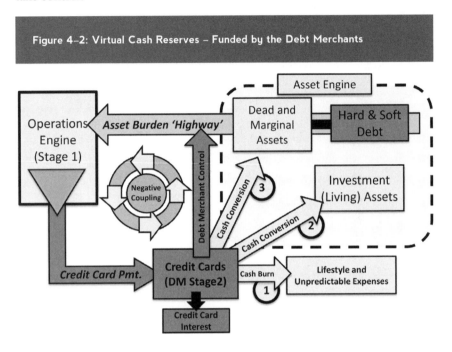

Figure 4–2: Virtual Cash Reserves – Funded by the Debt Merchants

When this occurs, our Asset Engine goes dark. We can no longer contribute to our investments or our future in any way. Our ability to fund our lifestyle begins to erode; we're left with no money for vacations, season tickets, or eating out, *unless we use the credit card*. Seemingly everything we need to buy winds up on the card and just adds to our balance. Our cash flow literally turns into payments on the credit cards. Even if we start working our way out, we have to use our credit cards and erase whatever progress we may have made when an unexpected and unavoidable expense arrives.

The combination of our routine use of credit cards, easily accessible credit, sky high interest rates, and low minimum payments make them the perfect trap. The Debt Merchants know this (they designed it, after all), and all they have to do is wait patiently for us to fall into their grip either by accident, bad luck, or poor management. They don't care how we get there; they're just happy we've arrived.

The first time we get into trouble with our Free Cash Flow and can't pay off our credit cards signals the beginning of the end of our financial freedom. Unless our Free Cash Flow rebounds quickly, the trap begins to close and we will continue to need to use our credit cards as our Virtual Cash Reserves. As highlighted in the graphic above, the Debt Merchants are now in control and they will keep giving us just enough credit until we are completely trapped. They prevent us from going bankrupt by carefully titrating allowable credit to us, but offer no help whatsoever to get us out of their iron grip.

How Debt Merchants Pave the Road to Becoming a Financial Drone

Debt Merchant Strategy 101:

Offer easy credit: We are flooded with offers for credit cards from banks, retailers, airlines–you name it. At everyone turn we are offered a branded credit card.

Provide incentives to use our cards: Points, Rewards, Gold, Diamond, Platinum, Preferred, etc.

Create the perfect (and perfectly legal) financial prison: Low minimum payments and very high interest rates (not to mention the impenetrable network of fees and hidden costs).

Utilize clever marketing: Convincing us that this is a 'normal' way to live–"We want to 'reward' you with additional credit," "We are **HAPPY** to have you as such a good customer!"

Maintain strong guardrails: The Debt Merchants are smart. They have clearly established parameters to protect their interests by preventing us from going so far into debt that we have to file for bankruptcy. They have fine-tuned their debt limit systems to ensure our continued payments on debts that in many cases are nearly impossible to pay off.

We all know that credit card debt is bad and the interest rate is high. But do we fully appreciate what is happening?

*Again, we are not saying credit cards are bad; rather, they are a useful financial tool. We just need to understand they have a '**dark side**' that is very real.*

Stepping back: When too much Asset Burden compromises Free Cash Flow, we *must* adjust the rate with which we are spending cash. This typically requires us to drastically reduce our spending on savings and Routine Living Expenses or Lifestyle Expenses with the goal of boosting Free Cash Flow and/or reducing our Baseline Cash Burn. When Asset Burden grows, what usually must give is our monthly living and lifestyle spending *and* our savings.

We frequently associate this lifestyle spending with the part of our lives that we enjoy the most. We are trying to achieve a lifestyle and asset ownership related balance that is defined by how much Asset Burden we have relative to how much we are allocating to our Lifestyle Expenses. This is a great example of how we can structure our Personal Finance Machine to help us live our lives in a more proactive, balanced, and directed way.

Chapter 5 will explore this question of balance further. We now can make a conscience decision: How much of our income do we want to allocate to asset-related expenses versus Lifestyle Expenses? Do we get more enjoyment from frequent vacations or from a bigger house or expensive cars? What balance point is right for each of us?

Who Do We Want in Control: Us or the Debt Merchants?

We can fund our Cash Reserves in one of two ways:

1. With our own cash

2. With Virtual Cash from the Debt Merchants

Option 1 puts us in control. We can decide how we want to operate our PFM. Option 2 turns control over to the Debt Merchants.

The primary impact of turning control over to the Debt Merchants is that we essentially destroy our ability to fund our lifestyle-related activities and save and build investments for our future. We wind up living paycheck to paycheck, trapped by a "budget" with no Cash Reserves and no easy way out.

Once our engines lock up, we cannot escape without a major effort and restructuring. Yet many of us resort to *managing* the situation with budgets, waiting for a miracle to get us out of this mess. The mechanism of getting in trouble is directly related to Free Cash Flow, Asset Burden, Cash Burn, and Cash Reserves. However, the motivation to get out of trouble requires that we realize that if we don't, we will forfeit control, financial freedom, and millions of dollars that we are earning over our lifetimes.

Again, Table 4–3 shows an example of our three families. The Joneses started out with $15,000 in credit card debt and then had to add another

$1,000 because they did not have the cash to pay for the whole $1,500 unpredictable repair bill. So now they have $16,000 in credit card debt.

Also note that to be able to pay the $250 (now $267) in credit card minimums, the Joneses have to get these funds from somewhere. Logically they will come from their baseline Lifestyle Expenses like eating out, vacations, hobbies, and other activities; or they will have to come from retirement savings. The loss of funds to support these highly enjoyable activities, or their future financial well-being will make them feel frustrated and poor.

Consider as well that the $267 is a minimum payment that covers the interest and a small portion of the principle. To pay off their credit card, the Joneses would have to pay $425/month to eliminate the debt within 5 years and $595/month to eliminate it in 3 years. This would require them to do away with virtually all lifestyle spending, all savings, AND never have a month where expenses exceed operating income (Gross Income – Taxes).

Table 4–3: Managing Cash Reserves

Managing Cash Reserves	Joneses (Drones)	Smiths (Laborers)	Millers (Builders)
Gross Income (GI)	$8,000	$8,000	$8,000
Net Taxes	$1,584	$1,520	$1,440
Asset Burden	$3,891	$3,114	$2,398
Routine Living Expenses	$1,550	$1,550	$1,550
Total Routine Operating Expenses	$5,441	$4,664	$3,948
Free Cash Flow	*$975*	*$1,816*	*$2,612*
Baseline Lifestyle Expenses (average)	$425	$710	$880
Savings/Investment	$80	$450	$900
Baseline Cash Burn	$505	$1,160	$1,780
Baseline Cash Reserves monthly change	$470	$656	$832
Average episodic Cash Burn (last 12 mo.)	$451	$594	$770
Average monthly impact on CR over time	*$19*	*$62*	*$62*
Total Cash Reserves Today	$1,870	$4,006	$31,132
Credit Card Debt	$16,000	$0	$0
Asset Burden (% of GI)	49%	39%	30%
Free Cash Flow Rate (MPG)	*12%*	*23%*	*33%*
Replacement Rate (mo.)	*11.6*	*7.1*	*4.7*
Cash Reserves (months of ROE)	0.3	0.9	7.9

This is not just incredibly difficult; it is also very painful from a lifestyle perspective. In the end, for most families like the Joneses, the task is too daunting and they simply remain trapped. Every once in a while, they buckle down and pay off some of the debt; but soon enough, some unplanned expense comes along and the credit card debt builds right back up.

Not only is this completely disheartening; it's a miserable and frustrating lifestyle. Even the most draconian budget has little chance of helping.

However, there is a solution to the Joneses' predicament. It is not an *easy* solution, but it will help. The answer is to *attack Asset Burden*. The Joneses must restructure their PFM to dramatically reduce their Asset Burden. This is really the only realistic path out of their financial prison.

The first step is for the Joneses to sell their cars and replace them with used cars for which they can afford to pay cash for. They need to get rid of the boat and the other toys and use the cash to pay off consumer debt. They may also need to downsize their house. These are difficult and potentially disruptive decisions, but this is the only real path out of being a Drone. They can also accomplish much if not all of this within the course of a year or less. The alternative of trying to "manage" one's way out of the situation can go on for years—even decades. But, think about how difficult it would be to have to tell their friends, the Smiths and the Millers that they are moving out of the neighborhood or further away and seemingly moving 'backward' from a lifestyle perspective. This is hard stuff and a predicament that is not easy to get out of.

Key Point: From our earlier analogy comparing Free Cash Flow to a car's MPG, there is no way to make a 10 MPG PFM operate like a 30 MPG PFM. When Asset Burden gets too high and our cash flow and cash reserves are squeezed or nonexistent, many people's first instinct is to start budgeting. But the only *viable* solution is to restructure our PFM to reduce Asset Burden, increase Free Cash Flow, and rebuild Cash Reserves.

The Smiths don't have to worry about paying off credit card debt. However, if they want to get out of the "watch every dollar and detailed budget because we have to" mode, they should also look at how they can adjust their PFM's structure to reduce their Asset Burden, increase cash flow, and build a larger Cash Reserves. This will get them out of the feeling of always living on the edge and point them toward the path of the Financial Builders.

The Financial Builders make it look easy. They use their significant Free Cash Flow, enabled by a manageable Asset Burden to save for retirement (build their Asset Engine), take vacations, have money to spend for the holidays, and to enjoy their lives without worrying about money.

> **Income Level Does Not Matter:**
> These risks apply at all income levels. It is easy to over spend, no matter where you fall on the income spectrum. As people increase their wealth and incomes, they begin to ratchet up their lifestyles. So regardless of what's coming in, there is only so much money to 'use' every month. The negative impact that AB imposes on the Operations Engine remains the same; it just happens on a larger scale. If we use *that* money AND maximize easy credit, we will wind up handing over much of our limited and precious income to the Debt Merchants. The difference between the financial flexibility, sustainability, lifestyle and *enjoyment* experienced by Financial Builders vs. the Financial Drones or even Laborers is profound, but what may **_not_** be different is their income.

Now that we understand how our PFM works on a monthly or operating basis and how to keep it healthy and productive, we need to consider another important dynamic: the long-term goal of our PFM. Keeping this in good shape will provide an opportunity to stop working *when we want to stop working* and have an enjoyable and sustainable lifestyle for the rest of our lives.

Chapter Summary:

- Our personal finances operate in a far different way than we have appreciated up to this point.

- The road to becoming a Financial Drone is slippery and smooth. It usually starts with a healthy Free Cash Flow and Cash Reserves, and it ends with the collapse of our Cash Reserves and reliance on the Debt Merchants to fund Stage 2 of our Operations Engine.

- Instead of focusing on our Gross Income, expenses, and a budget, we should focus on our Cash Reserves and the factors that help us manage and protect it (Asset Burden, Free Cash Flow, and Baseline Cash Burn).

- Our income does not matter; what matters is *how we manage our income*. We can be Financial Builders at almost any level of income.

- By losing control and becoming a Financial Drone, we will have even less to spend than if we had taken the Builder path in the first place.

- The cost of becoming a Financial Drone forces us to give up the spending that tends to make us happiest and feel most financially free—our lifestyle spending.

- We cannot simply budget our way out of being a Financial Drone.

- We are managing a system or flow of money. The decisions we make can disrupt and constrict that flow, making us much more vulnerable to unexpected expenses and erosion of our Cash Reserves.

- We only have so much money, and we simply can't spend more than we have. All we can do is overextend to the point that our lifestyle choices are constrained by the Debt Merchants and then we are much worse off than if we had just lived within our means from the beginning.

- Erosion of our Cash Reserves and loss of our ability to replenish it is the process that leads to locking up our engines and sends us down the road to becoming a Financial Drone.

Personal Finance Machine (PFM) - New Term Review

(Note: A complete list of term definitions can be found in the Glossary.)

- **Virtual Cash Reserves (VCR)** = The use of consumer credit to fund your Cash Reserves. This is a classic situation for many Financial Drones. This is one way the Debt Merchants maintain their iron grip – often for decades.

CHAPTER 5:

THE ASSET ENGINE

- YOUR PERSONAL MONEY MANUFACTURING MACHINE

C hapters 3 and 4 covered the details of the Operations Engine. We also discussed how Asset Burden controls Free Cash Flow and how Cash Reserves are balanced by *incoming* Free Cash Flow and by *outgoing* Baseline and Episodic Cash Burn. We also highlighted the central focus of the Operations Engine: cash flow and cash reserve management.

This is the reason we have given these engines these particular names. The Operations Engine is all about managing our financial *operations*, including all expenses, bills, and cash management, in a structured and controllable way. However, aside from our Cash Reserves, the Operations Engine has no intrinsic value. It is simply the mechanism by which we process our monthly income and expenses. This results in excess cash that we can then use to sustain our Cash Reserves and fund the all-important Asset Engine, whose job is to manage our assets in a structured and controllable way. Both engines have very clear inputs and outputs and key structural and operating measures that help us control them. In this chapter we will cover the inner workings of our Asset Engine and the factors that contribute to Net Worth and drive Net Worth Gain.

Too often people think of money in terms of income—when the real focus needs to be on how we build assets over time.

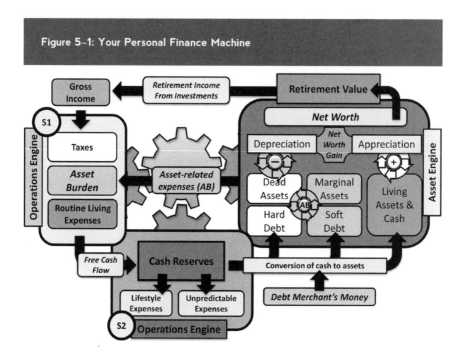

Figure 5–1: Your Personal Finance Machine

The Asset Engine is the financial repository (or the *financial sum*) of all our hard work and decisions we have made over many years. *Unlike* the balance sheet of a traditional business, the Asset Engine represents the status and actual accumulation of the multimillion dollar potential associated with our lifetime earnings. In many ways, it is the measure of our financial success. This is why it is very important for us to understand how it works, so that we can control it and capture far more than a paltry 1 or 2 percent of our multimillion dollar Lifetime Economic Value. Said differently, it does not matter how much money flows through our Operations Engine; we already know it's going to be millions. What matters, in terms of our future income stability, is how much of it we use to build our Asset Engine and how effectively we tune our Asset Engine for growth.

Understanding the Asset Engine's relationship with the Operations Engine allows us to effectively harness these tools and capture as much of this economic potential as we can. Remember, personal finance is not all about paying the bills; that's the Laborer's point of view. Properly building and managing a

PFM is about unlocking, capturing, and retaining the awesome potential our PFM holds. *That's how a Builder thinks.*

Our Asset Engine operates much differently from our Operations Engine. While the Operations Engine enables and manages a *flow* (Operations Engine Stage 1) and a *pool* (Stage 2) of cash, the Asset Engine generates (or *manufactures*) two important things:

1. **Asset Burden (-)**

2. **Net Worth Gain (+)**

We have already talked quite a bit about Asset Burden, and we'll talk more about it in Chapter 7. This chapter focuses on Net Worth and Net Worth Gain.

Net Worth and Net Worth Gain (NWG)

Chapter 2 defined all the components of our Asset Engine: Dead Assets, Marginal Assets, Living (investment) Assets, Cash, Hard Debt, and Soft Debt. At the highest level, when we simply add all these components together, we are measuring our Net Worth.

> Net Worth = Total Assets – Total Liabilities

Calculating our Net Worth is certainly important and informative as the status or snapshot of our Asset Engine. But what is more important are the changes in Net Worth over time. Net Worth Gain (NWG) measures the growth in our Net Worth over the course of a year. This also reflects the "health" of our Asset Engine as well as the complex dynamics and processes that are happening under the hood.

Net Worth Gain is driven by three factors:

1. Appreciation and depreciation of our assets (Asset Maturation)

2. Dynamics of debt and paying off our debt (Debt Resolution)

3. The composition of our assets and debts (Asset Mix)

Asset Maturation

Asset Maturation is essentially what happens to our assets over time. All our Assets are driven by two fundamental forces: appreciation and depreciation. Over time, each of our assets is maturing in some way. Some are growing in value (appreciating) and others are losing value (depreciating). We can calculate the result or current status of this process by taking the current value of our assets and subtracting their value since we acquired them. The difference is the cumulative amount of appreciation (positive) or depreciation (negative) they have experienced over time. If we know the number of years we have owned the assets, we can calculate the annual rate of appreciation or depreciation. Table 5-1 contains two examples. One where we purchased $1,000 of stock seven years ago, and the other where we purchased a car seven years ago. In the first case, we see that the stock appreciated in value by 50 percent overall and the annual rate of appreciation is 6 percent per year. However, the car lost $15,000 in value, but this represents a loss of value of about 8 percent per year.

Table 5–1: Asset Appreciation and Depreciation

Appreciation/ Depreciation	100 Shares Company A	New Car
Purchase price	$1,000	$35,000
Price today	$1,500	$20,000
Years held	7	7
Total Appreciation/Depreciation	$500	($15,000)
Rate	6%	-8%

As you can see in this example, the results can be dramatic. We will explore these differences further in this and the next chapter.

There Are Two Asset Maturation Forces:

- **Intrinsic Appreciation:** This is when underlying market forces—such as increasing demand, access to new markets, innovation, or increased competitiveness—over time exert upward pressure on an asset's value. Appreciation does not include improvements, contributions, or additions to assets (from us)—just *growth* of the intrinsic value of the asset.

All Living Assets are expected to have some level of intrinsic appreciation—which is why we call them *living*.

- **Intrinsic Depreciation:** This is the natural decline in value of an asset typically associated with assets that wear out or get used up over time. All Dead Assets have intrinsic depreciation, which is why we need to think of them as dead—even on the day we are buying them.

An asset with Intrinsic Appreciation or Intrinsic Depreciation can fluctuate in value either up or down from one year to the next; but over time, the overwhelming force of intrinsic appreciation or depreciation is expected to move the value of the asset either up or down.

Living and Marginal Assets

Our Living and Marginal Assets have a *dynamic intrinsic value*; that is, they can go up and down in value, sometimes significantly. Our Living Assets (investment assets) frequently comprise partial ownership of ongoing commercial businesses that are working to sustain and grow their sales and profits. They don't all succeed, but their focus and objective is growth and appreciation in value. If we own a diversified portfolio of these businesses, the value of our living assets will tend to move with the market.

However, we all know that the value of our investments at any moment in time can be volatile. Most of us have experienced the plunge of the stock market and its impact on our investments. But, we have also seen that the market over time tends to "right itself," and over the long run has generated a positive appreciation rate. This is because the combined value of the companies that comprise the market is not eroding; in fact, it's growing, driven by innovation and growth in the population and standards of living across the globe. Ultimately the markets are expected to *on average* reflect that fact.

Our Marginal Assets, such as our home or our art/antiques, also have a dynamic intrinsic value that generally helps them maintain their value or appreciate over time. The key difference between these two classes of assets is that *we* have to take care of (spend money on) our Marginal Assets if we expect them to maintain or increase in value over time. If we don't protect and maintain our Marginal Assets, they will *lose* value in absolute terms compared to similar marginal assets that have been well maintained.

For example, if we let our house go into disrepair and our neighbors are meticulous in maintaining both their homes and yards, the value of our neighbors' homes will undoubtedly be higher than ours. Picture an abandon Victorian home versus a beautifully maintained old Victorian that gets a $20,000 new paint job every five years (just to keep the outside nice).

On the other hand, we don't have to spend money to *maintain* our investment in a mutual fund or a stock that we own. We simply have the investment sitting in an account. However, there are expenses associated with many of our investments. We will be discussing this further in Chapter 6.

Cash

Ironically, cash has intrinsic depreciation. If we put our cash in a safe, under a mattress, or even in a bank account, it will *lose* value over time. Banks certainly pay an interest rate for the privilege of holding our money, but this rate is very low and generally well below the rate of inflation. This is part of the "price" we pay for the perceived benefit of safety of our money.

If we put our money in a bank, it is federally insured up to a certain amount against the bank going bankrupt or malfeasance. In this regard, a bank is protecting our money from theft, swindle, fire, or insolvency of another bank. However, the bank keeping our money is not protecting it from the ravages of inflation. So while a bank is safer than a mattress for protecting our money from theft, it does not protect the erosion of the value of our money through inflation (and to be fair, neither does the mattress).

Dead Assets

Dead Assets are actually *designed* to depreciate over time, and they usually lose significant value every year. This occurs because they get used up over time. Most of these assets perform some physical function and frequently can do so for a long time (utility value), but eventually they no longer work or are replaced by better-performing versions.

Many types of Dead Assets (think cars) are intended to be replaced long before they actually wear out. The auto industry has a long pipeline of new features that they strategically bring out in each new model year. These newer cars—with features and performance not available on older models—have a negative impact on the demand for older cars. The stuff that we bought five years ago is much less desirable in the market (even though it might still work just fine) than a newer version—consequently lowering demand and market value.

> **Things with Motors**
>
> In general, the Dead Assets we buy with motors are notoriously hard on our Asset Engine. They are a lot of fun, and many are necessary, but they tend to be expensive to own, operate, and maintain and tend to depreciate very rapidly.

What is surprising is just how quickly Dead Assets can decline in value. We need look no farther than the side of the highway to see all those ten-year-old cars, boats, and snowmobiles with For Sale or Best Offer signs with shockingly low prices.

Many other dead assets like electronics, furniture, tools, or appliances have planned obsolescence (designed to wear out in a certain period of time). This is a strategy developed many years ago by manufacturers to design and produce products with a certain usable lifespan. This was done after manufactures realized that if they made products too well, then after everyone had one, their sales would plunge. Now, nearly every product we buy has a specific planned obsolescence. Some things are designed to last less than a year, others for five years or more. But the point is these are all Dead Assets *by design*.

Asset Mix

For many of us, the aggregate of our Asset Maturing calculation/process is negative. This means that even though our investments and even our Marginal Assets might be appreciating or stable, our Dead Assets are doing what they are supposed to do over time—depreciate—such that the sum of our total asset appreciation and depreciation may be negative (or only slightly positive). This, of course, gives us a negative Net Worth Gain.

This doesn't make Dead Assets inherently bad. We need and depend on them to get us to work and enhance our lifestyle and enjoyment in countless ways. We just need to understand and balance their negative impact on our PFM.

The central upward driver of Net Worth Gain is our Living (investment) Assets. The larger this asset class is and becomes as a percentage of our total assets, the larger our Net Worth Gain will be. While it's true that our investments can have good and bad years, our Dead Assets *always* have bad years.

When our Marginal and Dead Assets represent the majority of our total assets, our Asset Engine (Net Worth) has almost no chance of growing over time. This is not to say that the intrinsic depreciation of our Dead Assets in some way limits the growth of our other Assets. Rather, we want to measure Net Worth Gain *inclusive* of all asset classes to increase our awareness and sensitivity to the mix or composition of assets that we have (by our own decisions) and their *overall* impact on our Net Worth over time. When we choose to purchase a Dead Asset, it represents not just an increase in Asset Burden and depreciation, but also an opportunity cost of not investing in Living Assets.

Cost of Debt (Gross and Net)

When we take out a loan to finance the purchase of an asset, we are simply paying a premium for the asset as represented by the loan's interest. This premium is for the privilege of purchasing an asset using somebody else's money. The bigger the loan, the longer the term; and the higher the interest rate, the more of a premium we are paying.

Of course, the true cost of a house involves much more than just the payment. The net impact of appreciation, expenses, and upkeep on our home is complex and may result in a positive investment return, but usually it does not. This is why we should not always think of our home as an investment— and why we call it a Marginal Asset.

The most likely situation is that, over time, our home appreciates in value and our equity grows (sometimes significantly); but after accounting for all expenses, owning our home frequently has a net monthly cost. We should simply hope that net cost of ownership is less than if we rented the same or similar property.

Debt Resolution

Debt Resolution is the change in debt owed from the annual debt service payments we make. As we all know, our Net Worth Gain can be affected by paying off the principle of some of our loans. The more of the principle that we pay off, the more of the Asset we own (equity)—and this can contribute to our Net Worth Gain. However, there is a big difference in the impact on our Asset Engine and Net Worth Gain when we pay off Soft Debt vs. Hard Debt.

Soft Debt

Remember, Soft Debt is typically mortgage debt or debt tied to Marginal Assets. As we make mortgage payments, some portion goes to interest and the remainder pays off some of the principle. Over the course of a year, the amount of principle that we paid off contributes directly to our Net Worth. If our home also increases in value (appreciation) that year, then we get an additive contribution to our Net Worth.

As a general rule, when we are paying off principle of Soft Debt, this reduction in what we owe adds to our Net Worth. This is why the term of our mortgage can be important. The shorter the term or time period—say fifteen years versus thirty years—the higher the monthly payment, the more principal is included in each payment, the faster the loan gets paid off, and the faster we are increasing equity in our home and the more we are adding to our Net Worth.

Another way to think about the principal portion of our payment is as a form of savings. We are simply saving into the asset that is our home versus investing that money in some Living Asset like a mutual fund. If our home appreciates more over time than another investment (net of expenses), then we will have made a good decision by investing in our home. If we choose a fifteen-year mortgage over a thirty-year, we'll increase the amount of Net Worth we allocate to our home versus other assets in our Asset Engine. This is because with each payment, we are contributing more to principle and less to interest compared to the thirty-year mortgage. Similarly, regardless of the term (years) of our mortgage, we can also make additional principle payments on our mortgage, which is the same as investing in our house as an asset versus choosing to invest that extra cash in Living Assets (we discuss more on this point in the next chapter).

Hard Debt

Hard Debt is all debt associated with Dead Assets. As we pay off the debt on Dead Assets, we get no durable contribution to our New Worth. Even if we pay off the debt quickly, any positive impact on our Net Worth is transient due to the drastic depreciation of Dead Assets over time.

As Figure 5–2 demonstrates, the actual amount of Net Worth that a Dead Asset we purchase using Hard Debt contributes to our Asset Engine is quite small. It can vary between negative and positive based on how much is financed and for how long, as well as the rate of depreciation and how long we keep the asset.

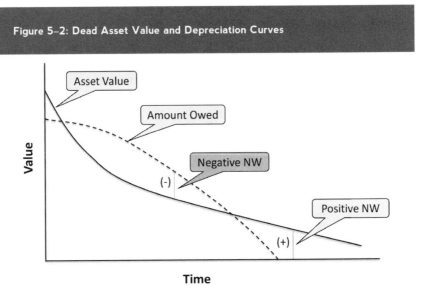

Figure 5–2: Dead Asset Value and Depreciation Curves

Source: Authors' estimation.

Intrinsic depreciation is generally not linear and not the same for all Dead Assets. But, it is typically much worse in the early years. As we all know, selling a financed Dead Asset can easily and frequently result in getting *less* money than is owed (e.g., sell it for $10,000 and at the same time we owe the bank $12,000). It is entirely possible that a Dead Asset can be worth less than the financed amount throughout the repayment plan, except maybe for the last year or so. For example, if you finance a new car for five years with a minimal down payment, and you sell any time before year four or five, you may still owe money on an asset that you no longer own.

Consequently, Dead Assets are *never* helpful in driving positive Net Worth Gain and building our Asset Engine. Debt Resolution for Dead Assets does not benefit our PFM. The assets' rate of depreciation simply vaporizes the equity we are building as we pay off the debt. Using debt to buy Dead Assets only increases the total cost of the asset and creates a much larger Asset Burden.

What if we pay cash only and incur no debt? Interestingly, when we are *acquiring* Assets and Debt, it has absolutely no impact on our current

Net Worth. At the moment of acquisition, we have simply *converted* cash into some asset with an associated debt. From a Net Worth perspective, they cancel themselves out. For example: If we acquire a boat for $20,000, we have the new asset of $20,000; but we paid either $20,000 in cash (trading cash for boat) or we used a combination of cash and debt ($10,000 in cash and $10,000 in debt). In either case, our Net Worth is exactly the same at the moment of the transaction. However, immediately after we make them, these decisions start having an impact on our Asset and Operations Engines.

Our Three Families

Let's look and see what is going on with our three families' Asset Engines.

As we already know, all three families have the same income, and each have around $400,000 in total assets. The Millers have the most with $456,000.

Asset mix is a critical differentiator among our families. Over the long term, it will determine who will be following their dreams later in life and who will be exhausted and exasperated by the stress of living on a meager retirement budget. In Table 5–2, even though all three families have similar levels of total assets, the Joneses have much more of their assets in Dead and Marginal Assets (> 98 percent) compared to the Millers (~70 percent). Notice how all three families' asset mix differs significantly based on how they used their Free Cash Flow over time. The Joneses and the Smiths both have much more invested in Dead and Marginal Assets compared to the Millers. Conversely the Millers have accumulated a significant amount of Living Assets (24 percent of total assets) compared to the other two families.

All three families have about the same level of Soft Debt, and the Joneses and the Smiths both carry some Hard Debt. Given these seemingly small differences between each family, it's a bit surprising that the Millers' Net Worth is significantly larger than either the Joneses or the Smiths.

Table 5-2: Asset Mix Comparison			

Three families - same income, different asset mix (at year 10)	Joneses (Drones)	Smiths (Laborers)	Millers (Builders)
Dead Assets	**$51,752**	**$36,052**	**$23,118**
Cars	$36,540	$26,100	$20,118
Toys (boat, ATVs, snowmobiles)	$9,212	$5,452	$0
Stuff (furniture, etc.)	$6,000	$4,500	$3,000
Marginal Assets	**$357,849**	**$324,695**	**$291,541**
Home	$337,849	$309,695	$281,541
Other Marginal Assets	$20,000	$15,000	$10,000
Cash	**$2,000**	**$5,000**	**$32,000**
Living (Investment) Assets	**$5,000**	**$30,000**	**$110,000**
Total Assets	**$416,601**	**$395,747**	**$456,659**
Hard Debt	$32,699	$9,624	$0
Soft Debt	$219,237	$200,967	$182,698
Total Debt	**$251,937**	**$210,592**	**$182,698**
Net Worth	**$164,664**	**$185,155**	**$273,961**
Appreciation	$7,477	$8,484	$12,855
Depreciation	-$7,763	-$5,408	-$3,468
Net Worth Growth	**-$286**	**$3,076**	**$9,387**
% Change	**-0.2%**	**1.7%**	**3.4%**

However, by adding together all the forces acting on each families Asset Engine, over time we can see that the Joneses have -$286 in annual Net Worth Gain today compared to $3,076 for the Smiths and $9,387 for the Millers. This is a powerful example and a *compounding* dynamic. So while it's important to know what our Net Worth is, it's equally important to understand what is happening to our Net Worth over time and how it is impacting our Net Worth Gain.

We can see how the dynamics are very different for each family by looking at the negative influence of depreciation for the Joneses and Smiths, which has a significant impact on their overall Net Worth Gain. While each family has a positive appreciation rate, depreciation counteracts all or most these gains for the Joneses and Smiths. Of course, the reason for these higher depreciation levels are related to the level (cost) of Dead Assets each family owns.

As the Millers' Living Assets continue to grow each year, this impact and difference in Net Worth Gain between the families will only get more pronounced; it will *accelerate* over time. In addition, the Millers' absolute level of depreciation is small compared to the acceleration of depreciation that the Smiths and Joneses will experience as their Dead Assets continue to erode in value.

For many of us, our Dead Assets rate of depreciation far exceeds the rate of appreciation of our Investment and Marginal Assets. It's very hard to consistently generate more than 10 percent annual growth in investments—and usually, our largest Marginal Asset (our home) appreciates at a much lower average rate than our Living Assets. Yet our Dead Assets have no trouble whatsoever in depreciating at 15 or 20 percent per year. Think about what last year's new couch and love seat are now worth online, or that seven-year-old car versus what you paid for it.

This does not mean that the appreciated value of our Living Assets is lost; it just means that our *total Net Worth* is a combination of the *equity* we have in all our Assets. If most of that equity is tied to Dead Assets, then we need to recognize that most of our current Net Worth is going to erode over time. This is the mechanism by which many of us get to retirement with nearly nothing. We bought lots of Dead Assets (with planned obsolescences) over and over again.

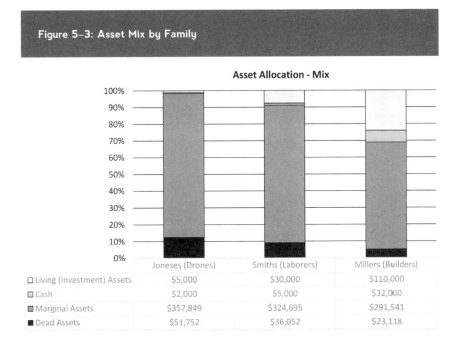

Figure 5–3: Asset Mix by Family

Asset Allocation - Mix

	Joneses (Drones)	Smiths (Laborers)	Millers (Builders)
☐ Living (Investment) Assets	$5,000	$30,000	$110,000
☐ Cash	$2,000	$5,000	$32,000
▨ Marginal Assets	$357,849	$324,695	$291,541
■ Dead Assets	$51,752	$36,052	$23,118

The more we accumulate Dead and Marginal Assets, the more difficult it is to build our Net Worth—because doing so depletes cash, increases intrinsic depreciation, and reduces investment contributions. In total, these negative impacts can overwhelm any investment gains we might otherwise be generating. Over time, our Net Worth needs to grow and be dominated by investment assets as we build our Asset Engine toward our chosen form of retirement.

Note how total assets are similar for each family, but Net Worth is showing some differences—and we see huge differences when we look at Net Worth Gain. Think about how different each family's Asset Engine will look in ten years. Looking at it this way, it's easy to see why Net Worth Gain is so important to understand and measure and why it helps reflect the health of our Asset Engine. It is also easy to see how these three seemingly similar families will have very different financial futures. This is driven *entirely* by the mix of assets that each family has accumulated over time and by the decisions they have made with their excess Free Cash Flow as well as how they chose to use Hard and Soft Debt.

So the triple negative of becoming a Financial Drone is being owned by the Debt Merchants *and* never having the chance to build a healthy Asset Engine *and* not having enough Free Cash Flow to enjoy life. Financial Drones are trapped, chained to an oar, and destined to work far beyond the age they had hoped to, in addition to forgoing any chance to have a chosen lifestyle that they could have otherwise afforded.

It's the *consequences* of the decisions that we make with our excess cash (Asset Engine Contributions) that we want to measure and track. If we can see how our decisions relative to cash impacts the direction of our PFM, we can be in a much better position—not only to change the direction, but to use this newfound control to harness our PFM to take us where we want to go. We can finally put our hands on the wheel and drive! This is why we call our PFM a "Wealth Manufacturing Machine."

Time is a critical factor in this equation. We can't easily "wake up" when we are fifty something and hope to create a powerful Asset Engine from scratch. In fact, in the next chapter we will explore the most powerful force in the universe and how we can harness it to drive our Asset Engine and Net Worth Gain.

Chapter Summary:

- The Asset Engine has a number of internal moving parts and unique dynamics at play and two important outputs: Asset Burden and Net Worth Gain.

- Net Worth Gain is driven by three factors: Asset Maturation, Debt Resolution, and Asset Mix.

- Our assets experience either intrinsic appreciation or intrinsic depreciation.

- Dead Assets have intrinsic depreciation and are a drag on Net Worth Gain. This drag is magnified by the use of Hard Debt to finance their purchase.

- Living and Marginal Assets have intrinsic appreciation, but their value and appreciation rates can be volatile in the short term. For Marginal Assets, their value greatly depends on how well we care for them.

- The higher our mix of Living Assets, the greater our year-over-year Net Worth Gain will be, and ultimately the larger our Retirement Value.

- The decisions we make relative to our assets are the most impactful decisions we can make relative to our PFM and its ability to work for us, versus the other way around.

CHAPTER 6:

THE MOST POWERFUL FORCE IN THE UNIVERSE

In Chapter 5 we covered the inner workings of our Asset Engine and the factors that contribute to Net Worth and drive Net Worth Gain. In this chapter, we will explore some of the tools that can supercharge our Asset Engine's performance.

Einstein is known to have said (paraphrased) that the most powerful force in the universe that he ever encountered was compound interest; money making money from itself. We only need three things for this to occur: money (of course), a *compounding engine* that can generate a growth or appreciation rate, and time.

Money: We need to establish a flow of cash into our compounding engine if we are going to have any chance of achieving our longer-term financial goals. This is our monthly *Living Asset Contribution* amount, including what we save into our 401(k), IRA, or any other amounts that flow into our investment accounts.

Compounding Engine: This is any investment vehicle that can generate an appreciation rate over time. As already discussed, we typically think about stocks, bonds, real-estate, and other forms of investments as having intrinsic appreciation rates. Fortunately for us, the stock market has been proven to be an extremely powerful compounding engine.

Over the last one hundred years, the stock market has delivered *on average* annual growth of about 10 percent.[21] But is not a consistent generator of growth. There were long periods of negative growth and other periods of very high growth. Some years, months, or even days experienced huge increases or decreases. Certain sections or industries within the stock market grew faster or slower than others. Some companies went bankrupt and others experienced tremendous growth and longevity.

However, if we assume average historical long-term growth rates are a reasonable predictor of potential future long-term growth rates, then we can expect to generate, on average, about 10 percent per year in average long-term growth. Roughly over this same 100-year period, inflation averaged around 3.2 percent,[22] so the NET, inflation-adjusted, compound annual appreciation rate of the stock market was about 6.8 percent. Do we know for sure that any 100, 50, or 20-year cycle will deliver exactly 6.8 percent? Of course not. But statistically speaking, our average inflation-adjusted return could reasonably be expected to be around 6.8 percent.

Fortunately, all of us have free and easy access to this incredibly powerful compounding engine. All we need is money and time to use this compounding engine to help us manufacture Net Worth Gain and ultimately Retirement Value.

Time: Because the stock market is volatile and does experience wide swings and long periods of both negative and positive growth, we need to be invested over a long period of time. If we put our savings in the stock market and plan to keep it there for only a few months—or even just a few years—this would be considered speculation or gambling, not investing. We have to give the market time to deliver its expected long-run average return.

In order to think about our PFM in a way that takes this powerful force into account, we need to look at four simple concepts to help us see the true power of this force.

- **Lifetime Economic Value (LEV) (as we have already defined):**

   o   This is the value, in today's dollars, of investing all our Gross Income over our entire working lives. We calculate this by taking our estimated average annual income across our working lives and investing the entire amount in the stock market over our entire working career.*

o   This establishes a context (or baseline) that we will use to understand the financial impact of our decisions.

o   This is a real number, but it is not a realistic value that we can expect to capture in retirement. It is just a simple quantification of the immense economic value that we control over our working lives.

- **Retirement Value (RV):**

    o   This is the projected value, in today's dollars, of our current retirement assets and future contributions that flow into our retirement accounts. It is calculated over the remaining time between now and age sixty-two (or our personal target retirement age) using our defined inflation-adjusted investment growth rate of 6.8 percent (see footnote).

    o   Retirement Value is not the same as projected Net Worth. Retirement Value is only associated with our retirement investment assets. Our actual Net Worth at retirement will be larger than our projected Retirement Value because it includes other things: the value of our home equity, cash, and our other Marginal and Dead Assets. Retirement Value is an important subset of our Net Worth because it is a critical or primary source of post-retirement income generated from our Asset Engine.

    o   Retirement Value is also a subset of our Living Assets. We may have other investment accounts that are not designated for retirement like a college fund for our kids. These are excluded from the Retirement Value calculation.

---

* Lifetime Economic Value and Retirement Value (and all investment-related calculations) are calculated using an inflation-adjusted compound annual growth rate of 6.8 percent. We will also use the average working career of 40 years and the average retirement age of 62 in these calculations.

o   Retirement Value is not intended to take into account social security or defined benefit pension plans or income from businesses that we may own (like rental property or a retail shop). It is simply a measurable output of our Asset Engine that we want to track, control, and grow to reach some target level of income generation in the future.

o   For most people, their investment assets and social security will make up the lion's share of their retirement income. This is why it is essential to establish a target for Retirement Value and understand what will be required to build it and track our progress against that target.

- **Retirement Income From Investments (RIFI):**

o   This is the calculated annual income that our retirement investments can generate. Since Retirement Value is calculated in today's dollars, Retirement Income From Investments (RIFI) is, as well. As a simple way to estimate the amount of income that can be generated from our investments at retirement, we will use a rule of thumb that has been used in the personal financial industry for years. Take the value of our investments and multiply it by 4 percent.

o   This is an amount that we can reasonably generate annually from our investments at retirement and not prematurely run out of money. For example, if we have $1 million in Retirement Value in today's dollars, we will expect it will generate about $40,000 per year in income ($1 million x 4 percent). *

---

*   To calculate our RIFI, we will also use a standard calculation of 4 percent of our Retirement Value to estimate the annual income our RV can generate (RIFI). There are many different strategies and formulas for structuring income-generating assets and estimating optimal RIFI. However, for our purposes, we will use the simple 4 percent of RV calculation throughout the rest of the book. This rate has been established through empirical studies and is one that financial planners frequently use to estimate the amount of retirement assets that can be distributed as income annually to minimize the risk of running out of money prematurely.

We may well have other Marginal Assets like rental property or ownership in a small business, and we would ideally include these in our retirement income o   We can look at Retirement Income From Investments in both absolute dollars of annual or monthly income (i.e., $40,000). We can also look at it as a percentage of our current Gross Income (in the case of our three families: $40K/$96K = 42 percent).

- **Retirement Value Impact (RVI):**

  o   Retirement Value Impact (RVI) is a way to objectively measure the impact of a financial decision on our Retirement Value.

  o   It can be applied to a fixed amount of money at a specific time or a flow of cash over an extended period of time. For example, what is the RVI of $10,000 when we are thirty-two years old versus what is the RVI of $400 per month for the next twenty-five years?

  o   It is calculated using our 6.8 percent compounding from our current age to our target retirement age (see footnote).

  o   RVI is a powerful tool to help us understand the impact of our decisions and better appreciate the opportunity cost of what we buy today versus if we had invested that money instead.

Our Multimillion-Dollar Machine

Recall from Chapter 1 that we calculated that a young couple just starting out making the average annual household income of $100,000 over their forty working years (assuming the earlier year's income might be a bit less and the later years a bit more) translates into a $20 million Personal Finance Machine in today's dollars. *This is the Lifetime Economic Value of a $100,000 average income.*

We know . . . this is a huge number. How can this possibly be true? The reason the average income household has about a $20 million PFM

---

calculations, as they are legitimate investments that can and do generate income. However, the many complex variables in these calculations are simply beyond the scope of this book and ultimately require professional assessments as to their future value and income potential.

is simply due to the power of compounding. We took $8,333 in monthly income ($100K divided by 12 months) every month for 40 years. We invested it in the stock market and used the historical inflation-adjusted compound annual growth rate of 6.8 percent. At the end of 40 years, this compounds to $20 million.

We, of course, don't actually *earn* $20 million over our lifetimes. In fact, we are earning only a fraction of that, about $4 million ($100,000 per year x 40 years). If we invested our $4 million lifetime earnings, they would theoretically become $20 million over 40 years (this is a 5x multiple on our actual earnings)—thanks to the power of compound interest.

This is crazy, right? We are not going to save and invest our entire monthly paycheck even once, let alone every one we earn over our lifetimes! So what is the value to us of calculating our Lifetime Economic Value?

This is so important because we often think about our financial lives in the context of our net monthly paycheck ($8,333 less taxes). People tend to say things like, "It's just a few thousand dollars; how can I possibly ever save a million?" or claim that "My income is just too low for me to have any chance at retirement."

This is not only the wrong attitude, it highlights a false understanding of the powerful economic engine that we all have and can control. The choices we make relative to that "paltry" monthly paycheck are the difference between financial freedom and hardship, regardless of income.

Notice in Figure 6–1 that about 75 percent of households make less than the average income of $100,000 and about 25 percent make more than the average. The Median income (50 percent above and 50 percent below) is closer to $50,000 per year. While $50,000 is a lot less than $100,000, the median household is still responsible for a $10 million Personal Finance Machine.

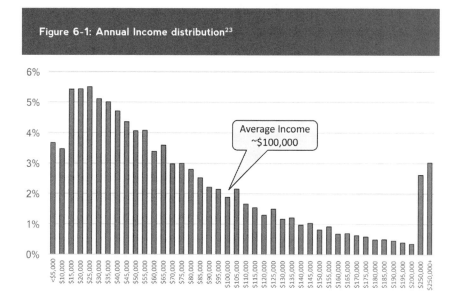

Figure 6-1: Annual Income distribution[23]

We want to be very clear here about the *value* of our lifetime earnings and the financial impact of our decisions. As we stated at the book's opening, we are all running a multimillion dollar enterprise—and every decision we make impacts the amount we are actually able to keep and use at retirement.

We have calculated the Lifetime Economic Value for a range of income levels. Figure 6-2 shows that not only do 50 percent of households have PFMs worth $10 million or more, those with incomes of $100,000+ have PFMs worth $20 million or more; and those with incomes of $150,000+ have PFMs worth $30 million or more!

Let's step back and take a breath here—these numbers are mind-bogglingly large and may seem utterly unrealistic.

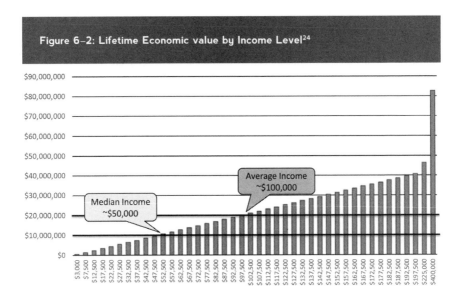

Figure 6–2: Lifetime Economic value by Income Level[24]

But if this is true, why can't we keep just a small piece of this incredible Lifetime Economic Value? Why don't 50 percent of us have at least one million at retirement?

Let's Look at a Simple Example: Say we have current retirement assets valued at $50,000, a Gross Income of $100,000, a Living Asset Contribution going into our retirement fund of 10 percent of our gross income from now until retirement. We are 32 years old with a plan to retire at 62. This yields a Retirement Value of over $1.37 million (in today's dollars assuming a 6.8 percent net of inflation, compounded annual growth rate). If we convert this to annual income (assuming a 4 percent annual distribution rate on our $1.37 million investment), this would deliver $55,000 in Retirement Income from Investments (RIFI) or 55 percent of our current gross income. If we add an estimated social security income (the average social security payment for retirees is about $16,000/year/beneficiary),[25] we could anticipate having a post-retirement income of 70 percent of our current annual Gross Income.

However, if we had only saved $25,000 so far and our future Living Asset Contribution was 5 percent, our Retirement Value would be about $683,000—and we would only be able to generate $27,000 in Retirement Income From Investments, or about 27 percent of our current income. If we add the average social security benefit, we might get to about 42 percent of our current income in retirement.

So we can see that in one case we can easily get to over a million in investment assets and can replace nearly all our pre-retirement income, and in the other case we don't even come close.

So the answer to the question of what happens to our millions: it's both simple and obvious—we just spend it all away!

The goal is not to capture all or even most of our LEV. It's to capture just enough of it to provide sufficient retirement assets to retire when we want with the lifestyle that we want.

Let's look at it from a Net Worth perspective (Figure 6-3). There are about 124 million households in the United States today,[26] and the top 10 percent of households hold 86 percent of the total U.S. Net Worth.

Figure 6-3: Household Net Worth by Percentile[27]

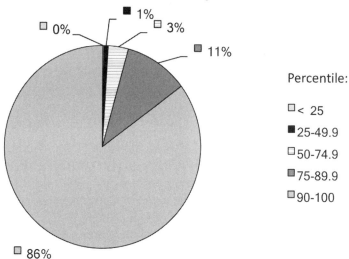

And if we look at the distribution of wealth over time in Figure 6–4, it is clear the top 10 percent just keep getting richer while the rest just keep . . . staying the same. Most households simply cannot break out of the low Net Worth rut. For example, we can see that even the 60 to 80 percentile group only have an average Net Worth of about $373,000—only about 17 percent of what those in the top 10 percent of households have.

Figure 6–4: Net Worth by Income Percentile by Year[28]

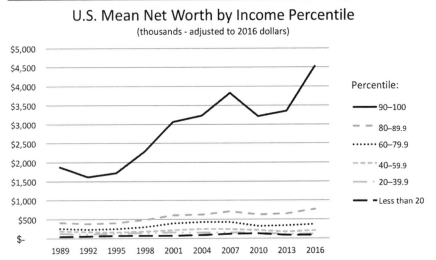

When we look at retirement account values by age group, in Table 6–1 we see that the typical working household age 55-64 has some very thin total retirement investments. These data show that the median retirement account balance for those 55-64 year olds in the 3rd (middle) income quintile is only $104,000! And, only 58 percent of these households have a 401(k). Those 55-64 year olds in the 4th income quintile are only somewhat better off with $335,400 in retirement savings, though only 62 percent of the people in this group have a 401(k). Turning to the highest income group, they have saved about $780,000—far below the $30 million or more in Lifetime Economic Value they have been managing for the last 30 to 40 years.

Looking across all income levels, the median retirement balance of this age group is $135,000. This shockingly low amount can generate only $5,400 per *year* in retirement income. To make this even more sobering, this is only for the 52 percent of households *who* have a retirement account.[29] The other 48 percent have no retirement account savings at all! These retirement values are less than 1 percent of the Lifetime Economic Value for *any* of these income levels. How is this possible? Is it a national crisis? Yes.

As stated earlier, like judging the weight loss industry on the obesity rate, these figures further highlight that after decades of work and access to all kinds of personal financial advice, we have failed spectacularly to leverage that advice to our advantage.

Table 6–1: 401(k) / IRA Balances for Working Households Age 55-64[30]		
Income Quintile	**Median 401(k)/ IRA Balance**	**% with 401(k)**
Lowest	$26,700	25%
2nd	$72,000	45%
3rd	$104,000	58%
4th	$335,400	62%
Highest	$780,000	70%
Total	**$135,000**	**52%**

These data are very sobering.

The Reason We Have So Little Is a Combination of Three Things:

1. We do not understand (and therefore control) our PFM.

2. We are not saving and investing enough (because we don't fully appreciate the impact of the decisions we are making).

3. We are not starting early enough. (The lure of the Debt Merchants is strongest when we are young.)

This compounding machine (that is, the stock market) works just fine. We are just not using it! Figure 6–5 shows the growth of the stock market since 1950. It looks pretty spectacular, and it is. Over the long term, the stock market is a very productive compounding machine. The key is to be in the market for the *long term*. We cannot just get in and get out of the market because we think it is going up or down or because we just lost or gained significantly.

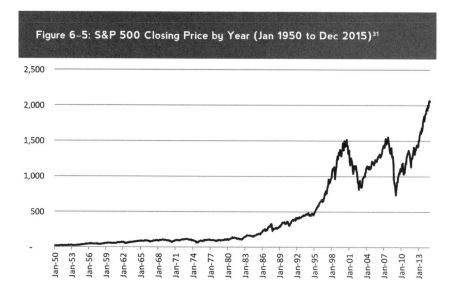

Figure 6–5: S&P 500 Closing Price by Year (Jan 1950 to Dec 2015)[31]

The Time-Value of Money

Take a look at this next chart (Figure 6–6). This shows the percent contribution of an investment from each individual year of a constant annual investment over 40 years, compared to the total value at the end of the 40 years. For example: If we look at our average household income of $100,000 and its associated Lifetime Economic Value of $20 million, the first year of income (after accounting for 40 years of investment at 6.8 percent interest) contributed 7 percent of the total $20 million (~$1.4 million). Conversely, the last $100,000 (at age 64) contributed only $100,000 or 0.5 percent of the total $20 million. The first year contributes the most, and each subsequent year contributes less and less, until the last year contributes only a paltry 0.5 percent of the total potential value. This is the power of compounding. The $100K we contributed in the first year has 15 times the value of the $100,000 contributed in the last year.

This same exact dynamic applies to any constant savings amount. So if the average income household is saving 10 percent of its Gross Income every year ($10K) into a retirement account, they would have accumulated a retirement savings of $2 million at age 65. About 7 percent of that amount would have come from the growth of the $10K contributed in the first year and 0.5 percent from the $10K contributed in the 40th year.

What is interesting is that over 50 percent of the $2 million comes from the contributions made in the first 9 years. Think about this for a minute. If we *start* saving 10 percent of our income *after* having worked 9 years, and then contribute 10 percent for the next 31 years, we will only accumulate 50 percent of what we could have if we had started saving and investing 10 percent in the first year rather than the 9th. Wow! Also notice that all contributions made *after* age 52 (the last 13 years) represent only about 10 percent of the total retirement savings potential.

Assuming no dramatic changes in inflation-adjusted income or savings rates, **what we do in the first eight to ten years of our working lives has the single largest impact on what our Asset Engine will be worth at retirement**. This chart dramatically highlights the importance of saving and investing *early and consistently*.

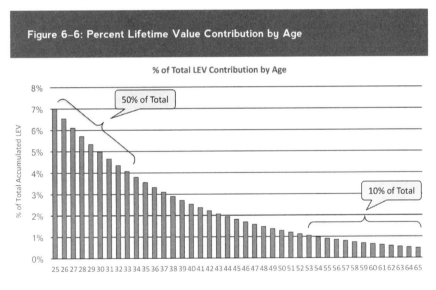

Figure 6-6: Percent Lifetime Value Contribution by Age

This is certainly not a new revelation. However, it reinforces Einstein's assertion that compounding is the most powerful force in the universe. But it requires time to do its magic and we have to put money into the compounding machine!

It Only Seems Like Our Incomes Are Going Up

These LEV calculations may seem simplistic because we think our incomes will be much higher as we advance in our careers. While this is certainly true for some of us, most incomes are not increasing, on average, relative to the underlying inflation rate.

By adding in an inflation rate of 3 percent per year, our average $100,000 Gross Income today becomes $332,000 in 40 years. This can lull us into thinking that our incomes are going up—when in fact, in real terms, they are not. Yes, our incomes do increase over time. But if they're increasingly at roughly the inflation rate, which they are, then in the context of buying power, they are not really increasing much at all.

As Figure 6–7 shows, some of us can increase our incomes much faster than the inflation rate. This is great, but it does not change the need for us to control our PFM and consciously decide how much to invest annually. Generally, our income goes through cycles of faster and slower growth, but in reality, for the vast majority of us, the long-term average will actually be pretty close to the long-run inflation rate.

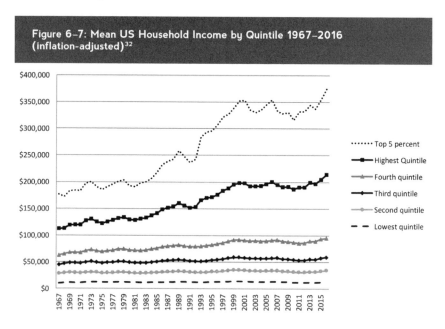

Figure 6–7: Mean US Household Income by Quintile 1967–2016 (inflation-adjusted)[32]

In fact, between 1967 and 2016, the inflation-adjusted mean income for the middle quintile has fluctuated around $50,000, but has not significantly increased over time. Middle quintile incomes have just not increased significantly since the late 1960s on an inflation-adjusted basis for any of the four lower quintiles (groups of 20 percent). Only the top 20 percent have seen their inflation-adjusted incomes increase significantly over this period from about

$112,000 to about $213,000. And within that top 20 percent quintile, the top 5 percent of wage earners account for the majority of that increase. Said differently, if you're not in the top 5 or 10 percent of income earners, expecting your income to grow faster than inflation is betting against the last 49 years of what actually happened, which is basically negligible real income growth.

Think about "how little" things cost twenty years ago and what incomes were back then. Our buying power is almost exactly the same today as it was back then. The only things that are different now are the prices and our income amounts (both, on average, increased by the same percentage).

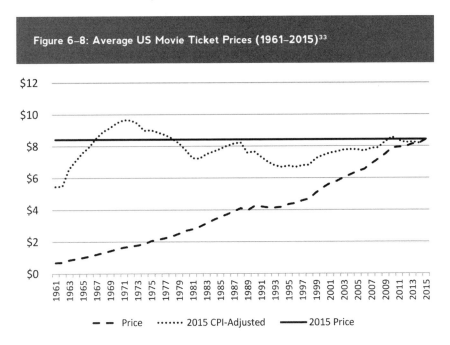

Figure 6–8: Average US Movie Ticket Prices (1961–2015)[33]

So if we consistently save and invest 3, 5, 7 or 10 percent of our Gross Income every year into our retirement account, then the % LEV contribution by age graph (Figure 6-6) we showed earlier actually is a fairly good representation of the absolute contribution to our Retirement Value from each of our working years, on an inflation-adjusted basis.

The implication is that if we don't start saving until we are 50, whatever we have when we are 65 is only 10 percent of the amount we could have had if we had started *consistently* saving from the beginning of our working lives.

This does not mean that we are *doomed* if we don't start saving until we are older. It just means that we have to save so much more of our Gross Income to accumulate even a modest amount of retirement savings because we have lost most of the power of compounding.

The Penalty of Ignoring Compound Interest

What if that average $100,000 income household took 10 percent every month of every year for 40 years and put it into mason jars and buried them in the backyard? They would actually have far less than the $333,320 ($8,333 x 40 years) they had stashed away because inflation would have eaten away its value or buying power. By retirement age, it would only be worth about $233,000 in today's dollars. Not to mention, they would have forgone the potential to have had about $2 million had they invested in the stock market.

This is the impact of compounding working AGAINST us. Even if we don't take advantage of the 9.8 percent average stock market investment return over the last 100 years, we still have to account for the *negative* impact of the 3 percent in inflation rate that is relentlessly eating away the value of our uninvested savings. If we stash our cash away in proverbial mason jars, our future savings will be worth about 30 percent *less* over the course of our working lives than what we actually saved—and almost 90 percent *less* than if we had invested it in the overall stock market. **If we don't invest our savings, over the course of 40 years, we will have thrown away ~90 percent of its potential value.**

The point is that we must not only consistently save cash to build Retirement Value, we have to invest it as well. Otherwise, it just erodes away to a mere shadow of its former self over time.

Said differently: **We must harness the most powerful force in the universe to avoid the corrosive effects of inflation working against us.** If we choose not to invest our savings, there is virtually a 100 percent chance that it will lose value—probably around 30 percent over the course of our working lives. If we do invest it consistently in the stock market, there is very good chance that it will be worth more than what we put in, probably about 5-6 times more.

The Road to a Million

We would be in a difficult predicament if we didn't have access to this most powerful force in the universe. Figure 6–9 shows that if we save and invest $281 per month starting at age 20, we will have $1 million in Retirement

Value by age 65 and a Retirement Income From Investments of $3,333 per month for the rest of our lives (in today's dollars). If we wait until we were 25 to start, it will require $403 per month to achieve the same result. At age 35 it requires a hefty $853 per month, and if we wait until we were 55, it will require an incredible $5,841 per month to get to the $1 million.

Here is the really interesting part: The precentage that we *actually contribute* out of our own pocket to that million dollar nest egg is very different. Starting Age: Age 20 = 14 percent, Age 25 = 19 percent, Age 35 = 31 percent, Age 55 = 70 percent. The end result is exactly the same: one million dollars. Why are we doing all the heaving lifting ourselves, when our money, time, and that fantastic compounding engine (the stock market) can do nearly all of the work, if we let it?

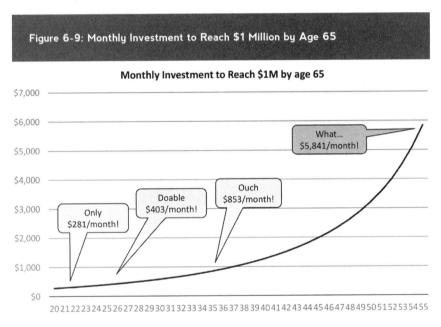

Figure 6-9: Monthly Investment to Reach $1 Million by Age 65

A Quick but Important Detour

The content in these next few sections is related to a common investing approach, called "passive investing," which can basically be found anywhere; therefore, it isn't part of what we had originally wanted to include in this book. However, we did want to reinforce a few key points here for one important reason: we humans collectively seem to have an aversion to using the stock market. Historically, and even today, participation in the stock market averages only around 54 percent of U.S. adults.[34] Even worse, there is evidence that participation is negatively correlated with age; that is, younger households have lower participation rates.[35] This fact reflects how we are literally throwing away the opportunity to use the most powerful force in the universe to our advantage. Avoiding the stock market, especially when we are young, essentially means that we're resigning ourselves to having a permanently weak Asset Engine and insufficient funds to achieve the financial freedom we seek. Effectively utilizing the stock market as a *compounding* engine within our Asset Engine is essential to a well-managed PFM.

But Investing in the Market Is Too Complicated!

Many of us look at investing as a game that is rigged against us. There is a certain truth to this when we look at the entire industry that has evolved to help us *manage* our investments. We're bombarded with messages from brokers, investment houses, and blogs, investment letters and strategies and an endless stream of "proven" strategies to *beat* the market. It is incredibly confusing and intimidating.

But it doesn't have to be that way.

Here are four basic concepts that are important to understand relative to successful investing:

1. Asset Allocation is proven to be one of the most important drivers of long-term growth.[36]

2. Very few individuals can consistently beat the market year after year—and we don't need to beat it.

3. Hidden expenses and fees can significantly erode your investment return over time.

4. There is a big difference between investing and speculating/gambling.

Let's look at each of these in detail.

Asset Allocation

The 1990 Nobel Prize in Economics went to Harry M. Markowitz, Merton H. Miller, and William F. Sharpe for their work in understanding and pricing capital markets. The result of their contributions is that the largest contributor to the rate of return of an investment portfolio is related to which classes of assets are selected and the mix you choose between them.

The individual companies or stocks that are represented within the asset class are much less relevant. For example, if equities (stocks) are an asset class, then it matters much less which companies within the asset class that you are invested in. What matters is how much of your total investment portfolio is invested in stocks versus other asset classes (like bonds, commodities, or real estate).

This insight greatly simplifies the challenge for everyday investors in making good decisions relative to their Living Assets. We should spend most of our time deciding the allocation of our Living Asset portfolio between traditional asset classes like: stocks (large, mid, small cap, domestic, international); bonds (government, corporate); and cash. Some investors also consider less traditional investment classes like: commodities (oil, corn, and precious metals), real estate (your home, rental property, Real Estate Investment Trusts—REITs), or venture capital (start-up companies). However, many investors just focus on the more common asset classes of stocks, bonds, and cash.

Because investing in individual stocks and across asset classes is so daunting for the average investor, the mutual fund was developed many years ago. A mutual fund is simply a group of individual stocks and/or bonds under some strategy or theme. For example, there are mutual funds of retail companies or gold mining companies or textile companies. There are as many different mutual funds as there are categories of companies you can think of. There are also international and domestic mutual funds. You can also find lifestyle, life stage mutual funds, green funds, and social funds. There are thousands of them—and for the most part, we think most of them should largely be ignored.

The funds that we focus on to achieve our goals and not spend endless hours trying to beat the market are index funds. These funds are designed to mirror the whole market. So, whatever the entire market does, these funds will do the same, and we should be happy with that.

Very Few Investors Can Consistently Beat the Market Year After Year Over the Long Term

The investment services industry is huge and hugely lucrative—and they want nothing more than to "help" us manage our investments. They offer us the value of guiding us through the complexity and risk of investing—that they created in the first place. They claim to be able to deliver better investment returns than the next guy, *and* keep our investments safe. But how can everyone be better than the average manager *and* better than the market. If you ask how this can be, you are 90 percent of the way there in recognizing that these are not the people you should be listening to.

There are thousands of actively-managed mutual funds in the market today. There are life cycle funds, social responsibility funds; there are even mutual funds of mutual funds. So how does one figure out what to invest in? How is this any better than having to pick from a sea of individual stocks and bonds?

In addition to the Nobel Prize-winning insight on asset classes, there is broad and compelling evidence to show that passively managed index funds deliver better results than actively-managed funds 80 percent to 90 percent of the time.[37] The longer the time horizon, the more likely index funds do better than any single or group of actively managed funds. The other piece of good news is there are only a handful of index funds to choose from—because there are only a handful of broad market indexes (S&P 500, Russell 5000, Dow Jones Industrial Average, and a few others) that exist.

Fund Expenses Can Quickly Erode Your Investment Gains

Not only do actively managed funds underperform index funds; they also are much more expensive. All mutual funds charge annual fees that are a percentage of the total amount we have invested. These fees are the way the fund managers make their money. They're based on the costs to manage the fund and how much the fund managers think they can charge.

Most index funds have expense rates far less than 1 percent per year; many charge as little as 0.05 percent (or about 5 basis points. There are 100 basis points in 1%) of invested funds. Conversely, most actively managed funds charge 1 to 2 percent per year, and some charge even more. So for the privilege of participating in many actively managed mutual funds they will charge you *30 times more* each year compared to the lowly indexed mutual fund. This level of expense is staggering when one considers that we get charged regardless of the fund's performance—and that the average (inflation-adjusted) long-term return is 6.8 percent. This suggests that if an actively managed fund takes 1.5 percent in fees, they are taking 20 percent of your total average long-term investment return—and that's only if the fund can deliver the same performance as the overall market in the long run. When you try to beat the market, you are more likely to underperform the market than match the market—specifically because you are attempting to do something different than the market and the ability to regularly select only those segments of the market that will consistently out-perform the overall market is nearly impossible.

Again, we want to keep things straightforward. Why fight against something as simple and effective as investing in low cost index mutual funds when the alternative is to wade into a sea of complexity and increased risk? There are lots of other places to invest our time and energy—like where we are going to go on vacation next!

Yes, there are a few investors who can consistently beat the market over the long term

Warren Buffet is the most famous of these rare individuals, and there are a few others as well. These individuals spend their professional lives digging into and understanding the details of every single company they invest in and then when they decide to invest, they invest for the long term. In addition, they manage their risk by investing in a broad range of very high-quality companies, because they know that even after incredible amounts of research, you just can't know everything and you can never predict the future with certainty.

Time Is the Most Important Factor in Determining Risk

When we consider investing in the stock market, we tend to think about the risk of stocks or bonds, or this or that particular industry or company. These considerations pale in comparison to *time* as a variable in the risk equation. Looking at Figure 6–10, we see that the stock market investment gains or losses can be huge over a one-year horizon. From this perspective, you might think the stock market looks like gambling, and you'd be right. Investing in the stock market and expecting to take our money out within a year or two is in fact just gambling. However, if we keep our money in the market for ten or twenty years, we have a much smaller risk of losing our original investment or failing to best the ravages of inflation.

Where Are Our Millions Going?

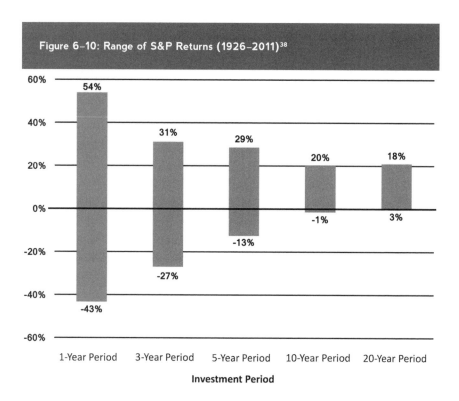

Figure 6–10: Range of S&P Returns (1926–2011)[38]

When we look at our collective financial situation in the context of our LEV, we can now see how much of our economic potential is just slipping through our hands. *Somebody* is getting our millions; it's just not us.

Every financial decision we make impacts how much of our LEV that we keep versus give away. It's absolutely true that we get something in return and something of value with every purchase that we make. But we also give up something of value, as well—specifically, the Retirement Value and the associated Retirement Income From Investments of that money we spend.

As we've stated several times, the amount of our income doesn't matter. What does matter is taking advantage of that compounding engine. You'd be surprised to find people with fairly modest incomes that are members of the top 10 percent in Net Worth club. You no doubt have heard stories of the unassuming janitor who dies with $2 million in the bank or the waitress who leaves $1 million to her cat. These people lived a frugal lifestyle, saved, and invested wisely and were consequently able to build a very sizable Asset Engine on a meager income. So if we make three or four or ten times what they made, we should be able to have something, maybe half or a quarter of these millions.

> Investing does not have to be so complicated. However, we are not investment or financial advisors. Find a competent **non-commission** advisor and work with him or her to help you understand the types of investments that might be right for you based on your time horizons and risk tolerances.

One of the primary reasons people don't have enough (or any) money at retirement is simple: **They don't realize the true cost of the financial decisions they make during their lifetimes.**

Opportunity Cost Index

The Opportunity Cost Index (OCI) is an easy-to-use multiplication factor that we developed. It reflects our money's Retirement Value based on the amount of time we could be leveraging compounding up to retirement. Said differently, our Opportunity Cost Index is a straightforward way to estimate the Retirement Value of the money we have to spend or invest today, based on our age and time to retirement. The bigger our Opportunity Cost Index, the more "valuable" our money is.

There are two versions of OCI. The first version—Spot OCI—is related to the Retirement Value of a one-time dollar amount at any given point in time. The second—Annuity OCI—is related to the Retirement Value for a constant contribution of money from any given point of time until retirement. For example, if we want to know the Retirement Value of $10,000 when we are 25 years old, we would use the Spot OCI factor multiplied times the $10,000. If, on the other hand, we wanted to know the Retirement Value of $3,600 per year ($300 per month) from the time we are 25 until retirement, we would use Annuity OCI.

You might wonder why we developed these OCI factors when it's fairly easy to calculate the Retirement Value of either a one-time amount or constant contribution of money. We did this because the OCI Index is a powerful and easy-to use-tool to help us understand and measure the impact of our financial decisions before we make them. OCI clearly shows us the multiplication of our money as a result of the incredibly powerful force of compounding and therefore the true impact of our decisions.

When we are 25 years old, our Spot OCI is 15.2. So if we spend $10,000 on a new ATV or a vacation, the Retirement Value Impact of that decision is about $152,000 (15.2 times $10,000). However, our Annuity OCI at age 25 is a whopping 207. So if we decide to put $300 per month ($3,600 per year) into our 401(k), we can expect to have about $745,000 ($3600 x 207) in today's dollars at age 65.

But, if we are 60 years old and buy the same ATV or vacation, the Retirement Value Impact of that $10,000 decision is only $14,000 because our Spot OCI is only 1.4 (we have only 5 years' time to invest that $10K). Similarly, for the $3,600 going into our 401(k), the value at age 65 would only be about $21.6K ($3,600 x 6).

Figure 6–11: Spot — Opportunity Cost Index

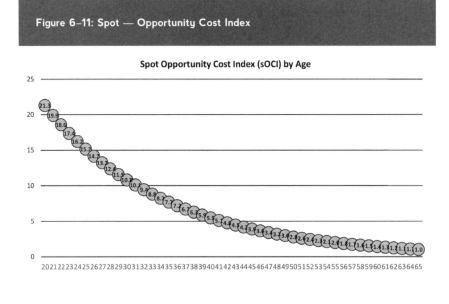

Spot Opportunity Cost Index (sOCI) by Age

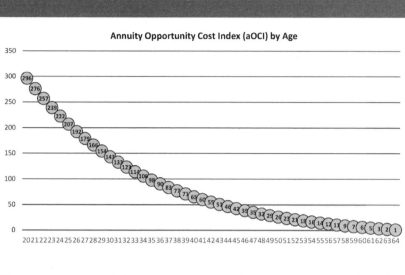

Figure 6–12: Annuity — Opportunity Cost Index

We can view a larger OCI as a cost when we think about spending, but also as a huge benefit when we think about it from saving and investing perspective. For example, a 60-year-old has to save and invest $108,000 all in the same year to equal the same $152,000 at retirement that the 25-year-old would have by a one-time savings and investment of $10,000. And to achieve a Retirement Value of the same $745,000 that the 25-year-old achieved by saving $3,600 per year, the 60-year-old would have to save and invest about $124,000 each year until age 65.

When we look at the Spot and Annuity OCIs versus age charts, we can see that our money's Retirement Value is incredibly large when we are young. It then falls off rapidly until we are about forty years old and then reverts to a slower rate of decline. Notice that the shape and relative impact of the two curves are similar. For example, notice that the Spot OCI is roughly three times larger at age twenty-five than it is at age forty, and the Annuity OCI is roughly three times larger at age twenty-five compared to age forty. So whatever age you are: take note of your spot and annuity OCI and remember it! Next time you make a big purchase, *do the math!*

The point of this is that we have a very limited window of time to have a large OCI. If we squander our opportunity to invest and leverage the power of compounding in our early years it is incredibly difficult, if not impossible, to offset. When it comes to investing and taking advantage of compound interest, time is the ultimate double-edged sword—it works for and against us!

If you are a grandparent, think about the OCI of your grandchildren. Setting money aside for them when they are young allows compounding to really work for them. For example, the Spot OCI for a newborn is over 80. If we make an investment on their behalf when they are born, it will multiply by a factor of 80 by the time they are 65. So if we put $12,500 in an investment account when they are born, and it will be worth $1 million when they retire (in today's dollars), which is more money than 90 percent of households retire with today.

> Our PFM simply cannot grow to achieve our long-term financial goals without using a compounding engine. **PERIOD!**

The Dark Cost of College Debt

One of the biggest challenges young households face as they begin their financial lives is college debt. It seems like a good trade-off: getting a college education for a little debt at the end. But this may not always be true. Those graduates with significant debt are left with a substantial burden that can put them at a major financial disadvantage for their entire lives.

We often think that the average post-graduation debt is large, but manageable relative to our future income potential. It may be true in that context; but in the context of OCI and the true cost of that debt on our Retirement Value, it can be devastating.

Consider that almost 70 percent of college graduates had college debt in 2014 and the average debt load was nearly $30,000.[39] Much of this debt is at interest rates (4–7 percent)[40] that are the same or higher than typical car loan rates (4-5 percent),[41] but with payoff terms of 10 to 15 years. The consequence of having debt this large so early in one's working life is considerable. Instead of being able to save and harness the incredible power of compound interest to help build Retirement Value, these young individuals and families have to prioritize paying off their college debts.

Earlier this chapter, we highlighted that 50 percent of our potential Retirement Value (at a constant savings rate) comes from the money we saved and invested in the first eight to ten years of our working lives. Instead of saving and investing this incredibly valuable money, people with college loans have to use those funds to pay off their debt.

In actual dollars, it looks like this: The theoretical Retirement Value Impact of that $30,000 debt is over $530,000. For the 70 percent of graduates with college debt, this is a significant burden and opportunity cost. Considering that the 2016 median 401(k)/IRA balance of working 55-64 year olds with these accounts is $135,000, graduates with average college debt are starting out $530,000 in the hole relative to their graduating counterparts without debt. Not only do these young households miss out on their most powerful compounding years, they frequently must delay their purchase of a home and other important financial and life decisions.

To understand the impact of student debt on your future potential Retirement Value and Retirement Income From Investments. Consider this simple rule of thumb:

> Take your total undergraduate student debt after graduating and multiply it by 0.7. This is the annual Retirement Income From Investments (RIFI) that you could have had at age 65 if you had been able to save and invest the money committed to paying off your student loans.

For the average student debt this is $30,000 x 0.7 = $21,000 in lost Retirement Income From Investments (or $1,750 per month) for the rest of your life! Coincidently, this is about 30 percent *more* than the average social security benefit per beneficiary being paid today (~$16K/year or $1,327/month). This is an incredibly significant long-term and hidden cost of excessive student debt.

Think carefully about how much debt you are willing to take on to earn a college degree. This is some of the most expensive debt you will ever own (from a Retirement Value perspective). If you have already graduated with significant debt, work really hard to get that debt paid off as soon as possible so you can engage a compounding engine (like the stock market) for as long as possible.

Note that we are not comparing the earning power or LEV of a college education to a high school education. We are comparing a college graduate with little or no debt to one with the average debt. While it may seem like a good idea at the time and that you will make it up later, this debt is a short, medium, and long-term financial headwind and lifetime burden.

In effect, colleges and universities, and the Debt Merchants that support them, are "helping us" by *mortgaging* a huge portion of our lifestyle and future Retirement Value.

Chapter Summary:

- The power of compounding cannot be overstated.

- Our PFM is worth millions, yet over our working careers, we keep almost nothing.

- There are potential millionaires at most every income level, because $400 per month over 40 years is worth $1 million in today's dollars, and even those with modest incomes should be within reach of saving $400 per month (or more!).

- The stock market is a fantastic—though inconsistent and erratic—compounding engine. It has delivered around 6.8 percent compound annual growth over the long term.

- We need significant time (more than ten years!) in the market to 1) fully benefit from compounding and 2) ride through the short-term ups and downs of the market.

- The first eight to ten years of our working lives are the most important in terms of building Retirement Value. They represent about 50 percent of the Retirement Value of a constant (inflation-adjusted) savings rate over our working careers.

- In inflation-adjusted terms, for most of us our incomes are not going up; so banking on increased incomes in our later years to fund our retirement is a risky proposition.

- Inflation is constantly eroding our cash–it's compounding working against us. Keeping too much cash because we are afraid of losing it in the stock market only guarantees that we will lose a significant portion of its value through inflation. There is no such thing as a safe investment or savings account—everything has a certain risk.

- The opportunity cost, as measured by OCI, is time-dependent and can be a huge number. The most valuable time for us to get into the saving and investment mode is when we are young. We can never go back and make up for that lost OCI effect. The Annuity OCI when we are

25 years old is 207. In other words, whatever amount we commit to saving annually from that point forward will multiply by 207 times by the time we get to retirement age—something to think about!

- Graduating from college with significant debt can cripple our ability to achieve our financial and lifestyle goals in the short, medium, and long term.

Personal Finance Machine (PFM) - New Term Review

(Note: A complete list of term definitions can be found in the Glossary.)

- **Annuity OCI (aOCI)** = There are two versions of the Opportunity Cost Index. Annuity OCI is an index or multiplier related to the Retirement Value for a constant contribution of money from any given point of time until retirement. For example, if we wanted to know the Retirement Value of $3,600 per year ($300 per month) from the time we are 25 until retirement, we would use Annuity OCI.

- **Retirement Income From Investments (RIFI)** = The annual income your retirement investments can generate in retirement. To calculate RIFI, you can use a standard calculation of 4 percent of your Retirement Value to estimate the annual income our RV can generate (RIFI). There are many different strategies and formulas for estimating the optimal RIFI, however this book uses the simple (and common) 4 percent of RV calculation.

- **Retirement Value Index (RVI)** = RVI is a way to objectively measure the impact of your financial decisions on Retirement Value. It can be applied to a fixed amount of money at a specific time or a flow of cash over an extended period. This is the result of applying either the aOCI or the sOCI to a sum or flow of money.

- **Spot OCI (sOCI)** = There are two versions of the Opportunity Cost Index (OCI). Spot OCI is related to the Retirement Value of a one-time dollar amount at any given point in time. For example, if we want to know the Retirement Value of $10,000 when we are 25 years old, we would use the Spot OCI factor multiplied times the $10,000.

SECTION THREE:

HARNESSING OUR PERSONAL FINANCE MACHINE

CHAPTER 7:

ACHIEVING FINANCIAL FREEDOM

Most of us dream about "financial freedom." It's why most of us work so hard, budgeting and saving, building our careers, sacrificing and scrimping—but, in the end, we find that the dream of financial freedom remains frustratingly out of reach. For many of us, buying lottery tickets is just a form of saying, "I can't get there on my own, so maybe I can get lucky."

However, financial freedom is nearly always right in front of us. What we need to do is exert sound control over our financial decisions and put our newfound understanding of how to control our PFM into practice.

We often think about financial freedom as having millions of dollars and the ability to buy whatever we want. That is certainly one way to see it, but not the only way. Financial freedom can be as simple as not having to worry about paying the monthly bills or covering holiday expenses or getting caught by some big unpredictable expense. It can be eliminating the need to worry about paying for our children's college education, or about retirement. It can be the ability to take a risk and start a business. It can be the feeling that whatever we want to buy or do (within reason) is within reach. In truth, financial freedom is achievable regardless of our income. And there are two types: Operational and Structural.

Operational Financial Freedom

Having a well-structured and managed PFM and Operations Engine—with several months of Routine Operating Expenses in Cash Reserves and a healthy and consistent Free Cash Flow—means that we've achieved the operational version of financial freedom. We don't have to worry about paying the bills or getting burned by some unforeseen expense, and we're in a strong position to weather a major financial setback like illness or even an extended layoff. In short, we will have an operational level of financial confidence, control, and freedom.

Said differently, *getting and keeping your Operations Engine in good working order is an immediate and material form of financial freedom.* No waiting for millions in the bank, no big raise or quarter million-dollar salary, no risk taking, no lottery ticket luck. All we need is a well-funded Cash Reserve, well-managed Asset Burden, healthy Free Cash Flow, and the discipline to keep things running smoothly. By doing so, most of us can achieve real financial freedom in months, not years. Operational Financial Freedom comes from *understanding and control.*

Structural Financial Freedom

The structural type of financial freedom is about building a targeted level of Retirement Value. Structural financial freedom requires that we establish the ability to have a sustainable target standard of living from our Asset Engine without the need to continue collecting a paycheck. Achieving structural financial freedom requires four ingredients: time, consistent and sufficient Living Asset Contribution, use of a compounding engine, and responsible management of our investments.

While it takes time to achieve Structural Financial Freedom, we can easily know if we are on track or not based on how much we are investing monthly and annually and the Retirement Value of that stream of cash. Again, understanding and control are what will deliver both forms of Financial Freedoms.

Today "Retirement" Is a Very Personal Concept

Everyone has different definitions, goals, timing, and lifestyle ideas for retirement. Therefore, we need to recognize that retirement may not be some hard date where we stop working and flip a switch to convert our Asset Engine into our primary income source. Many of us may want (or need) to have more of a transitional or partial retirement where we may still be working, or working part time. Or, we are pursuing some other endeavors that we always wanted to do. The point is that we want to be financially prepared for whenever and however we want to enter the next phase.

In a partial retirement mode—which could last for several years—our investments can frequently continue to grow as we are transitioning into full retirement by keeping our Living Assets in more of a growth mode versus converting them straight into an income generation mode.

So how do we get to Operational and Structural Financial Freedom? How do we manage and balance our short and long-term needs? How do we deal with these competing priorities without getting lost in the tangle of our finances? What big decisions have the biggest impact on our PFM? And which ones are screwing us up?

> *Operational Financial Freedom is all about building a healthy Operations Engine.*
> *Structural Financial Freedom is all about building a healthy Asset Engine.*

Primary Asset Allocation - Structuring Our PFM

Recall from Chapter 5 that our Asset Engine has two important outputs: Asset Burden and Net Worth Gain. Our Net Worth Gain is driven by appreciation, depreciation, asset mix, and debt resolution. And as we just discussed in Chapter 6, we have a great opportunity (and need) to leverage the incredibly powerful compounding engine to help us maximize the appreciation rate of our Living Assets and build Retirement Value. However, we need to structure our PFM to ensure that we have enough Free Cash Flow and a large enough Living Asset Contribution rate to achieve both our short and long-term financial goals.

The Importance of Our Decisions

We make decisions every day that impact our PFM's operation and performance. With all its moving parts and the many dynamics within our Asset Engine, it can be overwhelming to determine what we should focus on. Fortunately, the answer is very simple and clear. The most important decisions we make are all related to the Asset Engine and its all-important outputs: Asset Burden and Net Worth Gain.

Primary Versus Secondary Asset Allocation

In Chapter 6 we discussed the term "Asset Allocation" to describe the allocation of investments across classes of investment assets like domestic stocks (large, mid, and small cap.), bonds, international stocks, real estate, commodities (gold, silver, etc.), and cash.

In this book, we will refer to this type of asset allocation as Secondary Asset Allocation—the allocation of Living (investment) Assets among the various investment asset classes with the intent of optimizing our investment appreciation rate over time.

We also want to introduce the term Primary Asset Allocation. Primary Asset Allocation (PAA) is a critical set of PFM decisions that involve the allocation of our excess cash among the four asset classes within the Asset Engine: Living, Marginal, Dead, and Cash. Primary Asset Allocation happens above the level of Secondary Asset Allocation (which is why we call it *primary*). Primary Asset Allocation defines the structure of our Asset Engine, and by extension the Operations Engine. As we make decisions about how much house to buy, how many and which cars to own, or how much to invest, we are making Primary Asset Allocation decisions that have a direct impact on Net Worth Gain and Asset Burden, and by extension, on our Operational and Structural Financial Freedom.

> It turns out Primary Asset Allocation is the **Biggest Lever** that we have and use—knowingly or unknowingly—to control all aspects of our PFM.

Primary Asset Allocation dictates all aspects of our Operations and Asset Engines. Remember when we talked about *structuring* our Operations Engine to generate '30 or 40 MPG' (Free Cash Flow as a percent of Gross Income)? Primary Asset Allocation is how we *structure* our Asset Engine. That structure, in turn, determines how *both* our engines will perform. *This is the essence of how our PFM functions and how we exert control over it.*

In simple terms, Primary Asset Allocation is *what we do with our excess cash*. If we look back to Chapter 3 and our focus on our Cash Reserves, we recall that there are effectively two options for our deploying excess cash:

A. **Non-Routine Expenses (NRE).** These include Lifestyle (fun) and Unpredictable Gotcha expenses (not fun). We make everyday decisions about how much of our Cash Reserves we want to dedicate to our lifestyle expenses like vacations, activities, holidays, etc.

B. **Asset Engine Contributions (AEC)**: Any *excess* cash, after Non-Routine Expenses, goes into our Asset Engine and the *decisions* we make about where to *spend* this cash is Primary Asset Allocation (PAA).

Primary Asset Allocation decisions fall into five basic categories:

1. **Buying Living (investment) Assets**. As previously discussed, these are traditional investments like mutual funds, stocks, bonds, etc.

2. **Buying Marginal Assets**. Buying a house, investing in a work of art, valuable jewelry, or buying antiques or collectables all fall under the category Marginal Assets. In addition, making major improvements to a house is also a form of *purchasing* a Marginal Asset.

3. **Buying Dead Assets**. Every car, boat, ATV, lawn mower, or piece of new furniture is a Dead Asset.

4. **Using Hard and Soft Debt** (to fund 1-3 above)

5. **Accumulating cash**

Primary Asset Allocation Impact on Asset Burden and Our Operations Engine

Remember from Chapter 4 that sliding into financial servitude is directly related to Primary Asset Allocation decisions and their impact on Asset Burden. Every time we use cash to acquire Dead or Marginal Assets, we *add* to Asset Burden. Additionally, every time we use cash + *loans* or credit cards to acquire Dead or Marginal Assets, we *magnify* their impact on Asset Burden.

The reason why using cash has a *smaller* impact on Asset Burden, of course, is because we have no monthly principal and interest payments to go along with our purchase. While using credit/loans preserves our Cash Reserves—and therefore seems like a good idea on the surface —it also changes the *structure* of our Operations Engine by increasing Asset Burden and *significantly reducing* our Free Cash Flow. And, as previously discussed, constricting our Free Cash Flow until it is a trickle *is the main factor* that leads to the eventual collapse of Stage 2 of our Operations Engine—our Cash Reserves. If the stream dries up, so will the reservoir.

So how do we avoid locking up our engines?

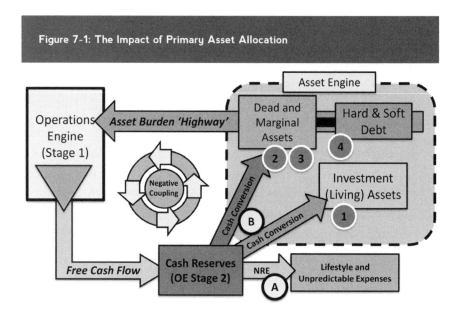

Figure 7-1: The Impact of Primary Asset Allocation

We see some interesting things if we look at Primary Asset Allocation from the perspective of Asset Burden. Looking at the Figure 7-1, there are two ways to put excess cash from our Cash Reserves to work: "A"—spending money on our lifestyle; going on vacation, enjoying the theatre, fun activities, etc. and "B"—converting that cash into assets. *Spending available cash on our lifestyle does not increase or impact Asset Burden.* Converting cash into assets is where things get tricky.

In looking more closely at "B", only one Primary Asset Allocation option *does not* increase or contribute to Asset Burden: Making **Living Asset Contributions (LAC)** (1). When we choose to dedicate a portion of our excess cash into our investments, we are, in effect, *controlling* Asset Burden and *protecting* our Free Cash Flow.

Alternatively, when we use our excess cash to acquire Dead or Marginal Assets (2 & 3) we are frequently* increasing Asset Burden, and when we use debt (4) to facilitate these purchases it *magnifies* the impact on Asset Burden. This gives us a clearer picture of how uncontrolled or misdirected *Primary Asset Allocation* can ripple through our entire PFM.

Important Implications of our PAA Decisions

1. Using most of our excess cash to buy Dead and Marginal Assets leads directly to increased Asset Burden and reduced Free Cash Flow.

    a. Keeping Asset Burden low and Free Cash Flow high is **central** to maintaining a healthy and resilient Cash Reserves and PFM. With a high Free Cash Flow rate (MPG), we can quickly replenish our Cash Reserves.

2. The fastest way to lock up our engines is to use consumer loans/credit to fund Marginal and Dead Asset purchases.

    a. *Protecting* our cash by using credit/loans seems like a good idea, but in fact it can be a really *bad* idea because this compromises Free Cash Flow and impairs our ability to recover from big or unexpected cash outlays.

3. The three ways to **_avoid_** increasing Asset Burden are to:

    a. *Invest* it in Living Assets

    b. *Accumulate* excess cash and don't convert it to anything

    c. *Spend* excess cash on Lifestyle Expenses, like a nice vacation or fun hobbies

4. The _need_ to budget our monthly expenses is a _symptom_ of increasing Asset Burden and falling Free Cash Flow.

---

* We sometimes use cash to pay for Dead Assets that do not have an impact on Asset Burden like that new table saw, flat screen, or kitchen table. These do not typically contribute to Asset Burden—unless we finance them.

a. No amount of budgeting can solve a structural Asset Burden and Free Cash Flow problem. We can't baby a 10 MPG PFM into performing like a 20 or 30 MPG PFM.

b. Financial Drones budget because they have already lost control of Stage 2 of their Operations Engine. That is, they have little or no Free Cash Flow and are using the Debt Merchant money as their Cash Reserves.

c. Financial Laborers budget because they are working hard *every single month* to make their 15 MPG PFM deliver 18 or 20 MPG so they don't wind up like the Drones. Instead, they need to re-structure their PFM.

d. Financial Builders—if budgeting at all—do so by choice to optimize/tune their PFM and maximize their Free Cash Flow.

e. There is simply no *need* to have detailed budgets if Asset Burden is manageable, Free Cash Flow is high, Cash Reserves are healthy and Living Asset Contributions are generating our target Retirement Value.

So let's say we have a well-functioning Operations Engine that is generating significant Free Cash Flow. One important way to protect and sustain that Free Cash Flow over the longer term is to *divert* a significant portion of our excess cash into investments and/or to use it to support lifestyle-related expenses, like vacations or hobbies or seasonal spending or donations and gifts. *Nice!*

Said differently, a well-functioning Operations Engine, facilitated by manageable Asset Burden, provides several wonderful gifts:

- **Operational Financial freedom** in the form of a large, stable and sustainable Free Cash Flow and Cash Reserves

    o No worries about having enough to pay the bills

    o No *dependence* on monthly budgets

- ○   No need for skimping or penny pinching

- ○   No worries about unexpected expenses

- **A significant flow of excess cash** that we <u>must</u> use on:

- ○   Investing for the future (Structural financial freedom) and/or

- ○   Enhancing our current lifestyle (vacations, hobbies, entertainment, etc.)

While this may seem counter-intuitive, it is an operational *fact*: Up to a point, the more we save/invest (and go on vacation) using our excess cash and limit our Asset Burden, the more Operational and Structural *financial freedom* we will both *achieve* and *feel*. This is because we are both *saving* for the future and *protecting* Free Cash Flow—therefore enhancing our ability to maintain and replenish Cash Reserves.

As we have mentioned, we must achieve and maintain a balance—and that balance point is unique for each of us. Some of us will prefer/tolerate a higher Asset Burden because we *love* a big house or new cars and are willing to more closely manage our other lifestyle expenses. Others will keep Asset Burden lower because they *love* to travel or fund their hobbies. Still others will prioritize Living Asset Contribution to maximize their Retirement Value and/ or accelerate their retirement date.

Whatever your lifestyle preferences, now that we are getting a better understanding of how the pieces fit together and interact, we can much more effectively and proactively *exert control* over our PFM. We can now *harness* it to meet our individual and unique lifestyle preferences as well as our short, medium, and long-term financial goals.

Asset Burden is the **Asset Engine** *output* that, more than any other, we need to focus on to ensure we don't weaken our Operations Engine and, by extension, our PFM. We *control* Asset Burden by the PAA decisions we make with our excess cash relative to acquiring Dead and Marginal Assets and how we use consumer debt to finance these purchases.

Optimizing Our PFM

Structuring our PFM (Primary Asset Allocation) is all about setting up guard rails or targets for our mix of Assets and Debts.

For example, when we contemplate how much house we can afford or when considering a new car purchase, we generally look at the payment and ask ourselves if we can *afford* it. The context in which we make these decisions is generally our Gross Income, our current expenses and what the Debt Merchant allows us to finance (red flag there!). But now that we understand our PFM more clearly, we can look at these decisions from another context— specifically, by asking: "Do they fit within the Primary Asset Allocation and operating targets we have established for ourselves?"

We can see when we look at Primary Asset Allocation decisions in the context of our two Asset Engine outputs (Asset Burden and Net Worth Gain) that they each have a unique impact. As shown in Table 7-1, accumulating cash is benign; that is, it has no positive or negative impact on our Asset Engine outputs (0). Acquiring Living Assets has no impact on Asset Burden, but a very positive (long-term) impact (+) on Net Worth Gain. Marginal Assets have a significant negative impact (-) on Asset Burden and a small or 'marginal' impact on Net Worth Gain. Dead Assets increase Asset Burden and represent a significant penalty to Net Worth Gain.

Table 7-1: The Impact of PAA Decisions

Primary Asset Allocation	AB Impact	NWG Impact
Cash	0	0
Living Assets	0	(+)(+)(+)
Marginal Assets	(-)	0/(+)
Dead Assets	(-)	(-)(-)
Soft Debt	(-)	(+)
Hard Debt	(-)	0

Soft and Hard Debt are also both significant negative contributors to Asset Burden. Paying off Hard Debt has no meaningful impact on Net Worth Gain because as the debt is reduced, depreciation effectively cancels it out. Paying off our Soft Debt provides a net positive contribution to Net Worth Gain related to the portion of the payment that is paying off the principle and therefore increasing our ownership of an asset that is not depreciating.

Note that the only Primary Asset Allocation decisions that keep Asset Burden in check are acquiring Living Assets and Cash and the only Primary Asset Allocation decision that positively impacts Net Worth Gain is acquiring Living Assets and the only decision that negatively impacts Net Worth Gain is acquiring Dead Assets.

Given this context, if we want to maximize Net Worth Gain, we need to think about decisions we make relative to Living Assets and Dead Assets. If we want to control Asset Burden we need to think about our decisions relative to Marginal Assets, Dead Assets, Hard Debt and Soft Debt.

So when we contemplate how much house we can afford and we look at the payments and other aspects of this decision's impact on our PFM, we are making a Primary Asset Allocation decision. When we buy a new car and decide how much we are going to spend and how much cash and financing we are going to use, we are making a Primary Asset Allocation decision. When we *decide* how much money we are going to deduct automatically from our paychecks to contribute to our 401(k) we are making a Primary Asset Allocation decision.

When we *decide* to take excess cash and pay off a student loan we are making Primary Asset Allocation decisions. When we *decide* to sell a car and not replace it, we are making Primary Asset Allocation decisions, or if we *decide* to down or upsize our house, we are making Primary Asset Allocation decisions.

All of these Primary Asset Allocation decisions will directly impact Asset Burden, Living Asset Contribution, Cash Reserves and the *structure* and performance of our PFM.

Dead Assets and Hard Debt

Dead Assets and Hard Debt are the wrenches we throw into our wonderful financial machine. These things can quickly and completely lock up our engines and send us into the arms of the Debt Merchants more than anything else.

Bottom line: We want to be sure we don't screw everything up by making Primary Asset Allocation decisions that generate excessive Asset Burden. Excessive Asset Burden will do many terrible things to our PFM:

- Choke off Free Cash Flow

- Weaken our Operations Engine resiliency (that is, our ability to maintain Cash Reserves when bad things happen)

- Diminish our ability to maintain our Living Asset Contribution at target levels

- Threaten our operational and structural financial freedom

- Force us to use and maintain a budget

- Force us to cut back on our lifestyle spending

- Lead us to become Profit Drones

So when we have the urge to spend our excess cash, we need to think carefully before acquiring and financing Dead Assets.

> ### This Cannot Be Stressed Enough
> *If there is one thing that can change the course of our financial future it is how we choose and finance Dead Assets.*

Have Cash? Go on Vacation!

There are only a few ways we can spend our excess cash that do not contribute to Asset Burden. One is taking a vacation—since this uses cash, but does not contribute to Asset Burden (unless you use a credit card to pay for it). It's an expense that can deliver a lifetime of memories and you can do it over and over and not contribute to Asset Burden.

Another great way to spend our excess cash is to increase our Living Asset Contribution. There are NO negative consequences to our PFM when we do this—but many positive ones. From a Cash Flow standpoint, Asset Burden stays the same; Free Cash Flow stays the same; Replacement Rate stays the same. From a Net Worth Gain standpoint only good things happen: Appreciation goes up; Net Worth Gain goes up; Retirement Value goes up, nearly *everything* gets better. *Think of investing not as a burden, but as a* **_necessary strategy_** *to protect our PFM from locking up and from becoming a Drone or Laborer.*

> This is how Living Asset Contributions play an incredibly important *dual role* in our PFM. By making a substantial and consistent Living Asset Contribution, we keep Asset Burden in check and therefore protect Free Cash Flow. This then delivers **Operational Financial Freedom** associated with a well-functioning Operations Engine **AND** we are building sufficient Retirement Value to ensure our **Structural Financial Freedom** is achieved!

The New Way of Thinking

The old view of our personal finances encourages us to focus on income, expenses and investments. We go through the motions of paying our bills, trying to save and living paycheck to paycheck. We focus on the details. We make budgets and try to limit our spending on things like clothes, entertainment or coffee. We use the extra money we do accumulate to reward ourselves with a nice vacation, new furniture or a new car. Many of us get sucked into using Debt Merchant money to artificially extend our lifestyle and purchasing power. In short, we have no idea what we are doing or how our decisions really affect our Personal Finance Machine.

The new way of thinking is all about structuring our PFM and making well informed Primary Asset Allocation decisions.

Structuring Our PFM

To re-enforce the idea that there are multiple ways to successfully run our PFMs, consider the following five basic approaches to managing our PFMs and living our lives:

1. Asset Lover: Focus on house, cars and toys.

    a. Higher Asset Burden, limited Lifestyle Expenses, steady Living Asset Contribution.
    b. Maximum house, nice cars and a few toys (boat, jet skis, etc.) too!

    c. Less focus on lifestyle and activities that don't involve our dead/ marginal assets.

    d. More discipline and focus required to protect Cash Reserves and fully fund retirement.

2. <u>Kids First</u>: Focus on our children.

    a. Higher Asset Burden, Routine Living Expenses, and Lifestyle expenses.

    b. Need to have a house, cars and maybe a few toys

    c. Spending on kids, education, sports, activities, etc.

    d. Possibly less motivation to retire early or with a higher Retirement Value.

    e. More discipline and focus required to protect Cash Reserves and fund retirement.

3. <u>Experientialist</u>: Focus on lifestyle and experiences.

    a. Lower Asset Burden, lots of Lifestyle Expenses, steady Living Asset Contribution.

    b. More modest house or apartment, older cars, no toys with motors

    c. Exotic vacations, frequent trips, theatre, eating out

    d. High level of Free Cash Flow facilitates both lifestyle and Living Asset investments.

    e. May be able to retire early or retire with a high Retirement Value

4. <u>Saver</u>: In control and with a focus on structural financial freedom.

    a. Low Asset Burden, low Lifestyle Expenses, lots of Living Asset Contributions.

    b. Modest house, older cars, no 'toys' doesn't eat out, reasonable hobbies.

    c. Enjoyment in Secondary Asset Allocation and watching Living Assets grow.

    d. Forgo now, enjoy later — longer term or early retirement focus

    e. Getting to structural financial freedom much sooner.

5. <u>Balancer</u>: In control with a balance of short and long-term financial freedom.

    a.   Balance between Asset Burden, Living Asset Contribution and Lifestyle Expenses.

    b.   Saving first with specific Retirement Value targets.

    c.   A house, cars and debt levels that keep Asset Burden in check.

    d.   Hobbies, entertainment, vacations, eating, but not at the expense of Living Asset Contribution targets.

    e.   Enjoying the journey _and_ ensuring the destination will be there.

While the first two of these lifestyles are pretty typical, they can sow the seeds of our financial undoing _if taken to extreme_. Of all the basic PFM structures, these two offer the greatest challenges and operating risk, because they force us to live much closer to the edge than any of the other approaches.

As we have highlighted previously, this is how our personal finances and our life are so completely intertwined. Once we understand and exert control over our PFM, we can use it to achieve what we want relative to our life and lifestyle.

Let's look again at our three families: The Jones have taken the Asset Lover lifestyle to the extreme and have fallen into the classic Financial Drone predicament. The Smiths are a _lite_ version of the Joneses with too much Asset Burden and therefore have essentially forgone the option of choosing lifestyle options 2-5. Finally, the Millers have the financial flexibility to tune their PFM structure to ANY of these lifestyle options.

As we go through different phases of our lives, we may gravitate to and transition through more than one of these PFM configurations. The key is to understand what we are doing, do it consciously and maintain control and focus on our short and long-term objectives.

An essential part of controlling and harnessing our PFM is establishing and maintaining a set of core measures or _dashboard_ that we can use to help us see what is happening. These core measures give us incredible insight and control and allow us to easily manage and tune our PFM to meet our life and lifestyle goals. As we continue to build our understanding of how our PFM works, we are also accumulating a core list of measures that will become our PFM Dashboard or Control Panel: **Asset Burden, FCF, Replacement Rate, Cash Reserves, Net Worth, Net Worth Gain, Retirement Value, RIFI, and others.**

The next chapter will explore the actual cost of the things that we buy and their impact on our Retirement Value. We are going to look at selected financial decisions and put them in perspective of the actual cost to our PFM from both an operational and structural perspective.

Chapter Summary:

- There are two types of financial freedom: Operation and Structural.

- We can achieve Operational Financial Freedom quickly and easily by Structuring our PFM to have manageable Asset Burden, a healthy level of Free Cash Flow, several months of expenses in Cash Reserves and a Cash Burn that is no larger than our Free Cash Flow.

- Structural Financial Freedom takes longer to achieve; but once we establish Operational Financial Freedom, it is easy to get on the road to Structural Financial Freedom by establishing a level of Living Asset Contributions that meets our retirement income goals (Retirement Income From Investments).

- We need to think differently about managing our finances. It's not about budgets and bills and investing; it's about making decisions that manage Asset Burden and optimize Net Worth Gain. *It's all about Primary Asset Allocation*

- When in doubt, use cash and avoid excessive use of Hard Debt to acquire Dead Assets. These two bad actors can quickly grind our PFM gears to a halt.

- Saving and investing are <u>*necessary*</u> to maintaining a healthy PFM by preventing the build-up of Asset Burden, locking-up our engines and turning us into Financial Drones.

- We can *tune* the structure our PFM with different emphases and focus that is geared to our preferred lifestyle and life stage needs.

Personal Finance Machine (PFM) - New Term Review

(Note: A complete list of term definitions can be found in the Glossary.)

- **Structural Financial Freedom** = This is about building a targeted level of Retirement Value. It is about establishing the ability to have a sustainable standard of living from your Asset Engine without needing to continue collecting a paycheck. This can take a long time to achieve.

- **Operational Financial Freedom** = This is about achieving a well-structured and managed Operations Engine with several months of Routine Operating Expenses in Cash Reserves and a healthy and consistent Free Cash Flow. This can be achieved in a reasonably short period of time.

- **Primary Asset Allocation (PAA)** = A critical set of PFM decisions that involve the allocation of your Asset Engine Contributions among the four asset classes within the Asset Engine: Living, Marginal, Dead, and Cash. Primary Asset Allocation happens above the level of Secondary Asset Allocation (therefore primary). PAA defines the structure of our Asset Engine.

- **Secondary Asset Allocation (SAA)** = If familiar with the term 'Asset Allocation,' you know it as the allocation of investments across classes of investment assets like domestic stocks, bonds, international stocks, real-estate, commodities, and money market funds. This book refers to this type of asset allocation as Secondary Asset Allocation.

- **Living Asset Contribution (LAC)** = Conversion of Cash Reserves into Living Assets (i.e., investment-grade assets).

CHAPTER 8:
THE BIG DECISIONS

Primary Asset Allocation decisions are the *BIG DECISIONS* that have the most profound impact on our PFM. They can quickly tie our PFM in knots and put our Retirement Value in peril. Often, these decisions put us at risk of *spending away* the majority of our Retirement Value.

Our Retirement Value is real money. It is not a mirage, fantasy, or some abstract calculation. It is not wishful thinking to say that if we (for example) save and invest $403/month every month during our 40-year working lives and invest in the overall market, we will have accumulated about $1 million in today's dollars. Just looking at the average income household making $100K over 40 years, we can see that that's $20 million in LEV that will go to someone —potentially us.

This chapter will look closely at the following Primary Asset Allocation decisions:

- Buying a house

- Buying cars

- Buying anything else with a motor

- Other Marginal Assets

- Soft Debt

- Hard Debt

An important note/context related to this chapter and the Retirement Value Impact analysis/calculations:

We have made these calculations under several generalized assumptions to facilitate simple comparisons and calculations. Most notably:

1. *We make these decisions and purchases starting at age 25 and then consistently carry them through for 40 years of our working lives.*

2. *Our <u>inflation-adjusted</u> income is constant throughout our working years.*

3. *Our inflation-adjusted investment returns will be 6.8 percent*

People tend to fall into patterns of behavior and it is not unrealistic that we will buy our first new car in our early 20s and replace it every 5 years and not think twice about this pattern of behavior for the rest of our working lives. Nor is it unrealistic that we will get our first apartment in our early 20s and start paying 30 percent of our Monthly Gross Income and at some point buy a house and continuing to pay 30 percent of our Monthly Gross Income. Of course, these assumptions won't exactly reflect our individual situations and experiences. Nor is it likely that we will start when we are 25 and set a fixed course for our finances over our 40 working years. We 'simplify' these variables to give ourselves a level view of an otherwise complex dynamic. If we attempted to be more detailed, we likely would have added unnecessary confusion and complexity that would obscure the key points of this analysis. We chose to use these simplifications to more clearly illustrate the incredible cost and impact of our decisions over time. The point here is that we have the opportunity to make decisions every day during our working years that have a huge impact on both our current lifestyle as well as our future Retirement Value.

Buying a Car

Let's begin with the most notorious Primary Asset Allocation Decision: **Buying a Car.** When we buy a car, we burden our PFM with four types of expenses:

1. Purchase expenses (thereby reducing our Cash Reserves)

2. Asset Burden-related expenses (payments, routine maintenance, insurance, gas)

3. Unpredictable Expenses (new tires, major repairs)

4. Depreciation

We also have two big Primary Asset Allocation decisions to make:

1. How much to spend

2. How much to finance

The more expensive the car, the higher the Asset Burden, Unpredictable Expenses, and Depreciation. The more debt we use, the more car we can 'afford' to pay—and the higher the impact on our PFM.

Let's say we purchase and finance a new car for $35,000 (which, shockingly, is the average price of a new car: $33,000, plus taxes, license and fees).[42]

Table 8-1 summarizes the impact of this decision on our Operations and Asset Engines. Assuming we have a trade-in worth $17,000 and put $2,000 down, we're left with $16,000 to finance. Given this situation, the annual payment plus insurance and operating expenses comes to $623/month. *This is the direct impact on Asset Burden of purchasing an average new car with $16K financed.*

In addition to Asset Burden, we have the additional allocation for Unpredictable Expenses associated with the car like new tires, brakes, or other expenses. Though small, these are real expenses that we will incur as we use the vehicle. And the more expensive the car, the more everything else costs as well.

Table 8-1: The Cost of Buying a New Car

New Car: (5 year replacement)		Monthly	Annual	Annual
Purchase price	$35,000			
Trade-in	$17,000			
Down Payment	$2,000			
Amount Financed	$16,000	First 5 years	First 5 years	Next 5 years
Payment (5%, 5 years)		$302	$3,623	$3,623
Insurance		$117	$1,400	$1,400
Gas & Routine Maintenance		$204	$2,450	$2,450
Total Asset Burden		**$623**	**$7,473**	**$7,473**
Allocation for Unpredictable Expenses		$17	$200	$200
Replacement of Down Payment		$33	$400	$400
Total Expense		**$673**	**$8,073**	**$8,073**
Retirement Value Impact (RVI)				**($1,682,127)**
Annual Depreciation Rate (average)			**($3,500)**	**($3,500)**

The $2,000 down payment is not free money. These are operating funds that were there and usable for acquiring the car that we must *replace* to replenish our Cash Reserves. We'll need to buy another car at some point, and we must save for the 'replacement' down payment. Even though we used cash, this is real money—and a real cost of owning the car that we must account for.

When we take these additional expenses into account, we see that our monthly cost of owning a new car is about $673/month—$8,076/year. If we assume we replace this car every 5 years and do this over the course of our working lives (historically, we purchase an average of 13 cars in our life-times),[43] *regardless of income level,* we will have devoted almost $1.7 million in Retirement Value to a *single* average priced new car (this includes the Retirement Value Impact of the first car where we have no trade-in).

If an *average* income household buys an *average* new car every 5 years, it will cost 8.4 percent of their Lifetime Earnings Value ($1.68 million / $20 million). This huge amount of money has a significant Retirement Value Impact. Do we really love new cars that much to give up almost 10 percent of the financial value of our *entire* working lives? Wouldn't we all want to have that $1.7 million in our investment account as we approach retirement? Note as well that our Net Worth is eroding by a very conservative depreciation cost of $3,500 every single year.[44] So we will need at least $3,500 in appreciation from our other assets just to stay even on our Net Worth Gain.

What about the impact on our Operations Engine? Well the $623 of Asset Burden is 8 percent ($623/$8,333) of the average family's monthly Gross Income. This represents a huge chunk of our cash flow, especially considering that we have yet to consider housing and our Routine Living Expenses.

So, owning and replacing an average new car every 5 years over the course of our working lives is a simple and powerful example of a multimillion-dollar decision that impacts the *structure* of our PFM and has significant implications for both our Operational and Structural Financial Freedom.

What if we had made a larger down payment? Would that change the impact on our PFM? The answer is both yes and no.

Let's use the exact same example above and say we paid $18K in cash with the $17K trade-in and financed nothing. You can see in Table 8-2 that this decision has almost no Retirement Value Impact compared to the first example, because the cost of the car is almost exactly the same. The total Retirement Value Impact is higher when we financed a portion of it because the total cost of the car is more because of the finance costs.

Table 8-2: The Cost of Buying a New Car (Larger down payment)				
New Car: (5 year replacement)		Monthly	Annual	Annual
Purchase price	$35,000			
Trade-in	$17,000			
Down Payment	$18,000			
Amount Financed	$0	First 5 years	First 5 years	Next 5 years
Payment (5%, 5 years)		$0	$0	$0
Insurance		$117	$1,400	$1,400
Gas & Routine Maintenance		$204	$2,450	$2,450
Total Asset Burden		**$321**	**$3,850**	**$3,850**
Allocation for Unpredictable Expenses		$17	$200	$200
Replacement of Down Payment		$300	$3,600	$3,600
Total Expense		**$638**	**$7,650**	**$7,650**
Retirement Value Impact (RVI)				**($1,621,545)**
Annual Depreciation Rate (average)			**($3,500)**	**($3,500)**

On the other hand, we do see a very different picture when we look at Asset Burden—avoiding financing has a significant *positive* impact on Asset Burden. When we pay cash for the car our Asset burden is only $321/mo. or about 50 percent of what would be if we financed the car. Importantly as a percent of Gross Income (for our average income family) Asset Burden drops from about 7.5 percent to 3.9 percent. This drop is very significant and helps prevent Free Cash Flow and Cash Reserves from being compromised. Also note that the total expense of both approaches is about the same ($673 vs. $638). This is because in the second approach we have to replace our $18K down payment if we hope to buy another car using this strategy!

So in either case Retirement Value Impact is the same and the total cost is the same, but the impact on *Asset Burden* is very different and the difference is completely due to how much debt we used to finance the purchase. When we use debt to purchase Dead and Marginal Assets, all else being equal it has much more impact on Asset Burden than on Retirement Value Impact. This is not the case if we use debt to buy a much more expensive Dead or Marginal Asset than we would have if we paid cash—in this case both Asset Burden and Retirement Value Impact are significantly impacted.

Note: When we look at these expenses, we are looking at them from the perspective of an established *routine* or a PFM management *strategy*. For example, one way we can manage our PFM relative to cars is to buy a new car every 5 years. This PFM management *strategy* has a certain impact on our PFM that we can calculate (Retirement Value Impact). Alternatively, if we chose the strategy of buying a 3-year old car every 5 years, this is also has a RVI on our PFM that we can calculate and *compare* to the new car every 5 years strategy. Throughout this chapter we will use this approach to assess and highlight the Retirement Value Impact (RVI) of our decisions. We can always change our strategies, but the goal of this approach is to help understand how various strategies will impact our PFM and our short and long-term financial goals.

Depending on where we live, we probably need to have a car. So how can we minimize this expense? There are several options or strategies we could use: we can keep our new car for much longer, like 10 years, we could purchase a 3 to 5-year-old car and replace it every 5 or 10 years, or we could purchase a much older car and replace it every 5 years or so.

As summarized in Table 8-3, if we assume these depreciation values and we purchase a used (5-year-old) car and replace it every 5 years or so, we can reduce the Retirement Value Impact to something like $1 million. It's possible to get by for less than $1 million in Retirement Value, but not without buying an older (> 5 years) car and doing some or most of the maintenance ourselves, which for some of us could be well worth the effort.

Table 8-3: Evaluating Different Car Buying Strategies

RVI Impact of Average Priced Automobiles	Ann. Dep.	RVI	Difference
New Car: (5 year replacement)	($3,500)	($1,682,127)	$0
New Car: (10 year replacement)	($2,800)	($1,436,074)	$246,053
Used Car (5 year replacement)	($2,000)	($1,073,812)	$608,315
Used Car (10 year replacement)	($1,600)	($1,045,085)	$637,042
Older Car (10 year replacement)	($1,000)	($687,188)	$994,939

Source: Depreciation rates based on authors' estimates.

Note that this is the Retirement Value Impact for **ONE** average priced vehicle. What if, like many families, we have two cars? That's easy math, but the result is even more harrowing. Also, we have not even considered the Retirement Value of more expensive cars. If for example, we were purchasing a single new car for $50,000 every 5 years, the impact on Retirement Value would go from $1.7 million to $2.6 million.

In general, Retirement Value Impact is *larger* than the percentage increase in the cost of the vehicle. In this example, we are increasing the price of the car by 43 percent (from $35K to $50K), but the Retirement Value Impact grows by 53 percent. The reason this relationship is non-linear is because of the higher financing costs associated with the more expensive vehicle (additional money that we are giving away to the Debt Merchants), higher maintenance costs, and the time value of money over our 40 working years.

Let's step back a second. A car represents a *significant* expense that, to make matters worse, is a largely *unavoidable* for most of us in the U.S. Unless we live in a city like New York with very extensive and accessible public transportation, a car is close to a necessity. However, we *can* do some things to reduce its impact on our PFM.

If we stick to buying used cars, keep them longer and limit the amount we spend and finance, we can more effectively manage this powerful and immensely impactful expense.

Cars: An Important Tool of the Debt Merchants

The impact of automobile ownership on Asset Burden and Retirement Value is so significant it can easily be the difference between financial freedom and enslavement. The Debt Merchants understand this and they work hard to 'help us' with our cars in many insidious ways.

First, they focus us on how *low* they can make our car payment. When we financed $16K in the example above, the payment itself is about 50 percent of the total impact on our Operations Engine ($302/$623). Because of the increasing competition for our limited incomes, we see loan terms today extending to 6-7 years (that's 72 to 84 months!). These extended terms lull us into buying much more car than we would have otherwise considered and keep us focused on the (seemingly low) payment, versus the total cost of ownership, which we now know is about *two times* the payment.

Extended loan terms do nothing but increase our total cost of ownership; the more expensive the car, the higher total cost (including interest), the higher every other cost is as well—from insurance to licensing to oil changes to new tires to depreciation. It also means that when we go to sell or trade in the car 5 or 6 years later, we will have paid more (interest) and yet *own* even less of the value of the car, because we will *owe* more than if we had a shorter-term loan.

Second, Debt Merchants entice us into a new car *sooner than we need one.* This is a way the auto industry maximizes their profits. They invest heavily in new features and saturation advertising, convincing us that we deserve an upgrade and have *earned* it. We've worked really hard and think of how nice that new vehicle will be. Extended terms and the constant drum beat of new features and advertising are clever tools the Debt Merchants use to ensure that they get their multimillion-dollar share of our PFM.

It is important to understand the impact that cars can have on our PFM in the short term (depletion of Cash Reserves), structurally (increased Asset Burden, reduced Free Cash Flow, increased Replacement Rate, increased depreciation), and in the long term (~$1-2 Million PER CAR in lost Retirement Value).

We also must deal with depreciation's *drag* on our Net Worth Gain. The average car loses almost 50 percent of its value in 5 years. That's like throwing away $15,000 (or more!) every 5 years *per car.* When we are working hard to grow our Asset Engine, this becomes a significant drain on our Net Worth *Gain* that severely limits our ability to generate positive Net Worth Gain momentum.

The Cold Hard Facts: The average American family making the average gross income of $100K/year simply cannot afford to purchase new cars every 5 years AND successfully build their Asset Engine. Yet many of us have not just one, but *two* cars that were purchased new. This puts many of us in a self-made trap that is difficult to escape. We think it's OK because we can *afford* the payments; but the reality is that we are giving away MILLIONS.

Nobody is *making* us do this. In fact, we do it willingly. It's simply a question of understanding the impact of our decisions. Buying two average new cars every 5 years is about $3.35 million in Retirement Value vs. buying two average 5-year-old cars every 5 years is $2.15 million.

If saved and invested this $1.2 million-dollar difference represents a Retirement Value almost nine times what households approaching retirement have in their retirement accounts.[45]

There are about 250 million registered passenger vehicles in the U.S. today. Since there are about 124 million households, each household has on average 2.0 vehicles. The average age of these vehicles is roughly 10-12 years old. From the RVI summary table above, this suggests that the typical household is spending between *$1 - $3 million* of their RV on cars.

Source: Jerry Hirsch, "253 million cars and trucks on the U.S. roads; average age is 11.4 years," LATimes.com, June 9, 2014, http://www.latimes.com/business/autos/la-fi-hy-ihs-automotive-average-age-car-20140609-story.html, U.S. Census Bureau, "Families and Living Arrangements," 2015, and authors' calculations.

Cars are amazing machines that give us tremendous enjoyment and freedom, but we need to be very smart about acquiring and owning them.

Let's look at our three families

Remember, they have the same Gross Income ($96K/year) and lived in similarly priced homes—on the same street, in fact. The Joneses buy *two new cars every 5 years* and pay $35K for each. The Smiths buy slightly less expensive new cars ($25K) every 5 years and make a larger down payment. The Millers buy *two 5-year-old cars, similar to what the Joneses are replacing* from the dealer and they pay cash. The Millers also invest the difference in their monthly automobile costs compared to the Joneses ($323/month plus the impact of the first car purchased without having a trade-in).

Table 8-4: The 3 Families—Examining Their Car Buying Strategies

Total Auto Expense	Joneses	Smiths	Millers
Number of cars	2	2	2
Average purchase price	$35,000	$25,000	$19,270
Trade-in	$18,270	$13,050	$10,059
Down Payment	$1,340	$2,008	$9,211
Loan Amount	$15,390	$9,942	$0
Loan PMT (Principle and interest)	$595	$384	$0
Insurance & License fees	$282	$200	$151
Operating Costs (gas + routine maint.)	$350	$400	$450
Asset Burden	**$1,227**	**$985**	**$601**
Replacement of Down Payment	$45	$67	$307
Unpredictable Expense allocation	$61	$65	$101
Total Expense	**$1,332**	**$1,117**	**$1,009**
Asset Burden as % of Gross Income	**15.3%**	**12.3%**	**7.5%**
Total Expense as % of Gross Income	**16.7%**	**14.0%**	**12.6%**

When the Joneses discuss their retirement plans after 40 working years, they realize that they have saved almost nothing. They expect to get social security of about $24K/year and cannot figure out what they are going to do. They were just not able to save enough. They plan to keep working part-time as long as they can, sell their house, move into an apartment (or with their children) and watch every dollar.

The Millers have exactly the same social security benefit ($24K/year) as the Joneses PLUS $1.2 million in investments (about $600K in Retirement Value they 'kept' for each car) *just from the savings associated with their Primary Asset Allocation decision relative to cars.* This $1.2 million will generate about $50,000 per year in income (52 percent of their Gross Income), plus the $24K/year in social security (Total of $74K or 77 percent of their pre-retirement Gross Income) *for the rest of their lives.*

> So what did the Millers give up (vs. the Joneses) to live the next 30 years as they please? *They drove the exact same cars*, enjoyed the exact same features, performance, and level of luxury as the Joneses. The *only* thing the Millers gave up was having the latest models in the year they were introduced—and that new car smell.

When we consider buying a car, in addition to the make, model, options and color, we need to very thoughtfully consider its impact on the health and performance of our PFM as well as our Operational and Structural financial freedom. "Can we afford it?" should take on a whole new meaning.

Other Dead Assets

These same breathtakingly large Retirement Values also apply to other notoriously Dead Assets including ATVs, motorcycles, snowmobiles, boats, riding lawn mowers etc. In general, anything we own with an engine may be costing us a fortune. A conservative estimate of the average price of a new recreational vehicle today is $17,600 (average of new ATVs, motorcycles, snowmobiles, boats (runabouts), and jet-skis).[46,47] *Nothing* in Table 8-5 is inexpensive from a Retirement Value perspective; however, each item seems reasonable or even affordable from a *monthly payment perspective* (20-40 percent of total monthly cost)—which is what lulls us into thinking we can afford them.

Table 8-5: The Cost of Things with Motors

Dead Assets	Purchase Price	Total Monthly Cost	Monthly Asset Burden	Monthly Payment	% Gross Income ($100K)	Retirement Value Impact (RVI)	% of Retirement value	Avg. Annual Depreciation
Avg. new car every 5 years	$35,000	$673	$623	$302	8%	($1,682,127)	12%	($3,500)
Avg. new car every 10 years	$35,000	$530	$430	$302	6%	($1,436,074)	10%	($2,800)
Used car every 5 years	$20,000	$450	$250	$0	5%	($1,073,812)	7%	($2,000)
Old car every 10 years, self repair	$10,000	$313	$208	$0	4%	($687,188)	5%	($1,000)
Avg. rec. vehicle every 5 years	$17,600	$318	$152	$49	4%	($811,674)	6%	($1,721)
Avg. rec. vehicle every 10 years	$17,600	$265	$186	$72	3%	($719,718)	5%	($2,073)

In addition, the depreciation of these assets is both relentless and significant. Most have double-digit depreciation rates even during the first 5 years of their lives, which continues in the second 5 years—to the point they have lost most of their value at 10 years. These are the vehicles that we see for sale on the side of the road—the types of Dead Assets that simply cannot avoid this fate.

Table 8-6: Example Vehicle Depreciation

Recreational Vehicles	Average New Price	5 Year Value	5 Year Depreciation	Average Annual Rate	10 Year Value	Average Annual Rate
Snowmobile	$15,000	$6,000	$9,000	-17%	$1,500	-21%
ATV	$8,000	$4,000	$4,000	-13%	$1,000	-19%
Jet skis	$15,000	$8,000	$7,000	-12%	$2,000	-18%
Speed/fishing boat	$25,000	$19,000	$6,000	-5%	$4,750	-15%
Motorcycle	$25,000	$14,000	$11,000	-11%	$3,500	-18%
Average Vehicle	$17,600	$10,200	$7,400	-12%	$2,550	-18%

Cars and all other Dead Assets—especially *anything with an engine*—can quickly and easily destroy our ability to create positive Net Worth; and, in combination with Hard Debt, lead us down the fastest, surest path to financial servitude.

Of course, these assets can bring tremendous enjoyment to our lives. We just need to understand the full impact these items have on our PFM and on our short and long-term financial and lifestyle goals *before we purchase them*. The next time you see a new $50,000 SUV towing a new $35,000 boat, consider that you are really looking at a *$3+ million* lifestyle decision.

Owning the American Dream

Buying a house is a big decision that very few people take lightly. Almost everyone appreciates this choice for what it is. While that's good, mortgage bankers are ready and waiting with open arms, smiles, and a proven self-serving plan to establish a direct and permanent pipeline from your PFM into their pockets.

Any good mortgage banker/broker can quickly calculate for you the maximum amount of mortgage you can 'afford.' They do so by looking at your assets, income and expenses. They consider how much you can put down, your other outstanding loans, look at your credit scores and then do some quick math and poof! You can suddenly, somehow afford a $400,000 house.

What this person fails to tell you is that this is the maximum amount you can afford based on *their* formula—which is designed to maximize *their* profit and minimize *their* risk of us going bankrupt. They are calculating the maximum monthly amount we can pay regardless of whether we have enough left over for our Lifestyle Expenses or to save for retirement, college or anything else. This *maximum* amount also happens to be at a level that may likely put us at risk of becoming Financial Drones.

Banks want nothing more than to have us as lifelong customers—for mortgages, credit cards, auto loans, etc. However, they don't want to lose their investment. They make sure that we do not exceed *their* guardrails for how much debt we can manage. A bank loan officer is a sales person, just like one at the car dealership. They will ask us many questions when we are considering a new home, but they will *never* ask what our financial goals are. They won't inquire as to what our retirement plans are, or how we plan to pay for our children's college expenses. They will only ask questions related to our ability to pay **them** — both now and into the future.

Keep This in Mind

When the banks look at us and our finances, what they see is a multimillion-dollar profit machine. They see our ability to generate income and pay them back. They look at our credit-worthiness and they then give us every opportunity to borrow up to the limit they have set for us. Once this occurs, we become tied to them—feeding them much of our potential RV. When we look back and ask: "Where did so much of our money go?" ... *It went to the Debt Merchants*!

To be fair, it is not a Debt Merchant's job to ask these questions—*it's ours*. *We* are in charge of our multimillion-dollar personal finance enterprise. We can choose to drive our Asset Burden up to the absolute limit, or we can take control and decide to structure and use our PFM in a way that will benefit us.

The decisions we make relative to our home or home ownership are some of the most important we make. Unfortunately, most people don't fully understand the cost of their home and the implications of buying the most expensive house our friendly banker says we can afford.

So what does owning a home actually cost? Just like our cars, *far more than we realize.*

Table 8-7: The Cost of Home Ownership

Total Home Expense	Joneses	Smiths	Millers
Mortgage (Principle and interest)	$1,288	$1,181	$1,074
Insurance	$141	$129	$117
Property Taxes	$418	$383	$348
Total PITI	**$1,847**	**$1,693**	**$1,539**
Utilities (gas & electric)	$169	$155	$141
Municipal exp. (water, sewer)	$28	$26	$23
Annual maintenance/up-keep	$113	$103	$94
Unpredictable Expense allocation	$84	$77	$70
Total Expense	**$2,241**	**$2,054**	**$1,867**
Asset Burden (Total - UPE)	**$2,156**	**$1,977**	**$1,797**
PITI as % of Gross Income	**23%**	**21%**	**19%**
Asset Burden as % of Gross Income	**27%**	**25%**	**22%**
Total as % of Gross Income	**28%**	**26%**	**23%**
Purchase Price	**$300,000**	**$275,000**	**$250,000**
Total as % of Purchase Price	**9.0%**	**9.0%**	**9.0%**

Let's look at our three families again: Each family lives in the same neighborhood and each bought a home at a price around $275,000. The Joneses paid the most at $300K and the Millers paid the least at $250K. Each family put 20 percent down and obtained a 30-year mortgage at 5 percent interest. Their expenses are outlined in the Table 8-7.

There is a significant difference in payment (Principle, Interest, Taxes, and Insurance—PITI) between the three families. The Joneses pay $308/month more than the Millers. They have a nicer house, but it's not *that* much nicer. In fact, the only difference is that the Millers' house is 17 percent smaller (i.e. one less bedroom and no den).

The difference between PITI and total expense is all the *ancillary costs* of owning a home: insurance, utilities, property taxes, maintenance, and Unpredictable Expense allocations. The Joneses, Smiths and Millers pay

$2,241, $2,054 and $1,867 respectively in monthly expenses; and again, the Joneses are paying significantly more ($374) than the Millers.

We see the key difference when we look at costs *as a percentage of Gross Income*. The Asset Burden impact for the Joneses is 27 percent vs. 25 percent for the Smiths and 22 percent for the Millers. Also notice that the total expense is only about 20 percent higher than the PITI.

Depending on our mortgage amount, interest rate and term (15 vs. 30 year), our total estimated *annual* 'cost of ownership' is typically in the range of 6-10 percent of the value of our home.[48] If we own our home without any mortgage, then we will assume total cost of ownership of about 4 percent per year.

The reason why a home is considered a Marginal Asset is that, by design, it does not usually depreciate like a Dead Asset. Even though it does it have intrinsic appreciation like a Living Asset (if we maintain it well), it may fluctuate in value from one year to the next. For example, in the not too distant recession and housing crisis, home values plunged across the U.S., and if we had to sell during the depths of the recession we would potentially have lost most or all our investment in our home. If on the other hand, we kept our house through the recession and don't sell for another 5 or 10 years, the recession might have had little or no impact on the *long-term* appreciation rate of the house. Like the stock market, we may need a long holding period to fully realize the intrinsic appreciation associated with our homes.

Another challenge with assessing a home's investment value is that we have to consider our operating costs as part of the investment return equation. If we assume an annual home appreciation rate of 3-4 percent per year, and our annual cost of ownership is 6-10 percent of the home's value per year (*after* accounting for paying off mortgage principle and the tax benefit on interest expense) then it's pretty easy to see that our expenses can frequently exceed the home's appreciation rate. But that is perfectly OK. After all, we have to live somewhere and we have to pay for it.

What is important to understand is that the Primary Asset Allocation decision to buy a house has a profound effect on our PFM. In fact, the equity in most people's home represents most their Net Worth. *Not because it was a great investment*, but because by focusing on maximizing the size of our home and buying Dead Assets, over time, for many people, most of what remains of their Net Worth is their home equity. The value of our Dead Assets just vaporizes over time, leaving us with our home equity as our *default* Net Worth. This does not mean that our house was a good investment. It only means that by being forced to pay our mortgage, we gained some *room* between what we owe and what our house is worth.

Let's look at what a banker might say to our three families making $96,000 Gross Income. It would not be a surprise if he or she advised that they could spend up to about 40 percent of their monthly gross income on the cost of their home and any other consumer loans (cars, boats, carried credit card balances, etc.)—which would be about $3,200/month.

Our families all have the same Gross Income ($96,000). The Retirement Value Impact of the bank's idea of what we can afford represents $8 million of their $20 million Lifetime Economic Value—40 percent of their Lifetime Economic Value.

What if we subtract their income taxes? While we can minimize these somewhat, they are largely unavoidable. If we assume that all income taxes (state, local, federal) represent about 20 percent of Gross Income (or $4 million in LEV) for our families, then the bank's idea of what we can afford in monthly debt payments is actually 50 percent of our LEV (net of taxes) ($8 million /$16 million). So before we take into account food, clothing, basic personal care, other living expenses, or even saving for retirement, we would have already handed over 50 percent of our available LEV to the Debt Merchants (less whatever our home equity is at retirement). This is a huge chunk of our amazing LEV.

Dead and Marginal Assets

These assets are extremely important to our lifestyles and our lives and impact every aspect of our PFM. From Asset Burden and Free Cash Flow to Replacement Rate, Dead and Marginal Assets directly impact our Operations Engine. They also can ravage our Asset Engine with relentless depreciation. We want and need these assets at some level and they are a significant part of our chosen lifestyle. We just need to be aware of and make conscience decisions about their impact on our short and long-term lifestyle and financial goals.

Furthermore, once we've made decisions relative to Dead and Marginal asset classes, it is more difficult to unwind them without considerable time, effort and financial risk/loss. This is why Primary Asset Allocation is such an important set of decisions and in particular why decisions around Dead and Marginal Assets are so critical.

As with almost everything else we've discussed, these dynamics apply *regardless of our incomes*. Most importantly, the *small* differences between

Drones and Builders are magnified even further at higher incomes. It is harder to be a Builder at lower incomes; it takes more creativity, more ingenuity and more discipline, because the *minimum* costs for housing and routine operating expenses eats up a much larger portion of our Gross Income. However, being a Builder is not just *possible*, but it is a far more satisfying lifestyle than being trapped as a Drone. It's always worth the effort to avoid excessive Asset Burden and paying interest to someone else.

Credit Cards

Credit cards are a wonderful convenience that most of us utilize. However, they can also be the financial wrench that quickly grinds our financial machine to a halt. Credit cards are also *an essential tool* of the Debt Merchants.

Credit cards are the perfect financial trap. They are broadly available to nearly everyone and accepted by nearly all retailers. Many people carry 3-7 credit cards and specialty incentive credit cards from different retailers.[49] They have replaced cash for many of us, which is exactly what the Debt Merchants want.

All of these credit cards have the same basic trapping mechanism: Incredibly high interest rates and incredibly low minimum payments, but with a specific credit limit that mitigates the bank's risk. This beautifully simple arrangement can facilitate our slide into more credit card debt that we can handle.

The Debt Merchants have engineered and refined this financial trap over many decades and it works incredibly well. Credit cards are the *mechanism* that pushes Financial Labors into the world of the Drones and *locks them in* with sky-high interest rates.

As classic Laborers, the Smiths are vulnerable to falling into the same predicament as the Joneses. However, they are also well positioned to become Builders, depending on how they manage their Asset Burden and Lifestyle Expenses going forward. Small changes in one direction or the other can make a huge difference in their financial health going forward.

If, for example, the Smiths drive Asset Burden up, their cash position will weaken and cash flow will decline. At some point, an unforeseen event will drain their depleted Cash Reserves, forcing them to use their credit cards to bridge the gap. Then the trapping mechanism of the credit cards will make them feel like they are still doing OK. They may even see their credit cards as an incredibly *valuable* safety net protecting them from something far worse. What a great tool! They can cover a large unforeseen expense and not have to pay it all back with cash they don't have. But the reality is that once credit card debt starts to accumulate, the combination of high interest and low minimums nearly guarantees that they will slide into the pit with the Drones/Joneses.

To see the powerful forces at play here, let's look at a simple example. Let's say we carry an average of $15,000 in credit card debt over our working lives, which, as previously mentioned, is about the average credit card debt for the nearly 40 percent of households carrying credit card debt today. The $15,000 of course goes up and down over time. We pay it down and then we use credit cards to purchase something that we need. Over time, it *averages* about $15,000. In essence, we are using the bank's money as our Cash Reserves.

This is exactly where the Joneses are. At 18 percent interest, that $15,000 in credit card debt costs $225 per month—or $2,700 in annual interest. This does not seem so bad; the Joneses get to use $15,000 of someone else's money that they *really need* for only $225/month. This is a great deal right? It's a great deal, except that it represents about $660,000 of Retirement Value. That $660K could generate almost 30 percent of the Joneses Gross Income for *all their retirement years.* That's a pretty high price to pay for the convenience of using the bank to fund our Cash Reserves. If we simply reduce our spending and used our own cash and invested the $225, we would have $660K when we needed it most.

As good stewards of our PFM, we should avoid all credit card debt. Credit cards are a wonderful *transactional* convenience, but beyond that they are financial chains and become the final and most powerful lock on the financial prison that can cost us our entire multimillion-dollar Retirement Value.... $225 at a time.

The Privilege of Using Debt Merchant Money

Over their 40 working years, the Joneses are paying the Debt Merchants $660,000 for the *privilege* of borrowing $15,000 of their money. And, after all of this, they still have to pay back the original $15,000 even though they already paid the equivalent of that $15,000 more than *44 times* over.

Primary Asset Allocation Summary

We have attempted to highlight the impact of these critical decisions on our PFM and on our Retirement Value. We all start with the potential for millions of dollars in Retirement Value, but we make decisions along the way that (unknowingly) can erode our Retirement Value to almost nothing.

To drive this point home a little further, Table 8-8 is a summary of the "Retirement Value of Stuff." This list is just an example of the true cost of the everyday decisions we make relative to our PFM. None of these are particularly earth shattering on their own. But taken as a whole, they can quickly add up to a stunning proportion of our Retirement Value—and often can be the 'tipping point' into sustained credit card balances and financial servitude.

Table 8-8: The RVI of Stuff

The RVI of Stuff	Monthly Cost	RVI
Average New Car	$673	($1,669,770)
Average Home	$1,888	($4,684,696)
Average Rec. Vehicle	$265	($657,357)
Premium Cable/Dish	$125	($310,240)
Season tickets + concessions (1 pers.)	$400	($992,768)
Coffee shop (1 per day @ $4 each)	$121	($300,312)
Beauty Salon (12/year at $80)	$80	($198,554)
Premium Exercise Club membership	$80	($198,554)
Eating out (3x/week @ $25 each)	$325	($806,624)
Smart Phone (full data/text)	$140	($347,469)
Saturday Nights Out ($50 each)	$216	($536,095)

Not to mention, we have not accounted for vacations, hobbies, entertainment, and the many other life-enriching opportunities we expect to be able to afford. Nor have we considered saving for college, retirement or other longer-term financial needs. This is how people wind up with the equity in their house at retirement and almost nothing else.

In the next chapter, we will tie all these moving parts together and see how, in the context of our three families, our Primary Asset Allocation Decisions can have a _dramatic_ impact on our PFM. We will also see how small adjustments that have little impact on our lifestyles can have large implications on our lives.

Chapter Summary:

- Primary Asset Allocation (PAA) decisions are the most important PFM-related decisions we can make. By *structuring* our PFM to have a healthy Free Cash Flow (our Operations Engine's MPG) we give ourselves both types of financial freedom and protect our status as Financial Builders.

- Houses and cars are much more expensive than their *payments*. We have to account for the total cost of ownership, including operating costs that impact Asset Burden—as well as replenishing the cash (for Dead Assets) that we will need to replace them in the future.

- New cars can kill our PFM. We can enjoy the same features and benefits of new cars simply by waiting three or four years and, at the same time, realize a profound impact on our PFM and our retirement years.

- Our house is not an investment, even though it represents the majority of our Net Worth for many of us. Our house can increase in value and our equity can increase over time, but the *rate of return* on this investment, considering all costs, is marginal to negative. With rare exception, there is a net *cost* to living in our home.

- There are many other things we take for granted that can have very large Retirement Value when extended throughout our 40 working years. When our monthly Living Asset Contributions are not delivering the Retirement Value and Retirement Income From Investments that we need, we need to think carefully about some of the truly discretionary stuff we are spending money on, like premium cable, expensive beauty treatments, over-the-top vacations, or daily espresso drinks. Individually, they are manageable, but *taken together* these can quickly add up to a $1 million in Retirement Value Impact.

- Dead Assets and Hard Debt can quickly destroy our PFM and cause us a lifetime of financial misery.

A note on income and income growth rates:

*This chapter discussed income growth rates. It remains a reasonable assumption many of our incomes are increasing at roughly the rate of inflation. Yet even if our incomes grow faster or slower relative to inflation, it would only skew some of these central points, calculations and conclusions one way or another; it would **not** invalidate them.*

As our income grows, for many of us, so will the amounts we are willing and able to pay for cars, toys, housing, etc. So in reality, the actual numbers simply go up in sync with each other (and can remain about the same as a percent of Monthly Gross Income) even as our incomes rise.

Lastly, while we consistently used 6.8 percent compounding for all our Retirement Value and investment calculations, we could have used almost ANY rate and the outcomes and insights would be the same on a percentage basis. So if we used 4.5 percent CAGR instead of 6.8 percent all the calculations would be scaled down by the same amount and therefore (for example) the cost of a single car would still be the same percentage of Lifetime Economic Value for each of our families. Also, the differences in their Primary Asset Allocation decisions would yield the same relative differences in Retirement Value between the families.

CHAPTER 9:
PUTTING IT ALL TOGETHER

Let's put all of these PFM concepts together now by looking at our three families.

Reminder: Here we are looking at a snapshot of the three families' PFMs at the 10-year point of their working lives. They have 30 more working years ahead and an additional 30 more in retirement.

We can see from the Table 9-1 that each family has made several different Primary Asset Allocation Decisions, but that their individual decisions are not radically different from the other families. The Joneses bought a somewhat more expensive house compared to the Smiths and the Millers. They purchase new cars every five years, but buy average priced, not expensive, cars, which they also chose to finance. They do have a used boat they financed and enjoy during the summer months and replace every 5-7 years.

By comparison, the Smiths and the Millers look just like the Joneses on the outside from a lifestyle perspective. They have similar houses, relatively nice cars—no junkers among them. The Smiths bought and financed the same car as the Joneses, but did not get all the bells and whistles that the Joneses did. They have an older boat that they paid cash for. The Millers don't have a boat or other recreational vehicles and they paid cash for their 5-year-old cars—that very well could be the Joneses' second-hand cars!

However, underneath these curbside similarities lie some stark differences. For example, the Joneses use their credit cards to cover some of their Non-Routine and Lifestyle Expenses rather than having significant Cash Reserves to cover these and other expenses. The Smiths have a modest level of Cash

Reserves, but have no credit card debt. However, the Millers have managed to accumulate a very healthy Cash Reserves and also have no credit card debt.

Table 9-1: PAA Decisions of the 3 Families

PAA Decisions	Joneses (Drones)	Smiths (Laborers)	Millers (Builders)
House	$300,000	$275,000	$250,000
Down Payment	20%	20%	20%
Mortgage Amount	$240,000	$220,000	$200,000
Car Acquisition Strategy	New Every 5 Years	New Every 5 Years	Used Every 5 Years
Number of cars owned	2	2	2
Purchase price	$35,000	$25,000	$19,270
Amount financed/car	$15,390	$9,942	$0
Toys (boat, 4-wheelers, etc.)	Yes	Yes	No
Purchase price	$15,000	$8,000	$0
Amount financed	$5,788	$0	$0
Carried Credit Card Debt	$15,000	$0	$0
Cash Reserves	$2,000	$5,000	$32,000

Primary Asset Allocation Impact on Free Cash Flow

As you can see in the Table 9-2, the Smiths and the Millers both have substantially higher Free Cash Flow compared to the Joneses. This is primarily due to lower Asset Burden from each of the seemingly small differences in Primary Asset Allocation decisions each family has made over time. All three families have the same exact monthly spending on Routine Living Expenses (food, clothes, insurance, healthcare, household supplies, etc.)—so it's only differences in Asset Burden that influence their Free Cash Flow.

Table 9-2: 3 Families—Relative Difference in Free Cash Flow

Asset Burden Impact of PAA Decisions	Joneses (Drones)	Smiths (Laborers)	Millers (Builders)
Housing	$0	$180	$359
Cars	$0	$242	$626
Toys	$0	$131	$158
Credit Card Debt	$0	$250	$250
Tax benefit from tax deferred savings	$0	$64	$144
Relative difference in Free Cash Flow	$0	$866	$1,537

Wow! How can this be? Compared to the Joneses, the Smiths have $866 MORE in Free Cash Flow and the Millers have a whopping $1,537 more EVERY MONTH. This is the simple cumulative effect of the Primary Asset Allocation decisions each family has made to this point in their working lives. While each family looks pretty much the same from the curb, *there is a world of difference inside their PFMs.*

As we continue to look at each family's PFM, we will see how these significant differences in Free Cash Flow result in very different Operational and Structural Financial Freedom. This is where we see the biggest divisions between Drones, Laborers and Builders emerge.

Table 9-3a: PFM Summaries of the 3 Families

Personal Financial Machine (PFM) Summaries	Joneses (Drones)	Smiths (Laborers)	Millers (Builders)
Gross Income (GI)	$8,000	$8,000	$8,000
Taxes	$1,584	$1,520	$1,440
After Tax Income	$6,416	$6,480	$6,560
Asset Burden	$3,891	$3,114	$2,398
Percent	49%	39%	30%
Routine Living Expenses	$1,550	$1,550	$1,550
Total Operating Expenses	**$5,441**	**$4,664**	**$3,948**
Free Cash Flow	**$975**	**$1,816**	**$2,612**
Percent	12%	23%	33%
Lifestyle Expenses	$550	$900	$1,140
Unpredictable Expenses	$140	$210	$180
Total Non-Routine Expenses	**$690**	**$1,110**	**$1,320**
Total Expenses	**$6,131**	**$5,774**	**$5,268**
Percent	77%	72%	66%
Asset Engine Contributions	**$285**	**$706**	**$1,292**
Tax deferred savings	$80	$400	$800
Non-tax deferred savings	$0	$50	$100
Cash savings to replace assets	$211	$234	$390
Remainder	**-$6**	**$22**	**$2**

The Joneses: Healthy on the Outside, a Financial Wreck on the Inside

For example, in Table 9-3a, we can see that the Joneses have pushed their asset purchases and use of debt to the limit and are trapped by the Debt Merchants. Their Asset Burden is 49 percent of the Gross Income, 39 percent of which is their total Principle, Interest, Taxes and Insurance (PITI) (house, cars, toys, credit card payments). The remaining 10 percent comes from utilities, maintenance, etc.

While the *maximum* debt from all sources can vary, most banks will limit *total* debt to 35-40 percent of Gross Income when considering us for *home* loans. However, *auto* loans differ in that the primary criteria here is a good credit rating and a reasonable down payment. Banks don't have the same concern about our total debt when we purchase cars, because it's easy to simply repossess and re-sell the car if we fail to make the payments.

So how did they qualify for their home mortgage with their total debt ratio of 39 percent? While this is high, if their credit rating is good, their incomes stable and their down-payment reasonably large, they may well qualify for their mortgage with a 39 percent 'Debt to Income' ratio. Or maybe they bought their home before they accumulated $15,000 in credit card debt or before they bought their latest new cars. The key is that total debt and payments can change (dramatically) after we purchase our home, depending on the Primary Asset Allocation decisions we make relative to cars and overall consumer debt.

Total debt payments are just one number banks can use to assess our credit-worthiness. Remember that Asset Burden includes other asset-related expenses that are not included in the bank's calculations, but that *we* absolutely need to consider. These are also unavoidable expenses associated with our owned assets that any calculations of what we can afford *must* include. The Joneses' difference between PITI and Asset Burden is 10 percent of their Gross Income (49 percent vs. 39 percent). Total debt payments are what the banks want to know to ensure they get re-paid. Getting paid *is their only concern*.

We, on the other hand, need to measure total Asset Burden to help us effectively manage our PFM. The Joneses' Primary Asset Allocation decisions have driven Asset Burden to the point of effectively locking up their PFM.

The point—as we have shown throughout the book—is that the Joneses are in over their heads. Their PFM is completely locked up. However—*They are fully functional*; they *can and do* pay all their bills, they eat out, go on vacations, and live a normal life. But, they are structurally and systematically giving away nearly all their $20 million in Lifetime Economic Value. *They are classic Drones.*

As a result, they cannot save for retirement. They cannot get out from under their ever-growing credit card debt. They have very little money for lifestyle expenses, and they can't save for their children's college or for other future expenses. They are the classic American financial train wreck. But they can live this way—barring a catastrophic event, and appear to be doing great for all outward appearances—*for all their working lives.* They just live paycheck to paycheck; and any little extra cash they accumulate goes to the next toy or TV or gadget or to pay down their ever-escalating credit card balance.

Looking at their Asset Engine, most of the Joneses' $416K in assets are in Marginal and Dead assets. Most of their Net Worth is the equity in their home. Their Net Worth Gain is negative and the Retirement Value of their current investments plus future contributions is a meager $132,000.

Table 9-3b: PFM Summaries of the 3 Families (cont.)

Three families - same income, different asset mix (at year 10)	Joneses (Drones)	Smiths (Laborers)	Millers (Builders)
Dead Assets	**$51,752**	**$36,052**	**$23,118**
Cars	$36,540	$26,100	$20,118
Toys (boat, ATVs, Snowmobiles)	$9,212	$5,452	$0
Stuff (furniture, etc.)	$6,000	$4,500	$3,000
Marginal Assets	**$357,849**	**$324,695**	**$291,541**
Home	$337,849	$309,695	$281,541
Other Marginal Assets	$20,000	$15,000	$10,000
Cash	**$2,000**	**$5,000**	**$32,000**
Living (Investment) Assets	**$5,000**	**$30,000**	**$110,000**
Total Assets	**$416,601**	**$395,747**	**$456,659**
Hard Debt	$32,699	$9,624	$0
Soft Debt	$219,237	$200,967	$182,698
Total Debt	**$251,937**	**$210,592**	**$182,698**
Net Worth	**$164,664**	**$185,155**	**$273,961**
Apprecaition	$7,477	$8,484	$12,855
Depreciation	-$7,763	-$5,408	-$3,468
Net Worth Growth	**-$286**	**$3,076**	**$9,387**
Percent Change	**-0.2%**	**1.7%**	**3.4%**
Retirement Value (Investments only)	**$132,065**	**$698,555**	**$1,702,968**
Monthly Ret. Inc. from Invest. (RIFI)	**$440**	**$2,329**	**$5,677**
Percent of Gross Income	**6%**	**29%**	**71%**
Est. Social Security Benefit (Income)	**25%**	**25%**	**25%**
Total Non-pension Income (% of GI)	**31%**	**54%**	**96%**
Estimated Net Worth at Retirement	**$510,966**	**$1,054,677**	**$2,049,627**

The Joneses simply cannot change their situation without *restructuring* their PFM. No amount of budgeting or skipping lattes will make any difference; their Asset Burden is just too high. When they reach the time they want to retire, all they will have is their accumulated home equity, a little cash, minimal savings, and the worthlessness of their increasingly shabby Dead Assets.

Actually, the Joneses' estimated Net Worth at Retirement looks pretty good relative to most households. The problem is that most of their $510K is tied up in the equity of their home. Their $132K of retirement investments can only generate 6 percent of their Gross Income. If we include social security, they might be able to replace about 30 percent of their pre-retirement Gross Income.

Basically, the Joneses (if they stay on the same path) have no chance at a reasonable retirement lifestyle. These seemingly small decisions (relative to the Smiths and Millers) they made (and continue to make) during their 40 working years has had a dramatic and irreversible impact on their roughly 30 years of retirement.

Over 50 percent of all households in the U.S. are Financial Drones or are at risk of becoming one. Revisiting our figures from the Introduction:

- *44 percent have credit card debt (average balance of $13K)*

- *46 percent live paycheck to paycheck and do not have the funds to cover a $400 unexpected expense*

They look very similar to the Joneses and they exist at nearly every income level.

The Smiths: Working Hard Just to Stay Even

The Smiths, as we already know, are classic Financial Laborers. As we have looked at the Smiths' PFM in earlier chapters, we highlighted that they have no credit card debt, but also struggle to maintain and build their cash position. They are saving about 5 percent of their Gross Income every month, but it's a struggle to do so. They use a budget to keep their spending on track and forgo some of the lifestyle things they would like to do or do more of (nicer vacations, entertainment, eating out more, etc.), because they feel they simply can't afford them.

The Smiths' total Asset Burden is 39 percent—a level that is just too high for the Smiths to get ahead of their Routine Living Expenses, Unexpected Expenses and basic lifestyle spending. This forces them to budget and have very little latitude to deal with the unexpected. The Smiths are always one major unplanned expense away from locking up their PFM.

But, if they can hold it together for 40 years, they will have accumulated a Retirement Value of almost $700K. Combined with social security, this can provide 54 percent of their monthly Gross Income during retirement. This level of income will help the Smiths keep their house if they want to and provide for a modest retirement lifestyle. But, in the end, they will have to keep budgeting and keep watching every dollar forever. The Smiths may be OK, but they have worked (and worried) really hard their whole lives to achieve this modest result.

The Millers: Carefree on the Outside and on the Inside

On the other hand, the Millers' total Asset Burden is 30 percent—a level that leaves the Millers with plenty of cash to fund their lifestyle expenses, save for retirement, and other long-term financial commitments like future college expenses. The Millers don't have a monthly budget; they follow more of a spending guideline than a strictly controlled budget. The Millers have such healthy Cash Reserves and cash flow that 'blowing' their budget this month or that month is just not relevant.

Looking at lifestyle spending, we see that the Millers are spending more than $1,100/month on the things they enjoy. The Smiths are spending about $900, and the Joneses are spending about $550/month. This difference between the Joneses and the Millers means that the Joneses probably *feel* much poorer than either the Smiths or the Millers. While they have the nicest house and newer more impressive cars, that may not translate into overall happiness when they look at their finances every month or when they decide what they can afford to do.

The Millers are also contributing far more to their Asset Engine than the Smiths or the Joneses ($1,292, vs. $706 vs. $285 respectively). The Millers are saving and investing over 10 percent of their Gross Income every month, the Smiths over 5 percent, while the Joneses are dedicating most of the AE contributions to be able to replace their Dead Assets—and only saving about 1 percent of their monthly Gross Income.

At $456K, the Millers' total assets are not much higher than either the Joneses or the Smiths. However, their *asset mix* is very different, in that they have 40 percent of their Assets in investments. Their Net Worth is almost twice as high as the Joneses and their Net Worth Gain is over $9,000 every year.

At retirement, the Millers' Retirement Value is about $1.7 million, which is able to generate about 71 percent of their pre-retirement Gross Income. By adding social security, the Millers are basically able to replace more than 95 percent of their pre-retirement income—*for the rest of their lives.*

What About Pensions? Every household situation is different. Some jobs offer a pension plan, but these are mostly going away and people are now changing jobs more frequently. The idea of working for the same company for 40 years and then retiring is a path that very few people can or do take anymore. Even if we are lucky enough to secure a pension, the pension can be negatively affected if the company's financial situation changes. The same is true of the future of Social Security. The safest bet is to assume that we are on our own, and anything we get above our own RIFI is gravy.

So in order to be so financially set for retirement, what did the Millers have to give up during their working lives that the Joneses didn't? Well, the Millers kept their housing cost down by buying a $250,000 house instead of a $300,000 home—not that much difference. The Miller's bought the Joneses' trade-ins from the dealer. So in the end they drove the exact same cars, enjoying the exact same features and performance—just 5 years later. All that took was some patience and a willingness to buy five-year-old cars. The Millers also gave up owning that boat. They just went out boating with Joneses once in a while, or they rented a boat when they felt the urge.

All the other differences between the Millers and the Joneses are favorable to the Millers. The Millers spent almost 3x more per month on lifestyle expenses and saved 10 times more per month. The Millers also were able to save for their kids' college costs or other future expenses like that once in a lifetime, around the world vacation.

Ironically, the Smiths have to change *very little* to become Builders like the Millers. In fact, even the Joneses could relatively quickly become Builders with some hard work and change. They have to restructure, but their Operations Engine could easily look like the Millers within a few years, giving them the same Operational Financial Freedom enjoyed by the Millers.

If the Joneses converted to Builders over the next few years, their situation would be much improved and they would have a much better retirement outlook. However, from a practical standpoint, the Joneses' Asset Engine will *never* be able to catch-up with the Millers. It is very difficult to make up time when someone else has a *compounding* head start.

Let's re-connect with our three families where we first met them, discussing their retirement plans, 30 years from now at the local coffee shop on Elm Street:

Joneses to the Millers: "*So all you did was make these small adjustments relative to what we did and this is where you wound up relative to us? We just can't believe it! We just never realized what buying new cars or owning our boat was really costing us. We liked having the new cars, but look at the hidden and real price we paid going forward! And yes, our house was a bit nicer with a bigger yard, but we love your house and how you decorated it and we never looked at it as a compromise or a significant step down from ours. If we only knew what the consequences of these decisions would be, we would have never made them the way we did. It just never occurred to us that we were living that differently than either of you. While we can't change the past, we can help our kids avoid the same mistakes that we just today realized that we've been making our entire working lives.*"

Smiths to the Millers: "*We feel so cheated. We worked so hard on following a budget and watching our spending and celebrating all the small wins, when in reality it was the big decisions that we should have focused on. Here we spent 40 years stressed out while we pinched our pennies, while you guys didn't spend a minute tracking expenses or managing to a budget. And now you have this wonderful retirement planned and we are resigning ourselves to another 30 years of restricted spending. We are so happy for you guys, but we just wish we would have known better. For us the changes we could have made were so small. It just hurts to think about it. Like the Joneses said, we can't change our situation, be we can help our kids avoid these simple and devastating mistakes. Thanks for sharing your insight. It has really been eye-opening.*"

Millers: "*Look, we are sorry to hear that we all wound up in such different places. When we first got married, we recognized that we had to really understand how our personal finances worked. There was so much pressure to buy-buy-buy. We also agreed that we needed to find a systematic way to put into practice all the good advice that was floating around out there like: 'Live below your means,' or 'Save early and often,' or 'Have an emergency fund,' or 'Don't get in over your head,' or 'Avoid credit card debt'. So we just built a system to focus on the big moving parts of our personal finances and we simply made decisions that kept us in the 'safe* *zone' where we had plenty of cash flow and a big cash buffer so we didn't have to worry about all the unpredictable stuff. We loved your cars and we were happy to buy them second-hand, but you must have realized how much less we were paying for them? Also, we invested our retirement money in index mutual funds, mostly because we don't know anything about investing, other than 'you can't beat the market in the long-run' and so we just left it alone. While we were off doing other things, our retirement fund, started small and then just grew and grew like a weed. It was painless and fun to watch."*

> The Millers just trimmed their Dead and Marginal Asset expectations down a notch from the Joneses and the Smiths; it was a SMALL difference. In the end, the Millers lived a great life, traveled widely, always had money for whatever came up, never had to budget and never had to worry about their financial future.
>
> *The key to the dramatic differences between these families is their Primary Asset Allocation decisions and the impact on Asset Burden and Free Cash Flow.*

Now that we see the incredibly powerful impact our decisions can have on our PFM and our lives, in the next chapter we can get focus on how we can *operationalize* these concepts and see how we can establish some practical guidelines for running our PFMs in a way that puts us and keeps us on the Builder's path.

Chapter Summary:

- Primary Asset Allocation (PAA) decisions are the most important PFM-related decisions we can make. By structuring our PFM to have a healthy Free Cash Flow or MPG, we give ourselves both types of financial freedom and protect our status as Financial Builders.

- Seemingly small differences in our Primary Asset Allocation decisions can have profound impacts on our lifestyles and the financial burden and stress we feel throughout our lives. The difference between Drones, Laborers and Builders can be deceptively small.

- Being a Builder does not mean giving up a great lifestyle compared to others in our income peer group. It simply means cutting back on a few strategic Dead and Marginal Assets and spending and investing the difference in a balanced way on things that don't increase Asset Burden. It also means taking advantage of compound interest.

- The Primary Asset Allocation decisions we make relative to our house and cars are the most important ones we can make and literally can define our financial destiny.

CHAPTER 10:

TAKING CONTROL

Winning the Battle for Your Money and Your Life

Now that we understand how our PFM works and more fully appreciate the impact of our decisions on its performance, we can wrap up by discussing how we can control and harness this incredible machine going forward. We can now establish control over the very thing that millions of people have struggled with, fought against, and literally given up on for decades.

The 3 Things That Really Matter:

1. Making sound Primary Asset Allocation decisions

2. Maintaining a healthy Cash Reserves

3. Making sound Secondary (Investment) Asset Allocation decisions

But how do we *operationalize* the first two of these three things? To begin, we need a simple set of measures to tell us what our PFM's status is. We also need some guardrails around these measures to alert us when our PFM is not aligned with our goals. This will let us know what is wrong and point to ways to get it back on track.

As shown in the Table 10-1, there are four core _operating_ measures that we need to focus on to fully control our PFM: Asset Burden, Free Cash Flow, Cash Reserves and Living Asset Contributions.

Why chose these four?

- Asset Burden is the primary factor that can cripple our Operations Engine

- Free Cash Flow is the primary factor in ensuring that we can maintain our Cash Reserves

- Cash Reserves is the lifeblood of our PFM. Without it our PFM is broken

- Living Asset Contributions is the primary factor in building our Asset Engine over time

By keeping these four parameters within _target ranges_ and _tuned_ to our personal lifestyles and needs, we can harness our PFM to achieve the balanced lifestyle that meets our individual short and long-term goals—and give us the Operational and Structural financial freedom we seek.

Table 10-1: The 4 Core Measures (MGI = Monthly Gross Income)						
Core Measures:	Description	Upstream Drivers	Downstream Impact	Standard Operating Ranges		
				Green	Yellow	Red
Asset Burden (AB)	Monthly expense associated with all owned Assets	Primary Asset Allocation (PAA)	FCF, CR, LSE	< 35% (% MGI)	35-40% (% MGI)	> 40% (% MGI)
Free Cash Flow (FCF)	Remaining cash after AB and Routine Living Expenses (OE Stage 1 output)	AB, RLE	CR, LSE	> 40% (% MGI)	30-40% (% MGI)	< 30% (% MGI)
Cash Reserves (CR)	Pool of cash required to effectively operate our PFM	FCF	Operational Financial Freedom, LAC	> 6 mo. (Stage 1 expenses)	4-6 mo. (Stage 1 expenses)	< 4 mo. (Stage 1 expenses)
Living Asset Contribution (LAC)	Monthly contribution to investment assets	AB, FCF, CR	Structural Financial Freedom	> 10% (% MGI)	5-10% (% MGI)	< 5% (% MGI)

Note: There are _many_ other insightful and interesting measures we can use to optimize our PFM and gain additional insight into its performance. We have provided a list of additional measures on the website and within the PFM Dashboard.

But what _controls_ or drives these measures? They are just the _result_ of our decisions and behavior—and it all starts with _Primary Asset Allocation_. As we already know, Primary Asset Allocation decisions _result_ in Asset Burden. Once we can control our Asset Burden, then we have to establish control over our Routine Living Expenses. Lastly, to protect our Cash Reserves, we have to ensure that our Cash Burn (what's going out of Cash Reserves) does not consistently exceed our Free Cash Flow (what's going into Cash Reserves). This requires us to exert some control over our Lifestyle Expenses. Once we do this, we need to optimize our Living Asset Contribution to fund our future cash and retirement needs and help keep Asset Burden in check.

The things we need to control to manage our four core operating measures within our target ranges are:

- **Primary Asset Allocation** => Asset Burden

- **Routine Living Expenses** => Free Cash Flow

- **Lifestyle Expenses** => Living Asset Contributions

- **Baseline + Episodic Cash Burn** => CR

You might be thinking—we've told you _all this_ just to come face to face with the fact that our _Behavior_ and our poor spending decisions are the source of our financial problems? But we already knew that, right? Yes, but we now have the understanding, framework and _tools_ to measure our status, see where we are going, improve our decision-making and _modify our behavior_ to keep our PFM on track. We have always known that we were in charge of the decisions; we've just lacked the understanding and near real-time measurement of the _impact_ of those decisions.

We can never have a better lifestyle than what our income allows— no matter what we do. Ultimately, we _choose_ one of the three paths we've described throughout the book:

1. **Financial Drone:** Overspend until the Debt Merchants own our PFM, its Retirement Value, and by extension, *us*.

2. **Financial Laborer:** Just keep managing our finances the old way, toiling over a budget, watching every dollar, hoping to avoid unplanned expenses to keep the Debt Merchants at bay.

3. **Financial Builder:** Assemble, structure and operate our PFM so that it can do the work and we are free to live our lives with confidence in our short and long-term financial goals.

Operating Ranges

Keep Asset Burden less than 35 percent of Gross Income

This may be the most important *structural* decision we make relative to our PFM. While maintaining a healthy Free Cash Flow is critical to our success, the primary thing that helps us achieve this goal is keeping Asset Burden in check. By doing so, we put ourselves *in position* to achieve both operational and structural financial freedom—and give ourselves a chance to keep much more of the millions we control.

This requires that we work hard to make smart Primary Asset Allocation Decisions. We don't buy too much house, pay too much for cars or use too much debt. We pay cash as much as possible and recognize that the total cost of ownership of many Dead and Marginal assets can be twice as high as their associated monthly payments. And most importantly, we measure and track our Asset Burden and ensure that we are keeping it in a healthy range.

As we will discuss in detail in the next chapter, the *optimal* range of Asset Burden for each of us will be different and is the result of all the other financial priorities we have set. Asset Burden becomes the last piece of the puzzle as we construct our PFM to meet our short, medium and long-term needs.

Keep Free Cash Flow more than 40 percent of Gross Income

With Asset Burden well controlled and tracking where we want it, the only thing that keeps us from our Free Cash Flow objective is being disciplined about our Routine Living Expenses. By *separating* our expenses into Asset

Burden, Routine Living Expenses and Lifestyle Expenses, we can much more easily achieve and maintain our Free Cash Flow targets.

We need a large Free Cash Flow because we want to have enough money to cover the three things that generally give us the most satisfaction and peace of mind:

- Enough money to 'enjoy life' (Lifestyle Spending)

- Enough savings to cover our retirement and other longer-term cash needs (Structural Financial Freedom)

- A large and sustainable Cash Reserves (Operational Financial Freedom) to deal with the unexpected and provide a financial cushion.

If we allow Asset Burden and Routine Living Expenses to get too large, we risk not having enough excess cash to cover these three incredibly important financial needs.

Keep Living Asset Contributions greater than 10 percent of Gross Income

With a healthy Free Cash Flow, we are in a great position to easily meet this savings and investment goal. However, we can undermine this objective by failing to maintain Lifestyle spending control. To protect our Cash Reserves, we need our Baseline Cash Burn—that is, the collection of expenses that steadily flow from Cash Reserves, including Living Asset Contributions—to be significantly less than our Free Cash Flow. This allows our Cash Reserves to grow over time so that our Cash Reserves balance can quickly recover when we have Episodic Cash Burn events—like a nice vacation. However, if our Baseline Cash Burn is not in control, we cannot *consistently* allocate our 10 percent to Living Asset Contributions without eroding our Cash Reserves.

Therefore, we have to keep our Lifestyle expenses under control—such that the total Baseline Cash Burn is well below Free Cash Flow. The key to doing so is to have a plan and manage to it. Decide at the beginning of each year how much you will spend on vacations, eating out, club memberships, and other lifestyle expenses and stay within your 'budget' for these expenses. Because we are using our Cash Reserves to cover these expenses, we can deal with larger fluctuations—*but there is no free money.* If our Lifestyle Expenses and our Living Asset Contributions consistently exceed the amount we have coming into our Cash Reserves, then CR will shift into in a natural decline. Then, any Unexpected Expense can completely disrupt our CR and force us to reduce our Lifestyle Expenses or our Living Asset Contributions—or force us to liquidate some Living Assets. We cannot have frequent or prolonged disruptions in our monthly Living Asset Contributions if we want to achieve our Retirement Value goals.

Keep Cash Reserves higher than 6 times Routine Operating Expenses (Asset Burden + Routine Living Expenses)

This is the last but most important measure in this 'cascade' of core measures. Cash Reserves is the result of all our other PFM decisions and our overall expense management discipline.

Our *individual* Cash Reserve target should be driven by several factors:

- How much *operating risk* we want to take on

- How much *variability* we have in our income

- The *size and frequency* of our planned Episodic Cash Burn events

- And the *time* associated with our calculated Replacement Rate

As stated above, the key to successfully maintaining our Cash Reserves is to ensure our Baseline Cash Burn is consistently well below our average Free Cash Flow. This keeps Cash Reserves growing until Episodic Expenses take it down a notch, but its natural upward trend will return it to its target level (based on our Replacement Rate—*measured in months of* Routine Operating Expenses).

Why is 6 months of Routine Operating Expenses in Cash Reserves the target amount? Well, we know that our Cash Reserves is _not_ an emergency fund. Thought it can act as one when needed, its primary function is to absorb the ups and downs of our Lifestyle and unpredictable expenses and act as a measure of how well we are managing our expenses and overall PFM. Six months' worth of Routine Operating Expenses creates a *flexible* buffer that allows us to absorb big negative expense events or big negative income or cash flow events (like losing a job). In the former situation, we can confidently continue our lifestyle spending and savings and investment rates without interruption, because we know how quickly our Cash Reserves will recover. In the latter case, we can clamp down on Lifestyle spending and suspend our savings and investments to significantly *extend* our ability to cover our expenses for well past 6 months.

Overall, how do we know these are the right ranges for each of us individually? These are broad ranges that are intended to reflect the *average* well-managed PFM—for each of us there will be a more fine-tuned target and range that makes sense for our specific situation.

However, after you work through setting up your own PFM, many of you will find these ranges to be generally reflective of your desired or *comfort zone* for these individual operating *targets* (your actual PFM today may not be there yet!). And when these ranges *do not* represent your personal PFM targets, this gives you great insight in how to modify, control and keep your unique PFM on track to achieve your goals.

Taking Control of Your PFM

Whether we are starting out as Financial Drones, Laborers or even Builders, the process and the goal is the same. These tools should improve our ability to manage our personal finances and, by extension, help us meet all our short, medium, and long-term financial goals. There are four important steps necessary to take control of our PFM:

1. Assembling our PFM

2. Develop a plan that reflects our needs, goals and desires relative to how we want to live

3. Structuring our PFM

4. Optimizing our PFM

Step 1: Organizing/Assembling Our PFM - We Have the Parts, But Not the Machine

We need to start with a reasonably good accounting of our expenses by type (food, clothes, mortgage, etc.) and their average monthly amount. We can then organize all these expenses into the major categories of Asset Burden

(AB), Routine Living Expenses (RLE), Unpredictable Expenses (UPE), and Lifestyle Expenses (LSE).

On our own this could be a difficult step and one that seems like just too much work. However, there are two things that actually make this step easy.

First, we don't have to be *exact or overly obsessive* about estimating these numbers. Of course, we should use exact numbers where we have them, like our mortgage or car payments. But where we don't—say, monthly grocery or gas expenses—we can and should roughly estimate them. Our PFM is *designed* to handle fluctuations in our monthly spending once we get it assembled and working.

Secondly, you can go to the website (www.manufacturingwealth.com) to easily input, organize and automate all the necessary steps to assemble and structure (customize) your PFM to meet your unique situation, needs and goals. The website also makes it easy to see your PFM's status and core measures. It literally brings your PFM to life *with a few well-spent hours of effort*.

> The beauty of our PFM is that we don't need to budget everything or document all of our spending all the time. Keeping track of our monthly or daily spending is an exhausting, frustrating, burdensome and a *completely unnecessary* task. However, many of us enjoy this level of documentation and control. By combining detailed documentation with assembling and using the PFM structure, we can exert even more control over our spending and maximize the RV of our AE (if that is our goal). However, choosing this level of detailed budgeting is a choice, but one that is not required to effectively manage our PFM.

Step 2: Developing a 'High Level' Plan

If you don't know where you're going, any road will get you there!

Of course, we have to have a plan if we are going to harness our PFM to help us meet our needs, goals and desires. Developing a plan is pretty simple, and can also be facilitated by the website PFM tool/dashboard. A key dimension of planning is to consider how our lifestyle, goals and what makes us happy are *interconnected* with our PFM. We need to *structure* or *customize* this tool to help us live the lives we want.

Short-term vs. Long-term Balance

We have to determine what is more important to us: living for today, saving for the future, or striking a balance between the two? Are we motivated by how much we can save or by experiencing life to the fullest right now? We need to make a conscious decision about the _balance_ we want to establish between our short-term and long-term lifestyle. The graphic below reflects the decisions we want to make to establish this very personal decision and then convert that _philosophy_ or approach into something we can measure and _operationalize_ within our PFM.

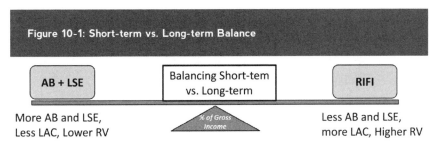

What portion of our income do we want/need to replace in retirement? _When and where_ do we want to retire? How do we want to retire (cold turkey, work part time for a while, volunteer)? What do we want to be able to do in retirement (travel, second home, volunteer abroad)? The further we are from retirement the less these decisions need to be worked out; but we should, at a minimum, have a target for Retirement Income from Investments (RIFI) and a target retirement date.

Once we work this out conceptually, we can then translate that into how much we want our Living Asset Contribution to be vs. Lifestyle Expenses or Asset Burden. The key is to make a conscious and personal decision about this balance between our short and long-term goals.

Lifestyle vs. Asset Balance

What is more important to us: a nice house and new cars or exploring the world (either around us or its distant corners)? It's an important question and one that people rarely contemplate proactively.

What energizes us? What do we look forward to? Many of us wind up with an asset-driven lifestyle by default. We just get sucked into the house and the cars and before we know it, the 'balance' is completely tilted towards Asset Burden whether we like it or not. Do we wind-up with a balance (in Figure 10-2) consciously or by default?

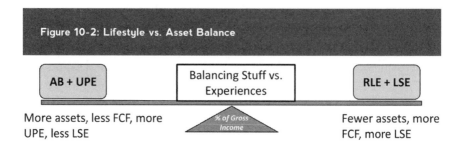

Figure 10-2: Lifestyle vs. Asset Balance

If an *asset*-oriented balance suits us, that's fine. If, on the other hand, we prefer to *experience* more, travel more, eat out more, then we should address this head on and (re)structure our PFM to accommodate the lifestyle we want—versus the one we wound up with. And we do this by establishing a plan, determining the balance between Asset Burden and Lifestyle Expenses and then revisiting that plan as needed. This is an individual decision, but an important one that we want to make proactively, rather than by default.

> Studies on happiness and feelings of fulfillment have shown that we gravitate to buying tangible things (Marginal and Dead Assets) to enhance happiness. However, it is *our experiences* that have a greater impact on both short-term and longer term feelings of happiness and fulfillment. So while it seems logical that buying 'stuff' would have a more lasting impact, the opposite is true. So if we want to increase our sense of happiness, we should spend less on stuff and more on great vacations!
>
> Source: Paulina Pchelin, Ryan T. Howell (2014), "The hidden cost of value-seeking: People do not accurately forecast the economic benefits of experiential purchases," The Journal of Positive Psychology, vol. 9, Issue 4, www.tandfonline.com/doi/abs/10.1080/17439760.2014.898316?journalCode=rpos20.

Cash Reserves Safety Margin

Another balance point we can consider is how tightly we want to manage our PFM from a Cash Reserves, Free Cash Flow and expense management perspective. At the safer end, we have more in Cash Reserves than we may need given the size of our Routine Operating Expenses and the more extreme Episodic

Cash Burn (ECB) fluctuations we may experience. At the other end, we can maintain a much smaller Cash Reserves than our Routine Operating Expenses expense and Episodic Cash Burn fluctuations may suggest. Like the other balance points, this is about our *personal* comfort and risk tolerance levels.

Figure 10-3: Cash Reserves Safety Margin

Step 3: Structuring Our PFM - The Millionaire's Roadmap

As kids, many of us played out some version of the fantasy of finding a treasure map that would lead to some long-lost riches. We even made our own maps and loved the many movies with the same theme. As adults, we often extend this fantasy of 'discovering' treasure into gambling, lottery tickets, get rich quick schemes or just plain dreaming about 'striking it rich.' Some of us keep looking and waiting for that lucky jackpot that will change our lives forever.

The great—and sad—irony is that we already have it in our hands. *We already are potential millionaires.* We've already 'hit the jackpot.' The treasure map leads directly to our doorstep; we just have to stop giving away the millions we already have (but don't realize we have)!

If the 50 percent of households that make $50K+/year invested 10 percent of their Gross Income every month ($416), they would have 10 percent of their Lifetime Economic Value at retirement—*at least* 7 times more than the typical pre-retirees hold today.

For those making *exactly* $50K/year that 10 percent translates into $1 million in Retirement Value. *Which will generate $3,333/month in retirement income—for the rest of their lives ($1 million x 4 percent divided by 12 months).* Said differently, if we save and invest 10 percent of our Gross Income every month, we will have accumulated enough investment assets to generate 80 percent of our gross monthly income when we retire. *We are already future* *millionaires*; we just don't see that we are and we just have to keep and invest a bit more every month to *stay* millionaires.

So, within Step 3, here is the simple process with five sub-steps or components for staying a millionaire. It's all about working backwards. We just finished discussing our core measures in 'top down' order, but we do our actual planning in <u>reverse</u> order.

3.1: Establish Our Desired Living Asset Contribution Level. After we develop our high-level retirement targets, we should be able to quickly calculate the Living Asset Contribution necessary to achieve it. As the saying goes—we must pay ourselves first. This is absolutely true and why we want to 'anchor' the structuring of our PFM to our Living Asset Contribution rate.

Remember, this can be a very low percent of our Monthly Gross Income if we begin soon enough in our working lives. By starting in our early 20s, *every 1 percent of Monthly Gross Income we allocate to Living Asset Contribution converts into a Retirement Income From Investments of 12 percent of our current Monthly Gross Income.*

3.2: Identify Other Long-term Savings Needs. We may have other savings priorities that we need to account for after beyond our retirement savings—a college fund for the kids, a wedding, or saving for a down-payment on a first home. Once we define the time and amount we need in the future, we can easily calculate the monthly contribution rate needed now.

3.3: Establish the Relative Importance of Experiences vs. Assets. Again, from our plan (Step 2 above), this will determine the relative importance of experiences vs. assets. Once this is clear, we can go on to 3.4. This is where we decide what our *philosophical* balance should be for Asset Burden and Lifestyle Expenses relative to each other and relative to our Living Asset Contributions.

3.4: Establish Targets for Average *Monthly* Lifestyle Spending and Other Medium-term (1-5 year) Cash Needs. This is all about developing targets for our Baseline Cash Burn. How much do we want to allocate for annual vacation? What will all our activities cost? How much do we want to spend on entertainment and eating out or other luxuries?

What about other future cash needs? Do we need new furniture in the next 5 years? How much do we want to spend? Are we planning on adding a deck or refinishing the basement? What will it cost? Do we need to replace a car in the next 5 years? How much cash will we need?

We need to establish some *average* annual budgets or savings rate for these expenses (how much will we spend each year for the next 5 years) and then convert this into an estimate of the monthly amounts (Cash Burn) associated with these expenses.

> Accounting for our 5-year cash needs is one of the most over-looked and important expense categories. We will have to replace our cars at some point in the foreseeable future. We will need cash for a down payment or to pay for the vehicle outright. However, if we don't plan for it and save for it, the money just won't be there. We will then have to make a very PFM-destructive move. We will have to **_finance_** our next car, cars, boat, or deck or whatever!

3.5: Determine Required Free Cash Flow to Sustain Our Cash Reserves.
Once we have established our monthly Baseline Cash Burn including Lifestyle Expenses, 5-year cash needs, our Living Asset Contribution and other savings, we then will know what our Free Cash Flow *must be* to sustain our Cash Reserves. Free Cash Flow must be *larger* than our estimated average Baseline Cash Burn. Once we know this, we can then look at what our Routine Living Expenses are or should be. This will leave us with our Asset Burden *limit*.

And just to be clear, when you do this, there is a good chance you will find your Asset Burden limit or target to be shockingly low (or far from what it is today). This is the fundamental reality for nearly all of us. *This is how we know we are being honest about our current and future expenses and needs.* When we don't understand our short, medium, and long-term expense needs, and don't understand how it all works together, it's easy (or inevitable) for our Asset Burden to become too large too quickly. Before we know it, we are laboring away with the Smiths or slaving away next to the Joneses.

Finally, we need to *iterate* this process until we are happy with the trade-offs we are making. This will result in development of *well-informed* targets for three of our core measures (Asset Burden, Free Cash Flow, and Living Asset Contribution).

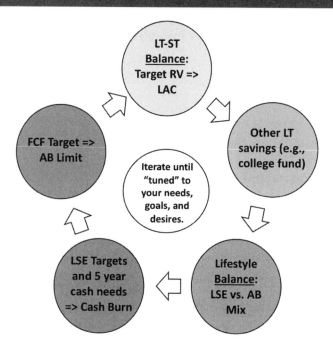

Figure 10-4: Managing Your Core Measures

Final step: we also need to establish a target for our Cash Reserves. Again, this should be informed by our plan as well as the answers to several other questions:

- How stable is our monthly income? (less stable = Higher Cash Reserves target)

- How secure is our job? (less stable = Higher Cash Reserves target)

- How long is our calculated Replacement Rate? (Longer = Higher Cash Reserves Target)

- How big do we expect our Episodic Cash Burn to be (relative to our monthly Gross Income)? (Larger and more frequent = Higher Cash Reserves Target)

To make it simple we have developed an algorithm within our PFM Dashboard that will help to estimate a target Cash Reserves and facilitate this iterative five-part process of establishing our PFM core measures.

Once we have developed and refined our *desired* PFM, we can now compare these targets to our existing core measures and develop a 'restructuring' plan to *migrate* our *existing* PFM over time to operate within the target ranges we have set for our *desired* PFM.

What If We Find a Big Mismatch Between Our Current Reality and Our Targets?

First, this is no reason to panic or give up. There is a very good chance that there is a significant disparity between how our PFM is structured today and how we want it to be structured in the future. However, not all mismatches are created equal. In general, the gap is driven by one of two primary issues:

1. **Asset Burden is too high**. This generally indicates that Free Cash Flow is too low and we cannot sustain our Cash Reserves no matter how much budgeting and skimping we do.

2. **Lack of spending discipline**. Our money just seems to evaporate every month. We get to the end of the month and there is nothing left.

When Asset Burden is Not the Problem

If Asset Burden is the problem, we are simply diverting too much of our monthly income into Asset Burden-related expenses which we are contractually obligated to pay for. We cannot skip or decide to pay only a part of our mortgage or car payments. We can't refuse to pay our utilities or property taxes, and we can't easily stop incurring 'usage' related expenses like gas. This is why Asset Burden is such a difficult problem.

If, however, we find that Asset Burden is not the problem, then we are dealing with a _behavioral_ challenge vs. a _structural_ challenge. Behavioral problems can also be very challenging. The big difference is that our non-Asset Burden-related spending challenges are typically much easier to modify. They are generally not contract driven, and if they are contract related (e.g., smartphone contract), we can usually get out of or modify them (perhaps with a cheaper plan).

Almost all behavioral spending issues revolve around our Lifestyle Spending—too much eating out, too much spending on our hobbies or activities, too much on lifestyle clothes, entertainment, etc. These are challenging problems, but our PFM can help us keep our spending in check (more detail on this in Step 4 below).

When Asset Burden IS the Problem

This is when we have to make some visible and potentially disruptive changes. Going back to our analogy of MPG, we simply cannot coax a car that gets 10 MPG to deliver 20 or 30 MPG. No matter what we do to nurse and manage and baby Stage 1 of our Operations Engine, if it's generating 10 percent Free Cash Flow, no amount of 'budgeting' will fundamentally change that. Skipping that morning latte or bringing our lunch to work is simply a waste of time and energy when Asset Burden is the problem.

In this case, *we need to reduce our Asset Burden.* We might have to sell our cars and replace them with ones that we can pay cash for, or sell the boat or the wave runners. We might have to cut off all discretionary spending to pay off the credit cards. We might have to move to a less expensive home. At some point, continuing to be 'house poor' is just a nice way of saying we are OK being Financial Drones. These are not easy decisions and they can have all kinds of ego bruising ramifications. But, in the end, there is no way to rationalize ourselves out of this problem. We just have to bite the bullet and restructure our Asset Burden. The only alternative is to be OK with being a Drone and give away our millions.

While this type of restructuring seems daunting and humiliating, we will be so much happier when we can re-establish control and *achieving* Operational Financial Freedom by having and maintaining healthy Cash Reserves. Imagine how energizing and freeing it will be when we can go on vacation AND watch our investments grow?

After reading this and assessing your current financial situation, you might be thinking "I just don't make enough money to do this." If you are, remember that we *simply cannot spend beyond our means* (for very long). If we do, we just wind up having <u>*less*</u> of our income (as compared to a Financial Builder making the same income), because we are simply giving <u>*more*</u> every month to the Debt Merchants and having <u>*less*</u> for ourselves—either to spend on our lifestyle or to invest for the future. **IT IS ALWAYS A ZERO-SUM GAME.**

You may also be thinking that you'll be able to 'work your way out' of this tight spot as your income increases. This may be true, but if we don't assemble, structure and *establish operational control* over our PFM, we will continue in the rut of a Financial Drone or Laborer.

Step 4: Optimizing Our PFM

The last step in the process of controlling our PFM is determining how we can *optimize* its performance. Think about this in three levels related to tracking our skill or competency relative to controlling, harnessing and optimizing our PFM.

PFM Management Level 1:

- Understanding the language and the fundamentals of how our PFM works

- Assembling and getting comfortable operating/using our PFM

- Tracking our core measures over time

PFM Management Level 2:

- Exerting *consistent* operational control (Operations Engine Stage 1 and 2)

- Completing a plan and establishing core measure targets

- Consistently keeping our core measures in target ranges (Asset Burden, Free Cash Flow, Cash Reserves, Living Asset Contribution)

PFM Management Level 3:

- Becoming highly comfortable with managing our PFM

- Using a broader range of measures to track and optimize its performance

- Employing higher level strategies to optimize and tune it

As we progress through these levels of comfort, confidence and competency, we can also increase our level of sophistication in how we control and harness our PFM to best serve our needs. On the website you will find several ideas and approaches to help you think about how to best optimize your PFM to suit your individual situation and needs. Your needs may be different if you are younger vs. older, have kids vs. not, and so on. Also, you may be in a different phase of life that requires some unique financial adjustments.

For example, we can optimize our PFM in various ways as we progress to Level 3. You'll recall from Chapter 7 that we can *structure* our PFM differently to emphasize different aspects of our life/Lifestyle approach like Assets, Kids, Experiences, Saving, or Balance. We can consider another strategic dimension as well:

Life Stage-Based PFM Optimization

We have different needs, challenges and expenses when we are in our 20s as compared to when we are in our 30s or 40s or 50s. Consequently, we will want our PFM to operate quite a bit differently in each life-stage that we progress through. While we will leave the details of life-stage PFM optimization to the website, it's worth touching on here.

We have defined 6 life stages from a financial perspective:

1. **Experiencing**

2. **Nesting**

3. **Managing**

4. **Maturing**

5. **Benefiting**

6. **Transferring**

Stage 1: Experiencing

This is when we are young and our priorities are all about 'the experience.' We are living in an apartment, building our careers, continuing our education and in general just experiencing life. From a PFM perspective, our Asset Burden is as low as it will ever be; at the same time, our Opportunity Cost Index (OCI) is as high as it will ever be. As crazy as it may seem this is *prime time* for setting up a retirement account to begin socking away at least 10 percent of our income. This might seem difficult when we are making seemingly so little. But this may be our richest stage for a while—making it an ideal time to establish and become comfortable with operating and controlling our PFM.

Stage 2: Nesting

We have now transitioned to ownership. This stage usually is marked by the purchase of our first home. So not only has Asset Burden taken a major jump, we are working hard to fill our nest with stuff, thereby severely stressing our PFM. After all, it just underwent the shock of going from a low to high Asset Burden. The question is: can we maintain our Free Cash Flow and Cash Reserves? Or will we slip and fall into the Debt Merchants hands? In this stage, we need to focus aggressively on our Operations Engine and ensure we don't lock up our engines. At the same time, we must focus on building our Asset Engine because our Opportunity Cost Index (OCI) is still very high and therefore the compounding engine *multiplication* of investments we make now is huge.

Stage 3: Managing

Not only do we have the house and the cars, but now we have the kids and the college fund and daycare and healthcare and braces and everything else—making this stage the *most* financially challenging. The demands on our PFM are at their peak. Not to mention we have to build our careers, save for our future, and *avoid* trying to keep up with the Joneses. If we managed to escape the Debt Merchants in Life Stage 2, they will be waiting with open arms here in Stage 3. One major slip up and they'll get their hooks into us. In Stage 3, we have to be managing our PFM with *operational excellence*—since this stage is the most difficult and the longest. But if we continue making good Primary

Asset Allocation decisions and staying focused on our core measures, we can successfully navigate it.

Stage 4: Maturing

After we have enjoyed and 'survived' Stage 3, the financial pressures are starting to subside. Our incomes are probably near their peak and we can see the light at the end of the tunnel. The kids are in high school or off to college. This is a great time to increase our Living Asset Contribution contributions if we've had to keep them a little light in Stage 3. While college is a big looming or actual expense, it's one that we have hopefully prepared and saved enough to handle. We also start thinking more about retirement and start to plan for what that will look like and what we will do. From a PFM perspective, we should be preparing and organizing for Life Stage 5.

Stage 5: Benefiting

Welcome to your version of retirement. Stage 5 is all about living off our fully developed Asset Engine. All the work that we did in the preceding stages is now paying off. We have achieved our Retirement Value goals and we are ready to go and do the things we have been planning for throughout stage 3 & 4. Or, maybe we have not achieved our Retirement Value goals and we need to keep working part time or we want to keep working.

For most of us, Stage 5 requires a major restructuring of our PFM. We will no longer need to save for retirement. Our Routine Living Expenses and Asset Burden should be significantly lower; and most importantly, our income from working will be dramatically reduced or zero. We may be shifting our priorities to Lifestyle Expenses that include more travel and entertainment. We may have a place by the kids or where it's warm and need to manage our time and PFM relative to this approach.

Notice that there are *no age ranges* for these stages. There is no 'rule' or absolute sequence to these stages. Stage 1 might last two years for one person and ten for another. These are *individual lifestyle choices*. The key point is that we can and should fine-tune our PFM to help us financially navigate and maximize our enjoyment of each stage.

Stage 6: Transfer

All of us will move on from this earth at some point and need to leave our worldly possessions behind. Because our PFM is *tangibly* what we are leaving behind, we need to organize and prepare it to be transferred to our heirs. This will include updating our wills and trusts and other estate planning documents. It will also include structuring our PFM appropriately. Stage 6 really begins as we *approach* becoming too old to travel, live on our own or have the mental acuity to manage our financial affairs.

When we can see that we are a few years from becoming dependents again, we need to get our PFM in shape. Our expenses will be low. We may need to get rid of some assets. We may have already begun the transfer process by gifting assets. The final steps include shutting down our Operations Engine and distributing the assets from our Asset Engine. In this final stage, we are just packaging things up for the next generation.

The power of our PFM is in both establishing operational control, but also in optimizing and tuning it _explicitly_ to support and achieve our personal and unique lives and lifestyle goals throughout these important live stages.

Chapter Summary:

- There are four core measures (Asset Burden, Free Cash Flow, Cash Reserves, and Living Asset Contributions) that we need to establish targets for and control over. Once we do this, we can harness our PFM to help us achieve whatever goals we desire.

- We need to have a plan that must consider our three structural balance points: Short-term vs. Long-term, Assets vs. Experiences and operating safety margins.

- We need to work backwards to structure our PFM to operate within the target ranges of our core measures.

- We need to migrate our PFM from its current structure to our desired structure.

- When Asset Burden is the problem, no amount of budgeting and scrimping will help. We must simply attack and reduce Asset Burden.

- We can optimize the structure of our PFM not just based on our personal operating balance points, but also based on our lifestyle emphasis, our life stage or other factors that might be important.

- We now have the knowledge and the means to achieve our goals.

Personal Finance Machine (PFM) - New Term Review

(Note: A complete list of term definitions can be found in the Glossary.)

- **Monthly Gross Income (MGI)** = Monthly Income from all sources.

CHAPTER 11:

ESTABLISHING FUNCTIONAL CONTROL OF OUR FINANCES

Where the Rubber Meets the Road

Now that we have developed a plan, defined our operating core measures and structured our PFM accordingly *on paper*, we need to apply it in the real world to our actual checking and savings accounts.

Establishing functional control over our Operations Engine is actually very straightforward. It essentially requires a simple system of two cash management accounts, both with automatic bill-pay and money transfer features. It also requires a debt or credit card associated with each account. **However, it does not require detailed budgeting or tracking every expense every month**.

Here is what we call the two accounts:

1. **Monthly Operating Account (MOA)**

2. **Cash Reserves Account (CRA)**

The Monthly Operating Account and associated **Debit Card** is our Stage 1 Operations Engine and has several functions:

- Receive our monthly income

- *Automatically* distribute our *target* Free Cash Flow to our Cash Reserves Account (Stage 2 of our Operations Engine)

- Cover all our Stage 1 expenses (Asset Burden and Routine Living Expenses)

    o Using electronic bill-pay

    o Using our ***debit card***

Our Monthly Operating Account should carry about 25 percent of our total Cash Reserves requirement that we estimated in Step 3 from Chapter 10. With a stable income, this should be an amount of cash roughly equal to 1.5X our Monthly Gross Income (MGI). Clearly our Monthly Operating Account will fluctuate *during* the month and *from* month to month. It's critical that a flow of cash into and out of Monthly Operating Account (as our Operations Engine Stage 1) is designed to be relatively stable with only small variations. It is stable because Asset Burden is fairly regular as are our true Routine Living Expenses, and presumably, our monthly income. Given this, a good starting point for Monthly Operating Account is about 1.5X Monthly Gross Income. If income is not stable, then your MOA needs to hold more cash, based on the amount monthly income fluctuates.

Our Cash Reserves Account (CRA) and its associated **Debit** or **Credit Card** is Stage 2 of our Operations Engine and has several functions:

- Receive (automatically) Free Cash Flow from Operations Engine Stage 1

    Note: the amount of this Free Cash Flow may have already been reduced by the amount of pre-tax dollars that you are moving into your retirement account.

- *Automatically* distribute funds (Living Asset Contributions) to:

    o Retirement Accounts (if not already deducted from your paycheck)

    o Other long-term investment accounts

    o Other designated savings accounts (e.g., cars, college, home down-payment)

- Cover all our Lifestyle and Unpredictable Expenses

  o   Using electronic bill-pay

  o   Using the *debit or credit card*

- Primary repository for most of our 'working' cash

- Act as our emergency fund (if needed)

As we already know, our Cash Reserves Account is the portion of our Operations Engine that—from a cash management perspective—deals with the unexpected, the discretionary, and the highly variable. It therefore needs to have a larger cushion of cash, and is why the majority our working cash should be stored in our Cash Reserves Account. However, because our Cash Reserves Account can fluctuate significantly, it's harder to tell if it is growing or declining over time. This is why we separate the more predictable and steady Lifestyle Expenses (our Baseline Cash Burn) from Episodic (and unpredictable) Cash Burn and only use Baseline Cash Burn to calculate our Replacement Rate.

This two account structure creates a simple check and balance. If we see our Monthly Operating Account (MOA) decline over time, it's a *clear red flag* that there is a problem we need to proactively dig into and correct. All we have to do is go back over our bill payment history and debit card transactions to uncover the problem. Even in the worst-case, if our Monthly Operating Account accidently goes to zero, we will have the majority of our cash in our Cash Reserves Account. We can then 'rebalance' between the two accounts as we investigate and correct the underlying Monthly Operating Account issue. The key to this approach is that we need to use the Debt card and bill-pay religiously. We can't take out a ton of cash every month, spend it and then have no record of where it went. If we use the MOA designated debit (or even credit card) in a disciplined and routine way, we will not have to budget or track expenses.

Our Monthly Operating Account is designed to be our stable, boring, work-horse account intended to cover all our Routine Operating Expenses (Asset Burden + Routine Living Expenses) and *consistently* move our target level of Free Cash Flow into our Cash Reserves Account. Our Cash Reserves Account is our *controlled* slush fund (OE Stage 2) so that we can effectively manage expenses that can vary widely is size and timing.

Using the Credit and Debit Cards

The purpose of having these cards is to establish an easy to use system of categorizing and tracking expenses without the need of a complicated budget or envelopes or other budgeting support tools. One of our biggest spending challenges we have is related to our *discretionary* spending during the month. Often, our money just seems to fly out the door.

Using these cards will allow us to do a much better job of tracking and controlling our spending. A debit card requires discipline because we are taking money directly from our account. This is why we use it for all Asset Burden and Routine Living Expenses. The debit card helps us 'protect' our Monthly Operating Account and our Free Cash Flow. By only using our debit card for Asset Burden and Routine Living Expenses we are ensuring that we maintain a healthy and consistent Free Cash Flow. The *disciplined* use of our debit card is how we engage our Operations Engine with the *real world* of our spending. We can cover the rest of our Asset Burden and Routine Living Expenses by electronic bill-pay or checks associated with the Monthly Operating Account. This keeps our Stage 1 Operations Engine expenses organized, trackable and in one place.

Our Cash Reserves Account is similar to the Monthly Operating Account, but more difficult to track due to higher and more variable expenses. We track our expenses in our Cash Reserves Account in the context of both the type of expense (Lifestyle Expenses vs. Unpredictable Expense), and whether it is a Baseline or Episodic expense. Using a single credit card helps us accomplish this; the 'WANT' card is dedicated for all lifestyle-related expenses like eating-out, hobbies, the local coffee shop, and vacations, as well as all the Gotcha-related episodic expenses like vacations or Unpredictable Expenses like a major auto repair or an unexpected need to fly somewhere for the weekend. The key is that we don't invade our Monthly Operating Account to cover Lifestyle or Gotcha expenses, nor do we use our WANT card for Routine Operating Expenses. Additionally, other lifestyle-related expenses not covered by the credit card can be paid using electronic bill-pay or checks specifically associated with your Cash Reserves Account (like cable, cell-phone, subscriptions, etc.). Likewise, all Asset Engine Contributions can and should be automatically transferred from your Cash Reserves Account into each appropriate savings or investment account every month.

Figure 11-1: Setting Up a PFM

Figure 11-1: Setting Up a PFM

NEED CARD
MOA - Debit Card

WANT CARD
CRA – Debit/Credit Card

- **Routine Living Expenses**
  - Groceries
  - Everyday clothing
  - Household expenses

- **Asset Burden-Related Expenses**
  - Gas
  - Oil changes
  - License tabs

- **Lifestyle Expenses**
  - Eating out
  - Personal care
  - Daycare/Babysitting
  - Hobbies
  - Seasonal expenses
  - Gifts
  - Fashion clothing
  - Coffee shop
  - Music/video/apps

- **Large Episodic Lifestyle Expenses**
  - Vacations
  - Anything > $1k

- **Gotcha Expenses**
  - Auto accident expenses
  - Major home repairs
  - Any insurance claim related expense

As a conceptual rule of thumb, we use the WANT card on everything that we *want*—lattes, pedicures, baseball games, seasonal expenses, vacations, weekend getaways, hobbies, gifts—and the NEED card on everything that we *need*—groceries, gas, basic clothes.

Then, at the end of the month, we can look at our WANT credit card statement and it will already contain all our Lifestyle Expenses spending (both Baseline and Episodic). It is not overly useful to know if we spent $125 this month and $275 last month eating out. What is useful is to know that that we are spending on average $450/month *in total* on our *baseline* Lifestyle Expenses, and it varies by +/- about $100 from month to month. We can also see whether this is consistent with our *target* for baseline Lifestyle Expenses.

Using this method helps us keep the integrity of our Stage 1 Operations Engine. We can now isolate and track all the harder to manage expenses and have a built-in cushion that lets us easily handle and recover from a bad month.

This method does not preclude us from having 5 other specialty credit cards from various retailers. And while we can choose to continue this practice, in the end it just adds complexity and risk. If we correctly allocate these additional cards to our Monthly Operating Account (e.g., where we shop for clothes) or our Cash Reserves Account (sporting goods store) and set-up automatic bill-pay, then it's certainly easier to manage. However, the more complex this becomes, the more we provide the Debt Merchants opportunities to undermine our Stage 1 and Stage 2 Operations Engine spending discipline. Wouldn't it be nice to just have two cards to worry about? Need and Want!

Now we can look at the output of our Cash Reserves Account—to find our monthly Total Cash Burn. Simply by tracking our Cash Reserves balance, we can measure the difference between our Free Cash Flow and our Total Cash Burn over time. This simple system helps us *deliver* our four operating measures every month and over time: Asset Burden, Free Cash Flow, Living Asset Contribution, and Cash Reserves. In addition, it's also easy to calculate our Replacement Rate and compare our Free Cash Flow and Total Cash Burn trends and their impact on overall Cash Reserves over time.

Having said all of that—no system can save us from ourselves. We must have a *system* to *alert* us when 'bad behavior' becomes a habit or when a Primary Asset Allocation decision structurally alters our PFM. This is how we'll know that we need to adjust everything else to maintain our four core measures where we need/want them.

What About All Those Specialty Credit Cards?

Many of us have multiple affinity/reward or specialty credit cards that give us special incentives to spend more than we should (yes, you know where this is going). We *should* work to get rid of these cards as much as possible. But even if we keep them, we need to correctly designate them as either NEED or WANT cards and pay them out of MOA or CRA as appropriate.

Macro Cash Management

Macro Cash Management is a concept and a tool to help us better manage our cash and our monthly spending and account balances. It is simply the immediate and automatic allocation of our monthly income between our Monthly Operating Account, Cash Reserves Account, and other saving/investment accounts. By allocating our monthly income *the second it comes in* we are in effect creating a 'macro budget' for Stage 1 (Monthly Operating Account) and Stage 2 (Cash Reserves Account) and our long and medium-term savings. This approach forces us to operate each month within that *macro* budget.

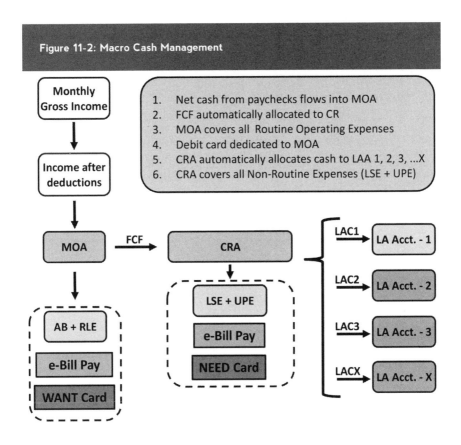

Figure 11-2: Macro Cash Management

1. Net cash from paychecks flows into MOA
2. FCF automatically allocated to CR
3. MOA covers all Routine Operating Expenses
4. Debit card dedicated to MOA
5. CRA automatically allocates cash to LAA 1, 2, 3, ...X
6. CRA covers all Non-Routine Expenses (LSE + UPE)

The vertical and horizontal black arrows in Figure 11-2 reflect our Macro Cash Management that occurs at the beginning of the month. This allocation of cash to Monthly Operating Account, Cash Reserves Account and to each of our savings or investment accounts creates a *forced* macro budget for Monthly Operating Account and Cash Reserves Account.

For example, when we transfer our expected Free Cash Flow from Monthly Operating Account to Cash Reserves Account at the _beginning_ of the month, then we will in effect guarantee that our Free Cash Flow will be X percent of our monthly income and *we are forced to manage our Monthly Operating Account within the limits we have set by our after-tax income and Free Cash Flow.* This is similar to the savings benefit that people experience when they elect to automatically deduct money from their paycheck into a 401(k).

Most of our Asset Burden expenses within our Monthly Operating Account are fixed and (hopefully) being handled through our electronic bill pay. Therefore, the expenses we are left with for the rest of the month, for the most part, are our Routine Living Expenses—now limited on one side by Asset Burden and on the other by our Free Cash Flow allocation. We will know very quickly if we overspend our Routine Living Expenses; there is just not much room for bad behavior. In fact, the only way we can disrupt our Monthly Operating Account balance is to start using our debit card or loyalty/retail cards inappropriately (for purchases beyond Routine Living Expenses)—which we can quickly see and correct.

When looking at Stage 2 (Cash Reserve Account), we see that our pre-defined incoming Free Cash Flow and automatic distributions out of our Cash Reserves Account to our retirement and other savings/investment accounts (Living Asset Contributions 1, Living Asset Contributions 2, Living Asset Contributions 3, etc.) creates a 'bracket' to limit our lifestyle spending each month.

However, because it is large, there is a lot of room for 'bad behavior' within our Cash Reserves Account. There is always the potential to blow it all on new cars, big vacations or a furniture spending spree. So how do we save ourselves from ourselves?

There are two tools that we have to help us protect our precious Cash Reserves.

1. ***Our commitment to ourselves.*** Our own self-discipline and the recognition that we have only two options: Keep our millions or spend them. By assembling and customizing our PFM to meet our needs and by being able to 'see' what is happening and the consequences of our decisions, we have set ourselves up for success.

2. ***Having and following a plan for our medium-term expenses.*** Remember that back in Step 3 (from chapter 10), we needed to identify and quantify our 1-5 year cash needs and then translate that into a monthly rate of cash required? One way to manage and track these future cash needs is to create separate savings account for each of these longer-term cash needs (Dead Asset Replacement Account, Vacation Account, Home Improvement Account, Furnishings Account, etc.) and then set-up automatic payments into each one from your Cash Reserves Account. This helps prevent us from having too much *unallocated* cash laying around.

If there is any version of a 'budget' related to managing our PFM, this is it. However, there is nothing that says we can't adjust on the fly and, for example, swap the European vacation for the new furniture. What we have to be careful about is taking the European vacation AND buying the new furniture.

Also, remember that our automatic transfers out of the Cash Reserves Account into Living Asset Contributions 1-X, in total should be far less than our Free Cash Flow coming into our Cash Reserves Account. First, we have to account for our average monthly Lifestyle Expenses and even after that amount is added to our automatic transfers (remember this is our Baseline Cash Burn) it should be less than our Free Cash Flow. So, over time, we should always have this upward trend on our Cash Reserves Account.

> This is where traditional budgeting can play an important role. It is important not to be frivolous or cavalier with our spending because we now have our PFM in order and a big healthy Cash Reserves balance to protect and manage. We have to keep our aggregate Routine Living Expenses and our Lifestyle Expenses in check and if we need to apply standard budgeting techniques to do so then we absolutely should. But the key is that we are doing *tactical* budgeting within the context of Macro Cash Management, which is key to helping us stay on track.

Managing Our PFM's Operations on a Monthly Basis Looks Like This:

- Establish Macro Cash Management—based on your target PFM core measures. You can easily set up the accounts at any brokerage house or bank. Set up automatic allocations for Free Cash Flow (Monthly Operating Account to Cash Reserves Account) and savings (Cash Reserves Account to various savings accounts).

- Use the NEED and WANT cards during the month based on the type of expense

- Pay the bills from the Monthly Operating Account and the Cash Reserves Account using electronic bill-pay (including the credit cards)

- A quick review at the end of each month:

- o Check Monthly Operating Account and Cash Reserves Account balances and trends

- o Check to see if the Cash Reserves Account has grown too large (as it should when Free Cash Flow > Baseline Cash Burn) and transfer a portion to whatever savings account we deem needs it the most.

- Any problem—and the reason for it—is quickly apparent. We address the problem by

  - o Moving money between accounts

  - o Adjusting MCM amounts

  - o Adjusting our spending habits

- Repeat next month!

- Once a quarter or whenever you are making Primary Asset Allocation decisions, visit the website, update your PFM and model the impact of significant changes you may be contemplating.

Using Our PFM Is About Keeping It Simple

We do not need to over complicate our financial life. Do we have money stashed away in 5 different places and investments in 5 more? Why? Are we investing too much time *micro-managing* our finances, when we could have more control with less effort? Are we tracking all our expenses? Are we budgeting every expense category and trying to reconcile the gaps and overages every month? Are we writing checks to pay our bills or are we using electronic automatic bill-pay systems? Are we tracking individual stocks and trying to decide to buy or sell this or that stock?

The more financial decisions and complexity we burden ourselves with, the less likely we will make informed decisions. In the end, *we need only four things*:

1. **A Plan** that defines:

    a.   Our Short and Long-term financial and lifestyle goals

    b.   5-year cash needs

    c.   Customized PFM balance measures

2. **A PFM Dashboard** to: (www.manufacturingwealth.com)

    a.   *Structure*, organize and measure our finances and guide our decisions towards meeting our plan (using the PFM model on the website)

    b.   Track core measures

    c.   Set Macro Cash Management (MCM) targets

    d.   Model Primary Asset Allocation decisions to ensure that they don't undermine our plans

3. **Functional Control** of our Operations Engine (Monthly Operating Account, Cash Reserves Account, credit and debit cards, and MCM)

4. **Effective Use of a Compounding Engine** to optimize our investment returns (Stocks, bonds, etc.)

Chapter Summary:

- Our current cash and bill-payment systems are essentially our Operations Engine. We need to reorganize them to match how our Operations Engine *actually works.*

- We need two primary accounts: Monthly Operating Account (MOA) and Cash Reserves Account (COA) and associated debit/credit card and bill-pay functionality. These two accounts represent our OE Stage 1 and 2.

- We can and should have other secondary accounts that our Cash Reserves Account allocates money to as needed.

- Macro Cash Management is how we functionally manager our Operations Engine. We set up automatic transfers of Free Cash Flow and Living Asset Contributions and then simply track and manage the *balance* of our Monthly Operating Account and Cash Reserves Account over time.

- We use the NEED card for all Routine Operating Expenses (ROE) and we use the WANT card for all Non-Routine Expenses (NRE) as our high-level budgeting and expense management and tracking tools.

- Now that we understand our PFM, know how it works, know how to operate and control and harness it, we can *effectively* put all the great financial advice that already exists to *great* use.

- Go to our website at www.manufacturingwealth.com to quickly build your own PFM and begin the process of becoming a Builder, or if you already are a Builder, taking your existing personal financial discipline to the next level.

Personal Finance Machine (PFM) - New Term Review

(Note: A complete list of term definitions can be found in the Glossary.)

- **Cash Reserves Account (CRA)** = Your CRA and a credit card are Stage 2 of your Operations Engine.

- **Macro Cash Management (MCM)** = This is how you functionally manage your Operations Engine. You set up automatic transfers of FCF and LACs and then track and manage the balance of the two accounts over time based on transfers and expenses over time in MOA and CRA

- **Monthly Operating Account (MOA)** = This account and the associated debit card is Stage 1 of your Operations Engine. While your MOA will fluctuate each month, it is important that the flow of cash into and out of MOA is relatively stable with only small variations.

FINAL THOUGHTS

A s we stated in the introduction, this book was never intended to offer any new financial advice. We are awash in a sea of websites and podcasts providing personal financial tips, recommendations, and advice. The exciting potential for our PFM is that we can now effectively organize, integrate, and put this great advice to work.

Our goal was simply to provide the *mechanism* that helps us put that good advice into practice. That mechanism is our PFM.

We can also now see how some of this advice applies within the framework of our PFM For example:

- "Live below your means"—A great platitude, but now we have a means to accomplish this by assembling and customizing our PFM to operate properly within our four core operating measures.

- "Penny wise and pound foolish"—We know that saving money on lattes when Asset Burden is killing us is not the answer.

- "Pay ourselves first"—Now we know that our PFM can calculate the benefit (Retirement Value) and cost (Opportunity Cost Index) of this payment, and how to structure our PFM to deliver a consistent Living Asset Contribution every month and how to use Macro Cash Management to make it happen—*every month*.

- "If you are struggling to manage your finances, make a budget"—If we *need* to budget and closely track our expenses, this just a *symptom* of a PFM that is not in control. The need to budget is responding to the consequence of the problem, not the underlying problem itself—which is why it rarely works.

- "Build an Emergency Fund"—It's not an emergency fund. It's a necessary and critical *operating* fund (Cash Reserves Account) that we *need* to effectively operate and manage our PFM.

- "Use debt wisely"—Yes, but what we need to focus on is the impact of debt on Asset Burden and Net Worth Gain.

- "Diversify your investments"—Investment decisions or Secondary Asset Allocation is probably the easiest and most 'data-driven' PFM-related decision we can make. However, it is worthless if we are not building our Asset Engine through consistent Living Asset Contributions and leveraging compound interest.

In the end, we truly appreciate how hard it is to accumulate wealth in our hyper-commercialized society. We know it's not as easy as it sounds to *just* save $403 or even $281 every month—*especially* when our incomes are near or below the median income, or we are just starting out, or are already in or 40s or 50s. The key to this challenge is to understand that we have a simple choice: Enrich the Debt Merchants or enrich ourselves.

We are all at risk of becoming locked into a *hidden* battle for our money and our lives. Our goal has been to make this battle with the Debt Merchants *visible* and to provide the tools and insights we need to understand, control and harness our PFM. This is ultimately how we will support and enhance our lives instead of a Debt Merchant's bottom line.

Yes, we could win the lottery. We could invent the next transformational technology, or we could attempt to climb our way to the top 1 percent income bracket. Or we can look *within* and realize we have something of significant value *right in front of us*. So while we are climbing the corporate ladder or inventing the next big thing, we can simultaneously ensure our future the old fashion way—by keeping and building on what we've *already earned*.

So there it is. We hope you agree and understand what a powerful thing a well-managed PFM can be. We also hope to have provided some useful tools and insights that can help you harness your PFM to achieve whatever goals you set. Viewed within the context of our 40 working years, we can now appreciate the immense impact our decisions have on our PFM—and the immense opportunity we have to change the course of our financial lives.

The End

EPILOGUE: BOOK SUMMARY

The 3 Things That Really Matter:

1. Making sound Primary Asset Allocation decisions

2. Maintaining a healthy Cash Reserves

3. Making sound Secondary (Investment) Asset Allocation decisions

The 10 Key Takeaways (To Help Achieve the 'Three Things'):

1. Our personal finances are a system—a machine, that once understood, can be harnessed and controlled to meet our needs.

2. We cannot easily utilize all the great financial advice in the world until we assemble and establish control over our PFM.

3. We have to stop thinking that we don't make enough or have enough. Ironically, if we are young enough (regardless of how much we have saved so far), *we are already potential millionaires*. Our job is not to earn a million-dollar salary or win the lottery, but to *manufacture wealth* and *prevent it from escaping* our PFM.

4. ***We can never live beyond our means.*** We can only choose to enrich ourselves or the Debt Merchants. By the simple act of having and maintaining a healthy Cash Reserves and by structuring our PFM to help us live within our means we *instantly* achieve Operational Financial Freedom.

5. ***Primary Asset Allocation*** drives every aspect of our PFM. In effect, our Asset Engine controls our Operations Engine, not the other way around.

6. We need to focus on four core measures: Asset Burden, Free Cash Flow, Living Asset Contribution, and Cash Reserves. If we do this, everything else will take care of itself.

7. Compound interest is the most powerful force in the universe—we just have to use it (or have it used against us!). This requires three things: money, time, and a compounding engine such as the stock market.

8. Financial Builders don't spend a lot of time on their personal finances. They ***structure*** their PFM to meet their needs and then let it do most of the work.

9. The ***need*** to budget our expenses is not a fact of life or a personal finance best practice; it's a ***symptom*** of not having *structural* control over our PFM.

10. Our finances are a means to an end, not an end onto themselves. Our PFM is a ***tool*** to help us live the life we want to lead. However, if we lose control of our PFM, we lose control over our lives. <u>**This is the hidden battle for our money and our lives**</u>.

It's time to take control and win this battle!

<u>Connect with Us Online and Next Steps:</u>

1. Visit our website at <u>www.manufacturingwealth.com</u> to engage in the PFM community and learn more about your own PFM.

2. Complete the PFM input tool on the website to help you organize, view and model your PFM quickly and easily.

3. Once you have completed inputting your PFM, it will be available in a de-identified form in the PFM database on the website. After the beta version of the website has been upgraded, you will have the ability to compare by income range or age range, stage or demographic, or customize your comparisons using many other available criteria. In addition, we have developed a variety of tools to help you make more informed financial and lifestyle decisions, including tools to help migrate or re-structure your PFM and model various 'scenarios' into the future to easily estimate the impact of your decisions on your Retirement Value and goals.

Note: our website does not ask for or store any of your specific financial account numbers or balances. Nor does it house any of your financial assets–that's what banks and other financial institutions are for. These tools, website and database use only de-identified 'pro-forma' information and are designed to help you *visualize, measure, assess, plan and decide*. The actual organization and movement of your cash and assets remains with and under the protection of your current financial institutions.

ACKNOWLEDGEMENTS

S pecial thanks to the following people who not only took the time and the care to read and provide constructive feedback on this book but also provided energetic support for the project over the many years of its development: Dave and Mary Jo Bangasser, Gary Borrell, Steve Carle, Chris Casey, Tracy Coenen Schaefer, Aileen and Charlie Craven, Joe Eskola, Grace and Nick Myre, John Galatowitsch, Mark and Mary Madaus, Chris Miller, Jeff Ruehl, and Sara Wegmann. Very special thanks to our wives who contributed enormously in all regards.

Last, but not least, thank you to Fred Martin for generously sharing his time and incredible expertise, wisdom, enthusiasm and encouragement.

GLOSSARY

Term	Description/Definition
Annuity OCI (aOCI)	There are two versions of the Opportunity Cost Index. Annuity OCI is related to the Retirement Value for a constant contribution of money from any given point of time until retirement. For example, if we wanted to know the Retirement Value of $3,600 per year ($300 per month) from the time we are 25 until retirement, we would use Annuity OCI.
Appreciation	An INCREASE in an asset's value over time.
Asset Allocation	The process of selecting which asset classes make up a portfolio and the mix you choose between those assets.
Asset Burden™ (AB)	Expenses associated with assets you own: mortgage interest and principle, auto loans, other consumer loans, all non-operating expenses (e.g., insurance, property taxes, association dues), and all operating expenses (e.g., gas, utilities or routine maintenance). If it is an expense that exists specifically because you own asset it belongs in Asset Burden.

Asset Engine (AE)	Your PFM's balance sheet. It contains all your assets and liabilities (debts) and therefore defines your Net Worth. The Asset Engine represents the status and actual accumulation of the multimillion-dollar potential associated with our lifetime earnings. It is the measure of your financial success.
Asset Engine Contributions (AEC)	The 'positive' coupling (wealth contribution) from the Operations Engine to the Asset Engine. Movement of cash from the Operations Engine into the Asset Engine. Often this includes the conversion of that cash into assets other than cash.
Asset Maturation	Assets are driven by two fundamental forces: Appreciation and Depreciation. Each of your assets is 'maturing' in some way. Some assets are appreciating and others are depreciating. You can calculate the current status of this process by taking the current value of your assets and subtracting their value when you acquired them. The difference is the cumulative amount of appreciation (positive) or depreciation (negative) they have experienced over time. If you divide this amount by the number of years you have owned the assets you can calculate the annual rate of appreciation or depreciation.
Asset Mix	The sum of your total asset Appreciation and Depreciation at a point in time.
Average FCF	Average Free Cash Flow over a set number of months.
Average CB	Average Cash Burn over a set number of months.
Balanced Lifestyle	Your PFM is designed to help you achieve two competing goals: One to support the lifestyle you want now and the other is to fund the lifestyle you want in the future. Taken together is a balanced lifestyle.
Baseline Cash Burn (BCB)	The sum total of your Cash Burn that is relatively predictable and stable. BCB example expenses include monthly savings/investing and most Lifestyle Expenses. These may fluctuate quite a bit month to month, but they are not usually large relative to out monthly gross income.

Cash	Any readily accessible liquid funds in accounts like money markets, checking, savings, etc. Though Cash is an asset and is counted as part of Net Worth, it is managed as part of the Operations Engine.
Cash Burn (CB)	The monthly drain of your Cash Reserves which includes Non-Routine Expenses (NRE) and Asset Engine Contributions (AEC). CB is the hole in the bottom of your Cash Reserves bucket.
Cash Reserves (CR)	A critical pool of cash required to support the healthy and smooth operation of your PFM. CR is used for two things: purchase assets (e.g., cars, furniture, lawn mowers) and fund your Non-Routine Expenses (e.g., Lifestyle Expenses like vacations and hobbies and entertainment as well as Gotcha expenses like a new water heater or significant auto repair).
Cash Reserves Account (CRA)	Your CRA and a credit card facilitate Stage 2 of your Operations Engine.
Compounding Engine	Any investment vehicle that can generate appreciation over time.
Dead Assets (DA)	Assets that depreciate by design. These include anything with an engine, furniture and furnishings, and most other 'stuff' you own that gets used.
Debt Resolution	Debt Resolution is the change in debt owed from the annual debt service payments made.
Debt Merchant (DM)	Banks, retailers, and other organizations that provide financing. These lenders have hundreds of years of understanding of how PFMs work and they work very hard, little by little, to get you to turn it over to them.
Depreciation	A DECREASE in an asset's monetary value over time.
Emergency Fund	Typically, a reserve fund that holds 4-6 months of monthly expenses.

Episodic Cash Burn (ECB)	Infrequent Cash Burn events. These events can sometimes be large and even exceed monthly Free Cash Flow (or even our monthly income). Sometimes you choose when they occur (vacation or new furniture) and sometimes you don't (broken water-heater, storm damage, or travel for a funeral).
Episodic Expenses	Infrequent, one-time or annual expenses that can be quite large. Sometimes you choose when they occur (vacation or new furniture) and sometimes you don't (broken water-heater, storm damage, or travel for a funeral).
FCF	Directly measures the output of Stage 1 of your Operations Engine and reflects the fundamental health of your PFM. It reflects the flexibility you have with your PFM.
Financial Builder	Financial Builders have plenty of cash. They don't budget expenses or worry about the details of monthly spending. They save for college, future needs, and retirement and have extra cash for new purchases. Unanticipated expenses are not a problem. Builders spend little time on personal finances and do not worry about money. Their lifestyle is comfortable and reasonable. Their Net Worth is healthy and growing and they invest for retirement every month.
Financial Laborer	Financial Laborers have some Cash Reserves. They see financial control as work. They budget and worry about monthly spending and are saving for retirement and new purchases. Unanticipated expenses are problematic, but they work through it. They spend a lot of time and energy on personal finances, thinking about money, budgeting and making sure they remain in control. They may have a significant amount of debt, but manage to stay one or two steps ahead of the Debt Merchants. Their hard work and diligence seems to pay off and they make slow steady progress, but worry they may be one big Gotcha away from the whole thing falling apart.

Financial Drone	Financial Drones owe a lot of money. They work for the Debt Merchants. They believe to be in control, but it's only an illusion created and sustained by the Debt Merchants. Their monthly payments and related expenses eat up huge chunks of their monthly income, leaving just enough to get by, but not enough to get out from under their debt. They have little or no savings or investments.
Financial Freedom	This term is highly personal. It can be as simple as not having to worry about paying the monthly bills or getting caught by some big unpredictable expense. It can be not having to worry about paying for your children's college education or not worrying about retirement.
Free Cash Flow (FCF)	Monthly cash left over once Taxes, Asset Burden, and Routine Living Expenses are paid. FCF then feeds and sustains your Cash Reserves. FCF is THE source of fuel for your PFM.
Gross Income (GI)	Income sources such as your paycheck, government payments, interest and dividends from income generating assets. This is usually a monthly measure (see also MGI).
Hard Debt (HD)	Consumer debt that includes credit cards, retail charge cards, auto loans, etc. Hard debt interest generally cannot be deducted for tax purposes and is usually tied to Dead Assets.
Intrinsic Appreciation	Underlying market force that, over time, exerts upward pressure on the value of an asset. Appreciation does not include improvements, contributions, or additions to assets.
Intrinsic Depreciation	The natural decline in value of an asset that is typically associated with assets that wear-out or get used up over time. All Dead Assets have intrinsic depreciation.
Liabilities	Debts that are contractually obligated to be repaid with interest. Liabilities are generally funds borrowed from a bank or other lender to purchase assets.

Lifestyle Expenses (LSE)	Expenses that enhance and reflect your chosen 'life-style.' They are unique to each of us, enrich our lives and help keep us happy. Examples include: entertainment, vacations, sports tickets, etc.
Lifetime Economic Value (LEV)	The theoretical untouched value of a person's total lifetime Gross Income plus compounded interest. It is calculated by taking your estimated average annual income and investing the entire amount in the stock market over your entire working career.
Living (investment) Assets (LA)	Investment-grade assets that include mutual funds, stocks, bonds, REITs, etc. These can be either tax advantaged (i.e., 401(k) or IRAs) or taxable (i.e. after-tax money invested in a brokerage account).
Living Asset Contribution (LAC)	Conversion of Cash Reserves into Living Assets.
Locking Up Our Engines	The melt-down of your Personal Finance Machine. The big risk you face in managing your PFM is in locking up your engines. Like any well-oiled machine, your PFM must be managed and maintained to avoid malfunction. This occurs when you have virtually no Free Cash Flow and very little or no Cash Reserves.
Macro Cash Management (MCM)	Macro Cash Management is how you functionally manage your Operations Engine. You set up automatic transfers of FCF and LACs and then track and manage the balance of the two accounts over time.
Marginal Assets (MA)	Assets that can appreciate or have a stable value over time. They include real-estate, valuables, collectables, jewelry, art, etc. They have a baseline value that can fluctuate and may have associated expenses (like insurance) to maintain or protect them.
Monthly Operating Account (MOA)	This account and the associated debit card is Stage 1 of your Operations Engine. While your MOA will fluctuate each month, it is important that the flow of cash into and out of MOA is relatively stable with only small variations.

Monthly Gross Income (MGI)	Monthly income sources such as your paycheck, government payments, interest and dividends from income generating assets (see also GI).
MPG (of Operations Engine)	MPG=FCF/GI. Free Cash Flow relative to Gross Income is like the fuel efficiency (or MPG) of your Operations Engine.
Net Worth (NW)	NW = Total Assets - Total Liabilities. Net Worth is simply the difference between Assets and Liabilities and includes all types of assets.
Net Worth Gain (NWG)	NWG = Year-over-year change in Net Worth. While Net Worth is an important status of your Asset Engine, what is more important are the changes in Net Worth over time. Net Worth Gain is the measure of growth in our Net Worth over the course of a year. NWG reflects the 'Health' of our Asset Engine.
Non-Routine Expenses (NRE)	These expenses need to be managed separately from Routine Operating Expenses. Non-Routine Expenses fall into two categories: Unpredictable Expenses (UPE) and Lifestyle Expenses (LSE).
Operational Financial Freedom	Achieving a well-structured and managed Operations Engine with several months of Routine Living Expenses in Cash Reserves and a healthy and consistent Free Cash Flow.
Operations Engine (OE)	The part of your PFM that deals with cash flow. This is your P&L or Profit and Loss statement. It is the part of our PFM that all your income and expenses (routine and non-routine) flow through.
Operations Engine (OE) Stage 1	The Operations Engine is a relatively simple part of your PFM. It is a two-stage 'cash flow' engine. Stage 1 is where Gross Income covers taxes, Asset Burden, and Routine Living Expenses resulting in Free Cash Flow that pours into your Cash Reserves.

Operations Engine (OE) Stage 2	Stage 2: Cash Reserves is a pool of cash required to deal with Non-Routine Expenses that are unpredictable, discretionary, and sometimes large. Stage 2 acts as a giant buffer that absorbs and covers all your highly variable, frequently large and often random Non-Routine Expenses (Lifestyle Expenses + Unpredictable Expenses).
Opportunity Cost Index (OCI)	An index or multiplication factor that reflects the Retirement Value of a sum of money today based on the amount of time that money could compound until retirement.
Personal Finance Machine (PFM)	The organization of your personal finances into a system that can be used to control and manage personal finances more effectively.
PITI	Principle, Interest, Taxes, and Insurance.
Primary Asset Allocation	Primary Asset Allocation (PAA) is a critical set of PFM decisions that involve the allocation of your excess cash among the four asset classes within the Asset Engine: Living, Marginal, Dead, and Cash. Primary Asset Allocation happens above the level of Secondary Asset Allocation (therefore primary). PAA defines the structure of our Asset Engine.
Replacement Rate (RR)	The number of months it takes to add 1 month of Routine Living Expenses to Cash Reserves.
Retirement Value (RV)	The projected value, in today's dollars, of your current Living Assets and future Living Asset Contributions. It is calculated over the remaining time between now and age 62 (or your personal target retirement age) using the inflation-adjusted investment rate of growth.

Retirement Income from Investments (RIFI)	The annual income your retirement investments can generate in retirement. To calculate RIFI, you can use a standard calculation of 4 percent of your Retirement Value to estimate the annual income our RV can generate (RIFI). There are many different strategies and formulas for estimating the optimal RIFI, however this book uses the simple (and common) 4 percent of RV calculation.
Retirement Value Impact (RVI)	RVI is a way to objectively measure the impact of your financial decisions on Retirement Value. It can be applied to a fixed amount of money at a specific time or a flow of cash over an extended period.
Routine Living Expenses (RLE)	All routine expenses associated with everyday living like groceries, cable, mobile, health insurance, basic clothing, household supplies, etc.
Routine Operating Expenses (ROE)	(ROE) = Asset Burden + Routine Living Expenses.
Secondary Asset Allocation	If familiar with the term 'Asset Allocation,' you know it as the allocation of investments across classes of investment assets like domestic stocks, bonds, international stocks, real-estate, commodities, and cash. This book refers to this type of asset allocation as Secondary Asset Allocation.
Soft Debt (SD)	Soft Debt is generally reserved for mortgage debt. Soft Debt has three features: 1) it is used to purchase marginal or investment assets 2) its interest is tax deductible and 3) it has a lower interest rate (compared to Hard Debt).
Spot OCI (sOCI)	Spot OCI (sOCI) = There are two versions of the Opportunity Cost Index (OCI). Spot OCI is related to the Retirement Value of a one-time dollar amount at any given point in time. For example, if we want to know the Retirement Value of $10,000 when we are 25 years old, we would use the Spot OCI factor multiplied times the $10,000.

Stage 1 (**Operations Engine**)	Where Gross Income covers taxes, Asset Burden, and Routine Living Expenses resulting in Free Cash Flow that pours into your Cash Reserves.
Stage 2 (**Operations Engine**)	Stage 2 acts as a giant buffer that absorbs and covers all your highly variable, frequently large and often random Non-Routine Expenses (Lifestyle Expenses + Unpredictable Expenses). Cash Reserves pays all Non-Routine Expenses and transfers AEC into the Asset Engine
Structural Financial Freedom	Structural Financial Freedom is about building a targeted level of Retirement Value. It is about establishing the ability to have a sustainable target standard of living from your Asset Engine without needing to continue collecting a paycheck.
Taxes (TX)	State and Federal income taxes from all sources.
Unpredictable Expenses (UPE) (Non-Routine)	Unpredictable (non-routine) Expenses such as replacing a broken appliance, major auto repairs, large medical expenses or other 'surprises' of life.
Virtual Cash Reserves	The use of consumer credit to fund your Cash Reserves. This is the beginning of the end and may precipitate financial collapse or financial enslavement.

NOTES

1. Lisa Greenwald, Craig Copeland, and Jack VanDerhei, "The 2017 Retirement Confidence Survey: Many Workers Lack Retirement Confidence and Feel Stressed About Retirement Preparations," *EBRI Issue Brief*, no. 431 (Employee Benefit Research Institute, March 2017), https://www.ebri.org/pdf/briefspdf/EBRI_IB_431_RCS.21Mar17.pdf.
2. Jesse Bricker, Lisa J. Dettling, Alice Henriques, Joanne W. Hsu, Lindsay Jacobs, Kevin B. Moore, Sarah Pack, John Sabelhaus, Jeffrey Thompson, and Richard A. Windle (September 2017), "Changes in U.S. Family Finances from 2013 to 2016: Evidence from the Survey of Consumer Finances," *Federal Reserve Bulletin*, Vol. 103, No. 3, Table 4, https://www.federalreserve.gov/publications/files/scf17.pdf.
3. Authors' estimate. The 2016 Survey of Consumer Finances (SCF) reported that 43.9 percent of "families" hold credit card debt. The "families" unit of measurement in the SCF is most comparable to the U.S. Census Bureau's definition of households. This 43.9 percent is multiplied by the 124,587,000 estimated 2015 households reported by the U.S. Census Bureau to estimate that there are 54,693,693 U.S. households that hold credit card debt. The New York Federal Reserve reported that in 2015: Q3 U.S. Households carried $0.71 Trillion in U.S. credit card debt. By dividing $0.71 Trillion by the 54.7 million households we estimate that the average outstanding credit card debt per debt-carrying household to be $12,981. See: Bricker et al., "Changes in U.S. Family Finances from 2013 to 2016," Table 4., U.S. Census Bureau, "Families and Living Arrangements," 2015, https://www.census.gov/data/tables/time-series/demo/families/households.html., Federal Reserve Bank of New York, "Quarterly Report on Household Debt and Credit," November 2015, https://www.newyorkfed.org/medialibrary/interactives/householdcredit/data/pdf/HHDC_2015Q3.pdf.

4. Federal Reserve Board, "Report on the Economic Well-Being of the U.S. Households in 2015," May 2016, https://www.federalreserve.gov/2015-report-economic-well-being-us-households-201605.pdf.

5. Bricker et al., Table 3.

6. Alicia H. Munnell, "401k/IRA Holdings in 2016: An Update from the SCF," Number 17-18, Figure 10, (Center for Retirement Research at Boston College, October 2017), © 2017, by Trustees of Boston College, Center for Retirement, http://crr.bc.edu/wp-content/uploads/2017/10/IB_17-18.pdf.

7. Trading Economics, "United States Personal Savings Rate," TradingEconomics.com, March 2017, https://tradingeconomics.com/united-states/personal-savings.

8. GO Banking Rates, "2015 Life + Money Survey: What Americans Think About Most," GoBankingRates.com, September 9, 2015, p.3, http://cdn.gobankingrates.com/wp-content/uploads/2015/09/What-Americans-Think-Most-About-2015-Life-Money-Survey-GOBankingRates.pdf.

9. Institute for Divorce Financial Analysts, "Survey: Certified Divorce Financial Analyst® (CDFA®) professionals Reveal the Leading Causes of Divorce," Institutedfa.com, August 2013, https://www.institutedfa.com/Leading-Causes-Divorce/.

10. This is a rudimentary test to quickly gauge retirement readiness. No simple test can adequately assess a person's specific financial situation. Therefore, this test should not be relied upon in place of proper financial planning.

11. Moneychimp, "Compound Annual Growth Rate (Annualized Return)," Online calculator using years 1915-2015 (Includes dividends), Moneychimp.com, http://www.moneychimp.com/features/market_cagr.htm.

12. Bricker et al., Table 1.

13. Ibid, Table 1.

14. Ibid, Table 3.

15. Compiled from GAO analysis of 2013 Survey of Consumer Finances data, GAO-15-419, Table 1, May 2015, https://www.gao.gov/assets/680/670153.pdf, and authors' calculations.

16. Ibid, Table 2.

17. Bricker et al., Table 4.

18. Ibid, Box 5.

19. U.S. Department of Commerce, Bureau of Economic Analysis, National Data, "Personal Consumption Expenditures (PCE)," December 2015, Table 2.3.5., https://www.bea.gov/itable.

20. Andrew Beattie, "Financial History: The Rise of Modern Accounting," Investopedia.com, http://www.investopedia.com/articles/tax/08/accounting-taxes.asp.

21. Moneychimp, "Compound Annual Growth Rate (Annualized Return)," Online calculator using years 1915-2015 (includes dividends but not adjusted for inflation).

22. Moneychimp, "Annualized Inflation Rate," Online calculator using years 1915-2015.

23. Compiled from the US Census Bureau and the Bureau of Labor Statistics, "Current Population Survey (CPS)," 2014, Household Income, https://www.census.gov/programs-surveys/cps/data-detail.html, and authors' calculations.

24. Authors' calculations.

25. Social Security Administration, "Research, Statistics, & Policy Analysis, Monthly Statistical Snapshot," SSA.gov, October 2017, Table 2, http://www.ssa.gov/policy/docs/quickfacts/stat_snapshot.

26. U.S. Census Bureau, "Families and Living Arrangements," 2015.

27. Compiled from Bricker et al., Table 2, and authors' calculations.

28. Data from Federal Reserve Board 2016 Survey of Consumer Finances.

29. Bricker et al., Table 3.

30. Table recreated with 2016 data by authors from Munnell, "401k/IRA Holdings in 2016: An Update from the SCF," Table 3.

31. Yahoo! Finance, Historical Prices, Jan 3, 1950–Jan 3, 2015, close prices adjusted for dividends and splits.

32. US Census Bureau. Historical Income Tables: Households, Table H-3, 1967-2016, https://www.census.gov/data/tables/time-series/demo/income-poverty/historical-income-households.html.

33. Compiled from US Bureau of Labor Statistics and www.boxofficemojo.com.

34. Gallup, "IN DEPTH: TOPICS A TO Z, Stock Market," Gallup.com, April 2017, http://www.gallup.com/poll/1711/stock-market.aspx.

35. The Economist, "How exposed are American households to the stock market?," Economist.com, August 26th, 2015, http://www.economist.com/blogs/freeexchange/2015/08/american-economy.

36. Harry M. Markowitz, *Portfolio Selection: Efficient Diversification of Investments* (New York: John Wiley & Sons Inc.; London: Chapman & Hall, Limited, 1959).

37. Jeff Cox, "Bad times for active managers: Almost none have beaten the market over the past 15 years," CNBC.com, April 12th, 2017, http://www.cnbc.com/2017/04/12/bad-times-for-active-managers-almost-none-have-beaten-the-market-over-the-past-15-years.html.

38. Graph recreated from the Schwab Center for Financial Research with data from Morningstar, Inc.

39. Christine DiGangi, "The average student loan debt in every state," USAToday.com, April 28, 2017, https://www.usatoday.com/story/money/personalfinance/2017/04/28/average-student-loan-debt-every-state/100893668/.

40. Federal Student Aid, An OFFICE of the U.S. Department of Education, "What are the interest rates for federal student loans?," Studentaid.ed.gov, July 2015, https://studentaid.ed.gov/sa/types/loans/interest-rates#what-are-the-interest-rates-of-federal-student-loans.

41. Bankrate, "Current Auto Loan Interest Rates," Bankrate.com, 2015, http://www.bankrate.com/finance/auto/current-interest-rates.aspx.

42. Kelley Blue Book, "New-Car Transaction Prices Rise Steadily, Up 2.6 Percent in April 2015, According to Kelley Blue Book," KBB.com, May 1, 2015, http://mediaroom.kbb.com/2015-05-01-New-Car-Transaction-Prices-Rise-Steadily-Up-2-6-Percent-in-April-2015-According-to-Kelley-Blue-Book.

43. Phil LeBeau, "Americans Buying Fewer New Cars in Lifetime," CNBC.com, November 14th, 2012, https://www.cnbc.com/id/49504504.

44. Meg Stefanac, "Car Depreciation: How Much Have You Lost?," TrustedChoice. com, February 14, 2014, https://www.trustedchoice.com/insurance-articles/ wheels-wings-motors/car-depreciation.

45. Munnell, "401k/IRA Holdings in 2016: An Update from the SCF," Figure 10.

46. Jessica Luff, "How Much Does A Boat Cost?," Carefreeboater.com, May 21, 2013, http://www.carefreeboater.com/how-much-does-a-boat-cost/.

47. Axle Geeks, "Q&A," AxleGeeks.com (accessed July 1, 2016).

48. U.S. Department of Housing and Urban Development, Office of Policy Development and Research, "U.S. Housing Market Conditions Summary: The User Cost of Homeownership," Huduser.org, 1997, http://www.huduser.org/ periodicals/ushmc/summer2000/summary-2.html.

49. Art Swift, "Americans Rely Less on Credit Cards Than in Previous Years," Gallup.com, April 25, 2014, http://www.gallup.com/poll/168668/americans-rely-less-credit-cards-previous-years.aspx.